AF646933

Globalisation WTO Policy and Its Impact on Indian Economy

Globalisation WTO Policy and Its Impact on Indian Economy

Vipin Mathur

2008

CYBER TECH PUBLICATIONS
4264/3, Ansari Road, Daryaganj, New Delhi-110002 (India)
Ph.: 011-23244078. Fax: 011-23280028
E-Mail: cyberpublicationsdelhi@yahoo.com

Globalisation WTO Policy and Its Impact on Indian Economy

© Reserved

First Edition 2008

Published by G.S. Rawat

For Cyber Tech Publications

4264/3, Ansari Road, Daryaganj, New Delhi - 110 002

E mail : cyberpublicationsdelhi@yahoo.com

Phone : 011-23244078,

Fax : 011-23280028

No part of the publication can be reproduced in any form or by means without the prior written permission of the publishers & author.

Printed at

Amit Enterprises, Moujpur, Delhi. Ph. - 9810878184

Preface

Globalisation influences every nation in different ways. Its impact also differs from country to country. The effects of globalisation in developed countries will be different from that of developing countries. In developed countries, globalisation has led to loss of jobs because many companies relocate production units to developing countries to reduce the cost of production. Unemployment is a common phenomenon in many European countries. In developing countries, globalisation affects the producers of foodgrains and manufactured goods. Globalisation has made it obligatory for many developing countries to purchase certain amount of goods from other countries even if they are produced within their own countries.

World Trade Organisation (WTO), an international organisation set up to promote trade among countries. It aims at conducting international trade in an open, uniform and nondiscriminatory manner.This gives an opportunity to India for trading with other member countries.

We may be able to export our goods and services to other countries with less restrictions from those countries.It is expected that the technology from developed countries will be available to India at a reduced cost. Since major share of world trade is taking place among the developed countries themselves, the benefit of being a member of WTO to the developing countries, particularly to India, is very limited.

Different sources scholars and institutions for their valuable contribution on this subject. While preparing this work for our readers.

Last but not the least my publishers who appreciated this book and brought this work out in a record time.

—*Editors*

Contents

Preface v

1. Impact of World Trade Organisation on the Indian Economy 1
2. Policy and Impact of World Trade Organization (WTO) 23
3. Theory of International Economy 73
4. Towards Globalisation and Liberalisation 134
5. Measurement of Poverty is Major Challenges Before Indian Economy 162
6. The Organisational Structure of Public Sector Banks in India 170
7. Implications of Globalisation for Agriculture Crisis in India 185
8. GATT and International Economy 213
9. Role of Insurance Market in India 224

Glossary 249

Bibliography 255

1

Impact of World Trade Organisation on the Indian Economy

World Trade Organisation was set up in 1995 by the member countries of the United Nations to promote trade among countries. The headquarters of WTO is located in Geneva. It has significantly influenced the liberalisation and globalisation processes in most of the developing countries, including India. WTO aims at conducting international trade among countries of the world in an open, uniform and non-discriminatory manner. While facilitating trade among counties, WTO expects countries to follow what it wants. Let us take three issues-bilateral agreements, import quotas and export quotas - which are crucial for the developing countries, particularly India. What do they mean? Whenever a country is involved in trade with some other country, it makes an agreement with each country separately. This is referred to as bilateral agreement. Bilateral agreements play crucial role in the trade relations among countries. In order to present competition from the producers of other countries with local manufacturers, it is common for countries to impose taxes on the imported goods. These countries also put a restriction on the amount of commodities to be imported. It is referred to as import quotas. In order to protect the local consumers. Governments put restrictions on exports that those goods cannot be exported beyond a limit. This is referred to as export quotas. WTO wants both the import and export restrictions to be abolished. Instead of bilateral agreements, it expects the countries to follow multilateral agreements. These are agreements formulated by a group of countries.

World Trade Organisation is not only regulating the international trade of goods, but also services. All the members of WTO have to adopt laws and policies in order to comply with the WTO rules.

Impact of WTO on the Indian Economy

This gives an opportunity to India for trading with other member countries. We may be able to export our goods and services to other countries with less restrictions from those countries.

It is expected that the technology from developed countries will be available to India at a reduced cost.

Since major share of world trade is taking place among the developed countries themselves, the benefit of being a member of WTO to the developing countries, particularly to India, is very limited.

Many of the present wto rules are biased against the developing countries. They are designed to force them to open their economies in the interest of developed countries. In India, it is feared that many industries may not be able to compete those international enterprises and survive, and are, thus, facing closure. This may reduce employment opportunities for our workers.

It is alleged that WTO is being used by the developed countries to support globalisation in areas that are not directly related to trade. As such, they interfere in the management of the domestic economy of a country. For instance, certain clauses in WTO agreement on agriculture put restrictions on the provision of subsidised food grains in India.

It is also feared that once India abides by the rules and regulations of WTO, the prices of many essential and life-saving drugs may go up.

World Trade Organisation is the largest and most comprehensive trade agreement in the history of International Trade, owing to the following facts and realities:

1. Raising Standards of Living.
2. Ensuring Full Employment.
3. Large and steadily growing volume of real income and effective demand.
4. Expanding Production and Trade in goods and Services.
5. Allowing for the optional use of the World's resources in accordance with the objective of sustainable development, seeking both to protect and preserve the environment and enhance the means for doing so in a manner consistent with their respective needs and concerns at different levels of economic development.

Further, to end local pessimism and acceleration of the path of global optimism depends upon the following factors:

* It has been observed that even where the Institutional underpinnings of a market system are weak, consistent policies, including liberalisation of markets, trade and the entry of new business, and reasonable price stability, can achieve a great deal.

* Country differences are important - "big bang" versus "gradualism" misses the point - What is required, are consistent reforms with a critical mass of support.

* Clear Intellectual Property Rights are required for an efficient response to Market processes and this will eventually require widespread Private Ownership.

* Major changes in Social Policies are needed to complement the move to the market to focus on relieving poverty, to cope with increased labour mobility, and to address the effects of reforms on the very young and the elderly; and

* Liberalisation and Stabilisation provide mechanism for economic growth, while economic growth in itself is

a means to meet the end of human development. Hence, the WTO bears an obligation to regulate the Trade Policies of Member-States.

It has been observed in the past that Outcome Oriented approach is the root cause of Trade War and creates conflict among States, while the Rule Oriented Approach is a sine qua non of global peace, Welfare and economic growth. The most important task and objective of WTO is to enhance the rule-oriented approach of World Trade.

World Trade Organisation (WTO) is a significant step for pulling out the developing countries from the paradoxical rapture of "No rule situation" on access to the International market, ensuring their comparative advantages and better Competitive Environment. It has taken almost 50 years to have such an organisation, after International Trade Organisation (ITO), the proginitor of the GATT failed to take off in 1947.

On 1st Janaury, 1995, the Marrakesh Agreement Establishing the WTO, entered into force. The Uruguay Round which started in 1986 ultimately consumated in 1995.

The establishment of the WTO places the International Trading System on a firm constitutional footing. For the first time, the pillars of the International Trading System rest on a full fledged International Organisation, with an International Legal personality.

The Marrakesh Agreement establishing the WTO sets out the purpose and objectives of the WTO and its institutional framework. The primary purposes of the WTO are two fold:

(i) to ensure the reduction of tariffs and other barriers to trade: and

(ii) the elimination of discriminatory treatment in International Trade relations.

The WTO is to ensure these primary purposes in order to facilitate in the economies of member State, higher standard of living, full employment, a growing volume of real income and effective demand, and an expansion of production and trade in goods and services. These National objectives corresponds to those of the International Monetary Fund (IMF) i.e. (i) the optimum use of World's Resources, (ii) Account must be taken of the need for sustainable development and protection and preservation of environment; and (iii) the objectives are to be pursued so as to ensure that Developing Countries, especially the Least Developed Countries (LDCs), obtain a level of share in the growth of International Trade that reflects the need of their economic development.

The following are the main functions of WTO:

1. The WTO provides a substantive Code of Conduct directed at the regulation of tariff and other barriers to trade, and the elimination of discrimination in International Trade Relations.
2. The WTO provides the Institutional framework for the administration of both all past trade agreements and the agreements under Uruguary Round of Trade Negotiations.
3. The WTO ensures the implementation of the substantive Code. It provides a forum for Dispute Settlement in International Trade matters, and conducts surveillance of National Trade Policies and Practices, and
4. The WTO acts as a medium for the conduct of International Trade Relations amongst member States. Particularly, it is to act as a forum for the negotiations of further Trade liberalisation, and improvement in the International Trading System.

The process of decision making in WTO is democratic, through consensus and voting. Voting on any issue may be through a show of Hands. Thus, there are three points particular to note, so for, the functions of the WTO are concerned:

(i) It is not clear what constitutes an "inter-pretative" decision.

(ii) The Authority to interpret the agreements is vested in the political organs; and

(iii) Interpreting the WTO normative framework is complex, involving a variety of sources as aids to interpretation.

However, there are a number of stress points at the level of basic constitution of WTO:

1. The purpose and objectives of the WTO are arguably limited in scops.
2. The WTO does not appear to have any effective mechanism to ensure that the development of International Trade Regulation in future will be responsive to the needs of the International Trading System (ITS) as objectively determined, rather than as defined by the influence of International lobbyists.
3. It is contended that the WTO, when seen as independent of the valuation of its membership, has a fairly rudimentary International personality.
4. The creator of the WTO has not been negotiated de novo but has emerged rather from the GATT. Owing to that WTO inherits some of the short-comings of the former GATT.

Basic Philosophy of the World Trade Organisation

The basic philosophy of the WTO covers the following aspects:

1. To open Markets,
2. Non-discrimination,
3. Most Favoured Nation,
4. National Treatment,
5. Global Competition, and
6. Rule Based International Trade Approach.

The rule Based System of International Trading System creates: global peace, prosperity and equal distribution of income. It highly assesses the counter-hegemonic role of the WTO to weed out protectionism, unilateralism, and monopolisation over

International Trade and Market. Likewise, WTO is considered as a significant step drowning-out the developing countries from the paradoxical rapture of "no rule situation" on access to the international market, ensuring their comparative advantages and better competitive environment.

Functions of World Trade Organisation

Following are the main functions of the WTO:

- Administrative Functions.
- It is a Platform for Negotiations.
- It is a Executionery Authority.
- It is a Administering Trade Policy Review Mechanism.
- Economic Coherence Function.

Developing Countries under WTO for Market Access

The WTO embodies a much stronger enforcement/dispute settlement mechanism than what existed under GATT. Trade Liberalisation has been an important component of economic reform programme undertaken by the developing countries. The Uruguay Round of Trade Negotiations was aimed at liberalising the World Trading Environment and thereby providing improved access to the Member Countries. The WTO since its establishment in 1995, has been enforcing various aggreements that were concluded in the Uruguay Round. As part of the agreement on Market Access, the Member Countries have made offers of reductions in the Tariff and NTBs to trade.

The implications of these offers of Trade Liberalisation depend upon the nature of the reduction in the barriers and the scope of the coverage of goods included in these offered packages. A detailed analysis of these implications is essential to understand the nature of the benefits and the costs accruing to the Member Countries. Such an analysis would-be of a great help to the developing countries in their task of identifying the strategies required to take advantage of the emerging opportunities of the New Trading Environment.

The Developing Countries (DCs) first of all have to understand whether the implementation of the present set of agreements of WTO has, in practice, really contributed to the expected improvement of Market Access to their Export Products or not. The Developing Countries have also to prepare balance sheet of the Market Access that they have gained in the Developed Countries in relation to the extent of the Market Access which they have offerred to the other Trade partners.

We know that in the Uruguay Round of the GATT, member countries agreed to the following points:

1. To provide tariff Liberalisation on a large number of Commodities/items; and
2. To remove all types of prohibitions or restrictions.

For Tariff Liberalisation, member countries submitted to the World Trade Organisation the "offer rates", also called "bound level" or "bound rate of duty", for agreed, commodities/items. The Member Countries are required to maintain the applied rate at or below the "bound rates". India has agreed to make adjustments in tariff rates to the level of "bound rates" for more than 3300 commodities.

We know that previously, India was having a Plan to phase out Quantitative Restrictions (QRs) on all commodities except for around 600 commodities by 2002-2003. Now, as per the recent report of the Appellate Body of WTO, India have to advance its phase out Plan to the end of 2000. Thus, India has to assess the position, whether the Developed Countries have given concessions for products where it has the Comparative Advantages.

India's Commitments in the WTO

The Government of India levies mainly two types of Customs duties on the goods imported into India i.e. the Basic Customs Duty' (BCD); and Additional Customs Duty (ACD). The Basic Duty rates are also called the "Scheduled Rates of Basic Customs, Duty," which in turn are known as *"Statutory rates".* There are two main categories of scheduled rates i.e. the standard rate and the preferential rate. The negative list of imports consists of three main categories as under:

(i) Prohibited;

(ii) Restricted; and

(iii) Canalised Items.

The UNCTAD has identified and defined the different types of trade Control Measures as under:

Tariff Measures

Statutory Customs Duties.

MFN Duties.

GATT Ceiling Duties.

Tariff Quota Duties:-

Low Duties

High Duties.

Seasonal Duties

Temporary Reduced Duties

Temporary Increased Duties:

Retaliatory Duties

Urgency and Safeguard Duties.

Preferential Duties under Trade Agreements.

Tariff Measures n.e.s.

Para - Tariff Measures

Customs Surcharges

Additional Charges

Internal Taxes and Charges Levied on Imports.

Decreased Customs Valuation.

Para-Tariff measures n.e.s.

Price Control Measures

Administrative Pricing
Minimum Import Prices.
Administrative Pricing n.e.s.
Voluntary Export Price Restraint
Variable Charges.
Anti-dumping Measures
Counter-vailing Measures.
Price Control Measures n.e.s.

Finance Measures

Advance Payment Requirements
Multiple exchange rates.
Restrictive Official Foreign Exchange Allocation.
Regulations Concerning Terms of Payment for Imports.
Transfer delays, Queuing.
Automatic Licensing Measures n.e.s.

Automatic Licensing Measures

Automatic Licence.
Import Monitoring.
Surrender Requirement.
Automatic Licensing Measures n.e.s.

Quantity Control Measures

Non-Automatic Licensing.
Quotas.
Prohibitions.
Export Restraint Arrangements:
Export restraint arrangements on Textiles outside MFA.
Enterprise-Specific Restrictions.
Quntity Control measures n.e.s.

Monopolistic Measures

Single Channel for Imports.

State Trading Administration.

Sole Importing Agency.

Single Channel for Imports for Sensitive Product Categories.

Compulsory National Services.

Monopolistic Measures n.e.s.

Technical Measures

Technical Regulations

Product Characteristics Requirements.

Marketing Requirements.

Labelling Requirements.

Packaging Requirements.

Testing, Inspection and Quarantine Requirements.

Technical Measures n.e.s.

Miscellaneous Measures

Marketable Permits for Sensitive Product Categories

Public Procurement for Sensitive Product Categories.

Voluntary Instrument for Sensitive Product Categories:

Product Standards

Eco-labelling

Voluntary Agreements or Covenants.

Product Liability For Sensitive Product Categories.

Subsidies for Sensitive Product Categories.

India's Export prospects with the Major Trading Partners

It has been observed that since the singing of the Final Agreement on the GATT in December, 1994 at Marrakesh, the Indian Export Sector has been facing more of challenges than opportunities from the Global Trading System. The major issues which are now emerging before India's Exports are:

- To identify the major products, which India is exporting to the Major Trading Partners at 6 digit HS Level.
- Demand for Indian exports in the Major Trading Partners Markets.
- To assess the Market Share and value to trade in these Markets.
- The evaluation of Price Competitiveness of Indian Exports in MTP's Markets.
- To assess the Increased Market exposure, under assumption, if India, keeps the export prices at the lowest/competitive level.
- It has been observed that even the recent Export-Import policy for the year 2000-2001 do not venture into the area of production. It does not support the economy to face the challenges by having closer integration with the latest development existing in the World Economy. What is radical in the Export-Import Policy is the removal of quantitative import restrictions on 714 items and the phasing out of special Import licences. This is owing to India's Membership of the WTO.
- The dispute settlement mechanism of the WTO had finally over-ruled India's appeals and required it to negotiate the phasing out of quantitative restrictions (QRS) earlier than the 2003 deadline the Commerce Ministry had earlier set for itself. After April, 2001, there would be practically no Quantitative Import Restrictions those imposed on grounds of security environment and morality. Once every commodity become importable, Special Imports Licenses Automatically will lose their relevance.
- India has extended the scope in the following areas:

- The Export Promotion Capital Goods Scheme.
- Re-introduced the Duty-free Replenishment Schemes for those sectors for which input output norms have been notified, rationalised and phased out the duty entitlement Pass-Book Scheme and its rates, simplified Export procedure, particularly in regard to applying for an export licence, which can now be obtained electronically.

  Offered some sector-specific schemes for Gems and Jewellery, leather, drugs and pharmaceuticals, agro-chemicals and the new thrust areas of bio-technology and electronic hardware.
- Export Promotions by offering them resources from a fund for the purpose of creating export-friendly infrastructure.
- The main problem is that these piece-meal measures come nowhere near adding up to a coherent strategy to tackle and solve the fundamental problems the Indian Economy has vis-a-vis trade.

India has chosen the path of imports substitution, Export Pessimism and dependence on aid for procuring the foreign Exchange needed for unavoidable imports and Debt-Service. Further, blocking out of Imports with physical controls and higher import duties has been the core of this strategy of development. Moreover, keeping out imports has also meant keeping down the exports. It has been observed that high protection make the Domestic Market, with its High Prices far more profitable than in the International Market. This automatically weakens Incentive to Export.

Further, the absence of Competition and Non-availability of Imported Inputs in a Protected regime to make for shoddy quality and high costs. This makes domestic products unsaleable in the competitive market abroad. Thus, from the Supply and the Demand side, there are only dis-incentives for exports in a highly protected market. This is the basic anti-export bias of the Indian Economy.

In such a situation, the only way to boost exports is to offer huge incentives for Indian Exporters to flog their products abroad at Cheap Prices. Some of these incentives - such as exemption from sales tax at two points of sale prior to export and exemption of export incomes from Income taxation-erode the tax base of the State Governments, making them relatively indifferent to Exports.

Now, these incentives are under pressure from the World Trade Organisation, which deem most of them actionable subsidies, calling for punitive duties in the Importing Countries. Ultimately, Trade Policy is not just about boosting exports, rather it is about re-organising all the processes of production and allocation of resources. The only way to boost exports is to make the economy more competitive across the board-by overcoming shortages of Social and Physical Infrastructures, removing lacunae in law that prevent flexible deployment and re-deployment of Capital and Labour and tightening law enforcement. Clearly, all this is well beyond the scope of the "New Trade Policy" of Government in the new Century.

Though, the WTO embodies a much stronger enforcement/ dispute settlement mechanism than what existed under the GATT. The Third Ministerial Conference of WTO at Seattle ended in failure owing to the following:

1. The members of the WTO not being able to agree on an Agenda for Millennium Round;
2. There were strong differences between the European Union (EU) and the USA on the issues relating to Agricultural Liberalisation;
3. Developing Countries were unwilling to accept inclusion of Labour Standards and Environmental Issues within the purview of the New Round; and
4. Small Countries were left completely in the cold.

Model of Trade Liberalisation for India

The last one decade of liberalisation and globalisation

policies in India has led to many visible and invisible changes in the country. Some of the visible changes are: better services in the communications sector, such as telephone facilities, availability of colour television sets and other electronic goods at low prices. Many food processing companies such as Pepsi, Coca Cola, have entered the country and taken over the market for soft drinks and some food prodcts. Some of the invisible changes in the economy are as follows:

* Indi's share in the trade of goods and services in the world has increased marginally. However, compared to other developing countries, our progress is very slow.

* Investment from other countries also known as foreign direct investment to produce goods and services in India had increased from Rs. 174 crore in 1991 to Rs. 9338 crores in 2000.

* We need foreign exchange reserves to pay for our imports. This had increased from Rs. 4822 crore in 1991 to 152924 crores in 2000.

* The price rise in 1990-91 was about 12 per cent and it has slowly/declined to around percent in the late 1990s.

* One of the objectives of the new policies is to generate employment. Though new jobs are being created in the economy. It is not sufficient to meet the increasing job

To gain and improve the Market Share in Trade, India has to do and to monitor the following things on a top priority basis:

1. Trade Policy should be development oriented, aimed on a selective basis. As a tool of development, Trade Policy is not necessarily synonymous with trade Liberalisation, and success in Liberalisation *per se* is not a guarantee of success in development.

2. Trade Policy may vary from one Country to another depending on its particular needs, objectives and socio-

economic characteristics.

3. Building up Supply Capacity and improving productivity requires selective Government Intervention in situations where no market yet exists, or the market is segmented or fails owing to the prevalence of dynamic externalities.
4. Since, resources are scarce, and all industries do not possess the same linkages and externalities, there is a need for establishing clear criteria in selecting those industries destined for development, upgrading and export expansion, particularly where, as in Least Developing Countries, the initial industrial base is very small.
5. Selective Investment Policy for building of physical assets (including infrastructure), human resource development, technological learning and innovation.
6. Selective measures to develop export intensive manufacture sectors.
7. External support in terms of finance, technical assistance and most important market access.

Baring recovery from recession in East Asia and from over all slowdown in Global Trade during the Asian Crisis. Domestic supply side constraints have not eased, though there appears to have some demand driven growth in certain sectors of the Economy. In Manufactured goods export India have done well in selected markets like the USA and Japan and to some extent in terms like iron ore, textiles and garments, Chemicals and Gems and Jewellery also To further promote the Exports Special Economic Zones (EPZs) will be converted into SEZs and 6 New ones will be set up, shortly. Success of SEZs is conditional on easing bottlenecks in infrastructure, procedures and Labour Laws. It has been concluded by the experts on Trade that an Export intensity of 10% translates an 18% Export growth which in turn contribute to Gross Domestic Product growth by 1.9%.

India and other developing countries; opposition to linking

trade and labour standards, is not so much anti-imperialism as pro-domestic business. Allowing exploitation of labour anywhere in the World undermines the rights of all workers around the World. It is possible to incorporate Labour Standards in Trade Agreements to help Workers, anywhere.

We know that the Core Conventions of International Labour Organisation (ILO) already deal with the following aspects in details:

1. The right to organise and bargain Collectively;
2. The elimination of all forms of forced or compulsory labour;
3. The abolition of Child Labour; and
4. The elimination of discrimination in employment and occupation.

Further, it is a hard reality that after a certain degree of Industrialisation, trade barriers can become a fetter to further development. Barriers to imports can make local industry technologically backward, producing lower quality commodities at higher prices than they would, if they were, exposed to International Competition and able to import technology. Barriers to Exports (that is, import barriers erected by other countries) can prevent Industries from expanding further. Moreover, for countries which have adopted an export - oriented strategy, the process of Industrialisation and the very survival of the Economy depends on access to Markets in Other Countries.

Developing Countries were expected to make substantial gains in terms of enhanced Market Access in the sectors like Textiles, Clothing and Agriculture. While restrictive practices for the removal of protectionist policies followed by developed countries in the proposed regime are limiting the market access of Developing Countries. But, in the areas like Intellectual Property Rights (IPRs) and Trade-Related Investment Measures, immediate gains could be reaped by the Developed Countries.

The proposed tarification of NTBs and reduction of levels

of Tariffs already existing in Countries is in keeping with the overall framework of the negotiations, which aim at:

(i) Progressive reduction in the Trade Barriers; and

(ii) Increased Transparency in the imposition of Trade Restrictions.

Thus, it is very clear that the Developing Countries have to evolve Institutional Mechanisms to safeguard their interests in the New Trading regime. These include mechanisms both to take advantages of the opportunities that are likely to be thrown up and those that would be essential to protect their own interests in the face of unfair Trade Practices. For Developing Countries, it may be difficult to bear the cost of making Trade Policy. Another threath to the Developing Countries from the Developed Countries/countries having marketable Surplus to Export by dumping their excess production in the developing countries. The impact of this dumping activities will be very ruinous for the Export Trade and Industries in Developing Countries.

Thus, Uruguay Round of negotiation is an ambitious endeavour with a keen sense of the profound changes taking place in the International economic landscape. This Round of Trade Negotiations has paved a perennial path drowning out monopolisation of trade policies. Some of the critics are of the opinion that it is a shift of Monopolisation of economic Power from the hands of State to the hands of Multinational Corporations (MNCs). In another words, we can say that the Whole sense of development is made ill-fated letting to the MNCs lap. While this development still contain the hope of re-distribution of Wealth and Power in favour of the Least Developed Countries (LDCs). Moreover, globalisation re-directs State action to providing better opportunities to the well-to-do in Developing Countries in their scramble for international standing.

To acquire real benefit from the WTO, irrespective of the Developed and Developing Countries, especially the Developing Countries have to change their whole pattern of State functionalism.

This is the main solution which saves from being marginalised and generates effectiveness to exploit opportunities arising from World Trade Organisation.

Further, it has been observed that the Internationalisation of Trade Rules has diffused a fundamental shift in the economic equilibrium of World, bringing all countries from all corners of the World and from all levels of development together on equal level as member of the WTO. Thus, this process of Globalisation has become undeniably irreversible. In this contest, the developed and Developing Countries, sit on an equal footing to write the rules of a Shared Trading System (STS). On this basis, even the LDCs can challenge the most powerful/Developed Country in defence of its trade interests, and not on the basis of economic power but on the basis of common and enforceable rules. We can conclude that WTO is the visible embodiment of th most profound development in International Trade where all countries have deep inter-dependence of all peoples and of all Nations.

If any country limit its economic relations, with World Exporters and Importers, that country will be limiting its possibilities to grow and achieve its commitment of Social equity after implementation of the Uruguay Round of Trade Negotiations i.e. in the WTO regime. We know that trade promotes growth of the economy by developing increased specialisation, having comparative advantage, increasing the diffusion of International knowledge and by having improved efficiency. Thus, Trade Liberalisation is a challenge and risk to the respective economy. For trade liberalisation, the states are required to remove lawlessness, obstacles to State reform, to avoid making fragmented policy making, to remove causes of corruption, and alienation from people. After the collapse of Ministerial Conference at Seattle, the WTO bureaucracy committed itself to getting member states to address some of the issues informally. Mr. Mike Moore, the Director General of WTO has also spoken of "tangible" and meaningful improvements in market access in favour of LDCs. Three commodities which are in India's interest are most distorted in World Trade. Rice is highly protected in East Asian Markets such as Japan, Korea, Philippines, Indonesia and so on.

The establishment of WTO has taken almost Fifty years since the concept of International Trade Organisation (ITO). In this process, the 8 Rounds of Trade Negotiations took place from 1947 to 1986. In 1986, the 8th Round of Trade Negotiations started, it was concluded in 1993 and on 1st January, 1995 the WTO came into existence with an International Legal personality. The primary purpose of the WTO is to ensure the reduction of tariffs, other trade Barriers and to eliminate the discriminatory treatment in International Trade relations. The process of decision making in WTO is democratic, which has been even evident from the failure of Third Ministerial Conference of WTO held at Seattle. It failed owing to the fact that the members of the WTO did not agreed on an Agenda for the Millennium Round.

Further, the spirit of the WTO agreement demands that removal of all NTBs. Raising of NTBs, will shut out Global price signals in the domestic economy. India and other Developing Countries' opposition of linking Trade and Labour Standards is not so much anti-imperialist as pro-domestic business. Being the rights of all worker around the World, it is possible to incorporate labour standard in Trade Agreements to help Workers.

With the establishment of WTO, Developing Countries were expected to make substantial gains in terms of Enhanced Market Access in the sectors i.e. Textiles, Clothing and Agriculture. While the restrictive trade practices of the Developed Countries are limiting the opportunities of Market Access to the developing countries specially LDCs.

The Developing Countries have to evolve institutional mechanism to safeguard their interests in the New Trading regime. It may be difficult for developing countries (dcs) to bear the cost of making Trade Policy. Another, threath to dcs, is of dumping surplus Exports goods by Developed Countries (DCs) in their markets. While these agreements seek to protect the interest of the present as well as future generation, under the circumstances it is obligatory on the part of India to enact laws and rules to protect environment and limit the use of energy.

Economic Impacts brings in capital from other countries.

as well as the latest technology and machinery. For instance, the information technology industry in India uses computers and other telecommunication equipment used in developed countries. About 15 years ago, this was unimaginable. The engineering graduates of some of the Indian institutions are most sought after in the USA and in many European countries. In many countries, governments own natural resources and utilise them efficiently in the interest of the people and provide them various services. Globalisation encourages the governments to privatise these resources that lead to exploitation of resources for profit motives and accumulation of wealth by the individuals privatisation also deprives those who do not have the capacity to pay to utilise these resources.

Globalisation shifts the power to regulate certain activities from governments to international institutions, which are indirectly controlled by multinational companies. For instance, when a country is engaged in the business activities of other countries, its government makes agreements with respect to those countries separately. These agreements differ from country to country. Now, international organisations, such as World Trade Organisation, frame rules and regulations for all countries and the governments have to enforce these rules and regulations in their respective countries. In addition, globalisation compels many governments to change legislation and constitution to facilitate the private sector. Governments often are compelled to do away with certain rules and regulations that safeguard the rights of working people and environment. Globalisation also brings about changes in the structure of the family. The joint family was the norm in the past. This has been replaced by nuclear family. Our eating habits, festivals, ceremonies have also gone under tremendous change.

REFERENCES

Daniel C. Esty, *Greening the GATT: Trade, Environment, and the Future,* Institute for International Economics, Washington, D.C., July, 1994.

Harry P. Bowen, Anbrahan Hollender and Jean - Marie Viaene, *Applied International Trade Aalysis,* Macmillan Press Ltd., 1998.

Surendra Bhandari, *World Trade Organisation (WTO). and Developing Countries*, Deep & Deep Publications Pvt. Ltd., 1998.

Dr. Dev Raj, *Economic Development: A Critical Appraisal of GSP,* Anmol Publications Pvt. Ltd., New Delhi, 1990.

2

Policy and Impact of World Trade Organization (WTO)

This chapter we will discuss what these terms need for such a till in policies, and how they were initiated, also discuss about World Trade Organization (WTO), which is one of the most important organizations that influences the implementation of new policies and their impact on the Indian economy. The Government has been following the policy of Liberalization, privatization and globalization since 1991. New policy regime took shape in the 1980s. Its main features were: deregulation of industries, decontrol of prices, liberalization of imports, tax reductions and increase in deficit spending. The contours of this policy regime had emerged immediately after the 1974 low conditionality IMF loan. But the ingredients of this policy seemed temporary as the Janata government tried in vain to modify the pat of development. In any case, it did not crystallize into a coherent package until 1982. The new package was instituted with the IMF loan in 1980 and consolidated in 1985. The logic behind this approach was that the industries which were critically important for the economy, such as coal mining, steel, power and roads, should be retained by the government. It was felt that the government control of critical industries would provide necessary resources to undertake developmental activities in different segments of the economy. The private sector was allowed to establish industries and business enterprises, but was subject to controls and regulations that came in the form of laws. This was also considered necessary, so that resources and wealth would not get concentrated n a few hands. Public sector, the government invested a considerable share of its revenues and started many public sector enterprises. The government outlay in these enterprises increased from Rs. 81.1 crore during the First Five year plan period (1951-56) to Rs. 34,200 crore during the Ninth five Year Plan period (1997-2002). The purpose behind this strategy was to eliminate poverty, reduce inequalities in the distribution of income and wealth and achieve economic growth with social justice. The continued mobilization of resources led to a situation where India's public sector became very large. Substantial proportion of government revenue went mostly in financing these public sector enterprises, rather than for other developmental purposes.

Bureaucracy and Development

The subject, Administrative Challenges of Planning and Development is of profound significance both for the academic seeking to unravel the developmental phenomenon in societies inhabited by nearly two-thirds of the world's total population and for the country as a whole. At the same time, the subject is multi-dimensional, being amenable to discussion from a variety of angles and perspectives. While not underrating the validity and worth of such disquisitions, the present chapter chooses a somewhat sharp though narrow focus; it seeks to address itself to questions, such as what peculiar challenges public administration in general, and bureaucracy in particular, are likely to face in India in the context of development as embodied in the nation's most authentic developmental blueprint, namely the Fifth Five Year Plan. One should, therefore, turn to the latter to gain a more stable appreciation of the changes demanded in, and challenges encountered by the bureaucracy as well as by the larger political system. The official document entitled "Approach to Fifth Plan (1974-1979)" made only a passing mention of public administration as a factor for consideration in determining the size of the plan including the scale of activities proposed to be taken up during the five-year period. This should be somewhat amazing. As the country has carried out five five-year plans, it is expected of this document to reflect the major experience gained since the launching in

1950, of the First Five Year Plan. Experience has invariably shown that public administration itself has been a severe limiting factor in the implementation of our successive plans. Indeed, as public administration has emphatically emerged as the dominant pipe-line for the carrying out of the policies and programmes, its revealed deficiencies, shortcomings and inadequacies in this respect ought to be of concern to all, more so to the planners themselves. Although the plan document makes a brief mention of this in its concluding part, it is more of a postscript or a tailpiece than an integrated thought. It observes: "An antiquated structure and the leisurely procedures are incompatible with the fulfilment of the plan tasks. Attention needs to be given towards evolving an administrative set-up and modes of functioning which can meet the challenge of the plan. Professionalism in administration must be promoted. The administrator must have capability and the initiative to provide active leadership rather than merely react to the views and actions of others. He must be accountable for results. There is need for visible improvement in the management and operation of the public sector."

Evidently, the plan document does not appear to bestow sufficient thought on administrative imperatives and implications of what it sets out to outline as the basic objectives of the fifth plan. It mostly takes public administration for granted while formulating them; it is assumed that the various objectives visualised in the plan are capable of being accomplished by the existing machinery of public administration. It tends to overlook—or, at any rate, does not recognise—that public administration itself might be a limiting factor in development and could be one of the scarcest resources. Implementability does not seem to be its concern; it has, for that matter, hardly bothered earlier plans either. Not very incorrectly, we as a nation, are sometimes accused of trying to bite more than we can chew!

Inadequacy of the administrative input in the plan could perhaps be explained, to a degree, by the background of the top planners and the highly selective consultation which *Yojana Bhawan* engages in with outside expertise. The Planning Commission is an experts' body, but it includes within its own fold but one kind of expertise—that is, economics. While it is unquestionably true that the economic component of our plan should necessarily be very large, the plan is evidently much more inclusive in its range and character. There are, in addition, distinct administrative, political and sociological dimensions of the plan as well, to mention only a few. The Planning Commission should have, therefore, consciously set out to seek the contribution which these disciplines too are capable of making. None of them has ever found any representation on the Planning Commission. While there has been a panel of economists to advise the Commission on economic aspects of the plan there is none seeking the counsel of other social scientists—political scientists (including students of public administration), sociologists, etc. Not unnaturally, this imparts an impression that there is an absence of awareness in the *Yojana Bhawan* of the possible contribution which these disciplines may make and of its own internal inadequacy in regard to the knowledge in these social sciences in general and public administration in particular. There are, to be sure, professional administrators on the staff of the Planning Commission. But they, as a rule, do not—nor are they expected—to *advise* on the administrative input of the plan. Similarly, the politicians have been associated with the Planning Commission but they, as a class, remain ineviatably engrossed in or pre-occupied with matters relating to the day-to-day politics. At any rate, being practitioners, their almost total passion for individual trees prevents them from acquiring a complete and objective view of the forest, *i.e.*, the social and political system. Those who are outside the wood and have been given to studying it in depth and in a perspective gain a fuller view of the forest than the pure practitioners who are in it.

Nevertheless, the inescapable truth is that no political executive may expect to accomplish more than its public administration permits it to do: it is too much on its part to move much beyond its public administration. Such a realization does not seem to be entirely non-existent in the Government—at least on certain occasions. The Prime Minister, while chiding her partymen for vying with one another in what came to be known as 'competitive radicalism,' queried: "Where is the organisational structure and administrative set-up to implement a more radical policy?" C. Subramaniam, the then Planning Minister, similarly asked: "The question is how far we are in a position to implement a more ambitious plan." Thoughts like these have not become an enduring consideration in determining the scale, variety and pace of our future planning, effort and at the same time compelling us to initiate timely measures calculated to raise and diversify administrative leadership and capability.

The challenging tasks of the 7th plan make exacting demands on public administration, much more on the country's polity. The plan demands total political support and discipline regardless of federal boundaries. Although the present paper is focussed on the administrative aspects of the plan, mention here must be made of the dependence, in multiple ways and in varying intensities, of public administration on the larger system of polity. The political leadership must set an example to others by its devotion to public interest, integrity, hard work, sincerity of purpose, austerity and firmness. As the government in a welfare state inevitably emerges as perhaps the biggest spender of money and dispenser of favours, and an elite glued to these propensities mushrooms threatening to render socialism a topic of public discussion but an instrument of private benefits. This ought to be guarded against. The political leadership must spell out clearly what it would like to accomplish, and in this articulation there must not be left any room for ambiguity or ambivalence. One may also suggest a suitable strengthening, both qualitative and quantitative, of the political wing of the government. Each ministry should have, in addition to the minister, a few junior ministrs, depending upon the nature, variety and volume of work. The political leadership should, with crusader's zeal, address itself to the task of laying down, in full consultation with the civil service, clearly defined policies, preparing time-bound programme compatible with these policies, and overseeing their implementation in accordance with the time-schedule. The point regarding need for utmost clarity in the enunciation of policies cannot be overemphasised. It is fairly well known by now that not much headway could be made in implementing the – much –talked-about land reforms in the country, the failure for this lying not as much in administrative ineptitude as political indecisiveness, irresolution or—which is even more probable—disbelief in the professed programmes themselves. At the same time, public administration can be expected to remain efficient and sensitive to popular aspirations only when it remains under constant political surveillance, control and guidance.

Full realisation of the objectives laid down in the plan document depends, in decisive way, upon the competence, participation and co-operation of all three levels of government in the country—the central, the state as well as the local governments. Although this should look self-evident—it is the age of co-operative federalism—its special mention is absolutely necessary in the present paper in view of not sufficient attention having been bestowed on this aspect in the past. It is absolutely necessary that each plan is firmly backed by an appropriate administrative plan detailing measures of strengthening of the administrative apparatus of the land.

The state level public administration is necessarily to be called upon to bear the brunt of the new tasks, and therefore, will have to be considerably strengthened, both in terms of quality and quantity, so that it becomes as apt instrument for undertaking programmes of development. A series of measures are imoerative; the states are well advised to scan the reports of the nearly twenty administrative reforms committees, set up by them from time to time since 1947, and to see that the urgent reforms are swiftly carried out. The well-known tenure system which operates rather erratically at present needs to be enforced more systematically. Not only should a civil servant coming to the central government on a tenure revert to the state (or, service) on his posting after completion of his spell of duty, the tenure system should also be applied in an orderly way within a state itself, ensuring regular exchange of personnel between the field and the headquarters. Meaningful training in programmes should be organised for state level personnel in various areas to improve their functional proficiency.

Nor should reform of local governments—rural as well as urban –remain shelved, as has generally happened in most states so far. Local government will necessarily have to be involved more meaningfully, more closely and more widely in the efforts at development. It would be good if the states go through the various reports, about twenty in number, having bearing on this subject and quickly implement the necessary reforms.

The seventh Plan more than any that has preceded it, demands a wide range of expertise, and skills in public administration. To recruit persons possessing these and to place them in positions without loss of time, suitable structural changes in the civil service would seem urgently called for. A much larger number of experts and specialists will necessarily have to be inducted into the civil service and their role and place in the generalists-dominated syndrome of bureaucracy has to be appropriately reorganised.

Measures towards enhancement of administrative capabilities at all levels of government and all along the hierarchy must be formulated and put in operation *right now* without any further waiting.

Stress may here be laid on the need for experts and specialists acquiring administrative experience and training to enable them to move into positions of administrative responsibilities in various areas and levels of government.

Bureaucracy, at any rate, a considerable segment of it is under an inescapable obligation to inculcate a disposition towards work in the field—more especially in the rural areas and amongst the vulnerable sections of the population. The rural and the social administrator bears a crucially important responsibility in putting through the various programmes of action. This demands structural and procedural changes in public administration and attitudinal changes in the bureaucracy. A broadening of the social base of the latter would also seem necessary.

As the plan calls for financial resources on an unprecedented scale, the extractive function of public administration—collection of taxes—is to be simultaneously accorded the highest importance. Tax administration at all the three levels of government must needs be streamlined and all possible loopholes—a more appropriate expression would be manholes—be plugged. Also, the prevalent system of financial control, which is evidently out of tune with the needs of a developing economy, stands in need of reform.

Popular urges and aspirations must be continually led into public administration at all levels. Significant in this regard is the need for increased and more meaningful participation of citizens and interest groups in the processes of governmental policy-making and its implementation.

Not the least pressing is the need for economy in public administration. Only one instance might suffice to indicate the gravity of the problem. The expenditure on Administrative services of the Central Government alone was Rs. 21.3 crores in 1950-51; it rose to Rs. 58.7 crores in 1960-61 and Rs. 75.2 crores in 1962-63. It would, thus, be seen that during the period 1950-51 to 1960-61, it galloped by no less than 27.5 percent. This expenditure, registered an increase of as much as 28 percent in just two years—1960-61 to 1962-63. Need a democratic government of one of the poorest countries in the world be necessarily so costly? The National Development Council at one time suggested that the growth of administrative expenditure on tax-collection general administration, etc., should be so controlled as not to exceed five percent per annum. In a sense, it looks rather tropical that the approach paper was published before the third pay commission submitted its report. The third pay commission has announced increase in pay of the central public personnel (including army personnel), which would, almost certainly set in motion similar demands on the part of the government personnel.

Finally and most importantly, political skill and administrative energy should be ceaselessly directed to convert what has been called 'soft state' into 'hard state'. As Gunnar Myrdal observes: "This stands out as significant feature among other conditions that together make a country underdeveloped. Without more social discipline, development will meet great difficulties and, in any case, be delayed. The term 'soft state' is understood to comprise all the various types of social indiscipline which manifest themselves by deficiencies in legislation and in particular law observance and enforcement, a widespread disobedience by public officials on various levels to rules and directives handed down to them, and often their collusion with powerful persons and groups of persons whose conduct they should regulate. Within the concept of the soft state belongs also corruption. These several patterns of behaviour are interrelated in the sense that they permit or even provoke each other in circular causation having cumulative effect."

The present chapter is concluded in the hope and expectation that the administrative aspects, issues and implications of an enterprise would me more carefully analysed and taken care of in the Five Year Plans. This is no less heroic task. Historically, this country has almost always tended to underestimate administration and overestimate objectives, thus lacking faculty to match the two.

Committees for Administrative Reforms

Jha committee reported in the possible scope for replacing direct measures of industrial control by indirect fiscal measures; another Narsimham Committee on industrial licencing and controls pleaded for the simplification of licensing procedures and relaxation of price controls; that on the monetary and credit policy argued in favour of the monetarist rule of a steady growth in money supply; the committee on the black economy showed the link between unreported income, tax evasion and controls; enquiries into the import and export policy considered import restrictions as important bottle-necks of industrial growth and exports and suggested the substitution of physical controls by tariffs for a 'growth-led exports' scenario; and investigations into the public sector suggested that the public sector should conform to the management practices of the private sector. These committees emphasized that the tax structure had become too complex to be effectively implemented, taxes were pitched too high to be realized, administrative controls were too unrealistic to be accepted by the pubic. and the industrial licensing system had become too discretionary to be relevant. They pointed out that the policy regime had become cumbersome and generated black income, and the industrial licensing system and bureaucratic discretion acted as important barriers to industrial growth. These committees also stressed that the public sector, initially designed to create the means of industrialization (power, transport and machines), had not only exhausted its potential, but had also become bureaucratized to the point of constraining industrial growth. It was resource-intensive without the capacity to modernize technology or generate surpluses. Instead of creating the conditions for a self-reliant and self-sustained process of industrial growth, the public sector, it was argued, had become a drag on the economy.

In sum, these committees provided the necessary building blocks for the new economic policy. By 1985 a powerful academic opinion also emerged against the policy regime of controls and regulations. The discussions on the post-1966 industrial slow-down converged on one aspect, namely, that economic development was inefficient in the sense that the returns on investment were inadequate. The low growth rte of national output, despite a high rate of investment, was attributed to the high capital-output ratio, which implied economic inefficiency. Isher Ahluwalia (1985) and I.G. Patel forcefully argued that the stagnant-high cost-inefficient syndrome was mainly fostered by the regime of subsidies, controls and licences which bred an alliance between the government and various vested interests, that thrived on the exercise of arbitrary power and often operated contrary to the consideration of economic efficiency.

Influential bureaucrats and politicians echoed these: opinions, The PM's closest adviser, L.K. Jha pointed out that the absence of competition was mainly responsible for the steady worsening of the capital-output ratio as weli as the slow-down of industrial growth despite the increase in domestic capital. That technological backwardness underlay the industrial stagnation of the 1970s was hardly contested, thought the opinions differed on its causes. A cabinet minister, Vasant Sathe, launched a scathing attack against the public sector. His ire was specifically directed at tits management.

The all-round debunking of the bureaucratic approach to economic growth—through licencing and public sector planning—was accompanied by the emergence of a new technocratic/managerial elite. The Indian government had set up several institutes of management and technology in the late fifties and early sixties. These prestigious institutes turned out graduates who were willing to compete within the Indian private sector and in the world economy. They had entered the public sector as well where the professional ethics they introduced ran counter to state patronage. Thee formally trained managers and technocrats were sharply critical of bureaucratic regulations and controls. It is not fortuitous that Prime Minister Rajiv Gandhi's close friends were not politicians but classmates from the Doon School, who had become businessmen, managers in multinational corporations and advertising executives with managerial and technical skills. They symbolized the rise of professional elites. Some of them might be wheeler-dealers but the majority of them were aspiring entrepreneurs in new fields involving high technology. By the end of 1084, then, verdicts of all official committees were in favour of liberating industries form bureaucratic controls. The intellectual opinion in the country had also veered against the licence-permit raj. In early 1985, significantly enough, several of the erstwhile employees of the IMF and the World Bank became advisers in the Planning Commission, the Ministry of Finance and the Prime Minister's Secretariat. Those who still emphasized the demand constraints on industrial growth were marginalized in policy-making committees.

This strategy has helped India in creating a large industrial base and increase in industrial production. Through poverty and unemployment, which are the twin problems of our economy, have not been eliminated completely. The proportion of population living below poverty line has declined substantially. Earlier, we were importing food grains because we were not able to produce sufficiently enough for all the people. But now, we have become self-sufficient in this field. Besides, a base for export-oriented industries has also been created. India has mobilized savings and has generated its own resources for development. The educational institutions have produced a large pool of scientists and technically skilled working persons. This has helped in industrial and technological growth and self-reliance.

Industrialization did not take place as expected. For instance, when the Indian economy was highly controlled, the growth rate of industrial production was not increasing appreciably. During 1965-1980, the growth rate of industrial production declined to 4 per cent per annum as compared to 8 per cent in 1950-1965. Laws that were formulated to regulate the private sector, were said to be responsible for slow growth of industrial sector. These laws have also failed to reduce he concentration of economic power in the private sector. Corruption, lack of efficiency in work and ineffective management became common features in the public sector enterprises. Many public sector enterprises started making losses. For instance, when the government invested Rs. 18,207 core in 1980-81 towards central public sector enterprises, in lieu of making profits, they incurred losses to the tune of Rs. 203 crore. It was also found that the official machinery, which was created to regulate and run the private sector smoothly had become a major hindrance to its development.

Reforms only the negative aspects that triggered the need for a change in policy, but also several other problems like rising prices, shortage of adequate capital, slow economic development and technological backwardness contributed to it. Government expenditure far exceeded its revenue. By 1991, our borrowings from abroad increased to such a level, that we were finding difficulty in paying even the interests; and we were not able to pay for imports. We had arrived at a severe financial crunch. This financial crisis forced the Indian government to borrow money from international banks such as World Bank and IMF. All these led to the framing of a new policy, which is known as the New Economic Policy, that aims at putting the economy on the track of rapid economic development. The new economic policy contains three strategies – liberalization, privatization and globalization.

Liberalisation contains two components. The first is to allow private sector to run those activities which were restricted earlier only to public sector. The second is relaxation of all the rules and regulations, which had restricted the growth of the private sector earlier. Many industrial activities, which were carried out by public sector enterprises are opened to private sector also. Earlier, a large number of goods, event if they were allowed to be manufactured by private sector. Were required to get prior permission from the government. This system has been abolished for all the goods, except for these: alcohol, cigarettes, hazardous chemicals, industrial explositives, electronic aerospace, and drugs and pharmaceuticals. The number of industries reserved for public sector has been reduced from 17 to 3. Now, private sector can also enter in core industries like iron and steel, electricity, air transport, ship-building, heavy machinery and some defence goods. The private sector has been freed from many regulations such as (a) licensing, (b) permission to import raw materials, (c) regulation on price and distribution, and (d) restriction on investment by large business companies. In fact, many formalities have been simplified to facilitate industrialists to produce goods in India.

Globalisation means integration our economy with the world economy. In this process, we become economically interdependent at the global or international level. This takes place at various levels. Many producers from outside the country can sell their goods and services in India. We can also produce goods and services and sell them in other countries. Globalisation also facilitates those who have capital to establish enterprises in India, produce goods for sale within the country. Or export them in the same way, entrepreneurs from India also can go and invest in other countries. Globalisation includes movement of not only capital, but labourers from one country to other country as well.

Earlier, the Indian government had put restrictions on import of goods to protect domestic producers. These restrictions helped to attain technological capability within the country. The new policy envisages the need for relating the Indian economy with the world economy, so that the unrestricted exchange of capital, technology and experience between countries becomes possible. In pursuance of this policy, the government has removed restrictions on import of goods, reduced taxes taxes on imported goods, and encouraged investors from abroad to invest in India.

The last one decade of liberalisation and globalisation policies in India has led to many visible and invisible changes in the country. Some of the visible changes are: better services in the communications sector, such as telephone facilities, availability of colour television sets and other electronic goods at low prices. Many goof processing companies such as Pepsi, Coca Cola, have entered the country and taken over the market for soft drinks and some food products. Some of the invisible changes in the economy.

India's share in the trade of goods and services in the world has increased marginally. However, compared to other developing countries, our progress is very slow.

Investment from other countries (also known as foreign direct investment) to produce goods and services in India had increased from Rs. 174 crore in 1991 to Rs. 9338 crore in 2000.

We need foreign exchange reserves to pay for our imports. This had increased from for our imports. This had increased from Rs. 4822 crore in 1991 to Rs. 152924 crores in 2000.

The price rise in 1990-91 was about 12 per cent, and it has slowly declined to around 5 per cent in the late 1990s.

One of the objectives of the new policies is to generate employment. Though new jobs are begin created in the economy, it is not sufficient to meet the increasing job requirement in the country. The new policy has failed to generate additional employment where 75 per cent of the population live.

Though the industry has shown some growth during 1991-2001, it has not yet reached the expected level.

The Union Budget

The union budget of 1985 reduced corporate income tax

from 57.7 per cent to 52.5 per cent, lowered wealth tax more sharply, pruned welfare expenditures and abolished estate duty altogether. It raised the exemption limit for personal taxation from Rs. 15,000 to Rs. 18,000, reduced the personal income tax rate by about 25 per cent, abolished the compulsory deposit scheme, which was introduced in 1974, and eliminated the licence fee for radios and TVs. These changes implied a large budgeted deficit, which was covered through borrowing. Subsequently, the government announced the long term fiscal policy to assure stability in the tax rates. The system of industrial liensing was substantially liberalized with a view to removing entry barriers and achieving economies of scale. These changes centered on redefining big business, delicensing, broad banding and automatic capacity expansion. The MRTP limits were raised to Rs. 100 crores of assets, beyond the expectations of industrialists. Twenty-live broad categories of industries, including electrical machinery, electronic components, machine tools and industrial machinery and eighty-two bulk drugs and related drug formulations were delicensed. Twenty-two industries, such as pig iron, air compressors and internal combustion engines, were delivensed for MRTP/FERA companies, provided they were willing to locate such industries in backward areas. MRTP companies were allowed to directly obtain licenses for twenty-seven industries without being subject to the provisions of the MRTP Act. Within the licensing regime, broad banding of product-mix was allowed for twenty eight industry groups. This provision was intended to facilitate diversification of industrial production. Capacity was allowed to expand automatically by one-third per year. Greater expansion in capacity was allowed in cases where economies of scale were possible. Controls were lifted for new or additional capacity in non-industry districts. The licensing procedure was simplified in instances of capacity expansion of up to 49 per cent arising from modernization. In respect of electronics, liberal imports of technology and foreign collaboration were allowed, with no limits on capacity in the non-consumer sector. A new textile policy removed long-standing constraints on textile production, especially of synthetic fabrics, by the mill sector. A new textile policy removed long-standing constraints on textile production, especially of synthetic fabrics, by the mill sector.

Trade barriers were lowered to stimulate exports and update technology. Imports of capital goods, raw materials and technology were liberalized by including hem in the open general licence (OGL) list. In the case of capital goods for projects, customs duties were drastically slashed from 105 per cent to 45 per cent ad valorem, with even sharper cuts for power (25 per cent) and fertilizer projects (reduced to nil). In respect of electronics, not only were the upper limits of imports raised substantially, but an open door policy of foreign investment was also declared. Export duties were removed on several commodities (such as iron ore, manganese ore and cotton). The 1985 budget also gave tax exemption to 50 per cent of the profits from exports. And the import-export trade policies were announced for a period of three years, long enough to assure the business community that the new policy regime was durable.

The NEP, it should be emphasized, was not a new policy package. It was a continuation of the liberalization policies initiated in 1974. Nevertheless, it marked an intensification of those policies and included several others affecting a wide range of economic activities. On the whole, it signaled a coherent economic design aimed at the restoration of market forces in determining economic activities. It implied a new recognition that the state should no longer shield public industry from competition.

The NEP in full swing sought to de-emphasize the growth of the public sector and provide an enlarged arena of operations for the private sector. Controls on industrial production and prices were either eliminated or relaxed. The planning process was diluted and market forces were allowed an increasing role in the allocation of the country's investible resources. The public sector was also whittled down. Its major component was delinked from the budgetary support, and a nascent segment with the new political patronage was integrated into the private sector, including the foreign sector as in the case of Maruti Udyog. In order to enable the further growth of the private sector, additional resources were to be made available through reduction in corporate taxes and expansion of the capita market. Technological backwardness was sought to be compensated through imports. The industrial policy of delivensing was, therefore, combined with a vigorous drive to import technology. Although these trends had been unfolding since 1981, they culminated into a radical departure in 1985. The FICCI welcomed the NEP with open arms.

The union and left politicians vehemently criticized the NEP. They opposed it because it gave short shirt to the public sector and opened the door for multinational corporations.

The NEP meant a continuation of the process of downgrading the public sector begun in 1966. This process was accelerated in 1977 when the price preference of the public sector vis-à-vis the private sector in biding for contracts was withdrawn; in 1980 its budgetary support was snapped and, subsequently, its claim on loans at lower rates of interest was discarded. In the mid-eighties, even the Planning Commission became niggardly in allocating resources towards its expansion. In its day-to-day functioning it was forced to conform to the management practices of the private sector, in line with the recommendations of the Arjun Sengupta committee (1984). (The prominent recommendations of this committee were: greater autonomy and accountability defined by 'Memorandum of Understanding,' uniform wages linked with productivity, 'golden handshake' to workers on their retrenchment when perpetual loss-making units close down, appointing directors and chief executives for a period of five years, reorganization in 'holding companies' and so on. Although all recommendations of this committee were not implemented, yet they became the reference points for improving the performance of public sector units.) The state had clearly changed its thrust; from the earlier entrepreneurial strategy focused on expansion and growth of the public enterprises to a managerial approach centered on consolidation and efficiency. An important implication of the NEP was the shift in the pattern of planned investment. Until the Sixth Plan, the allocation of the public sector had been higher than that of the private sector. This was reversed for the first time in the Seventh Plan; the share of public sector investment in total planned outlays declined from 53 per cent in the Sixth Plan to 48 per cent in the Seventh Plan. Nevertheless, it is noteworthy that the government could not go the whole hog in its attempts to subordinate the public sector, much less privatize it. The government's inability or reluctance in this respect was due to the strategic importance of the public sector and the clout of pressure groups ranged in its favour.

The size and strategic importance of public sector units as producers of machinery, intermediate products and infrastructure confer tremendous power o their managers and workers. The public sector moves like a leviathan in he Indian economy. Even excluding railways, communications, air transport, defence enterprises and financial institutions, it had 48 units amongst the 100 largest companies ranked according to sales in 1984-85; it controlled 93 per cent of the paid-up capital, 80 per cent of net assets, 74 per cent of sales and 76 per cent of profits before tax. The paid-up capital of just one public enterprise, SAIL, was more than three-and-a-half times that of the top52 private companies taken together; the sales of Indian Oil corporation and ONGC were nearly equal to he aggregate sales of the same top 52 private companies.

More than its size, the public sector was significant for its state-building role. Its role was perceived as:

(1) Preventing the penetration and domination of the economy by multinational corporations.

(2) Transforming the agro-based industrial sector to a well-diversified, sophisticated and complex industrial system.

(3) Advancing political autonomy.

(4) Contributing to investment in technology adaptation and development.

(5) Promoting social justice by serving as a model employer through better and inflation-indexed wages and job security, setting up units in backward areas and reserving jobs for scheduled castes and tribes

In his detailed study of the political economy of the public sector, Baldev Raj Nayar (1990) shows that by 1985 the pressure groups in support of the public sector had become too powerful to be dislodged. The employees of the public sector constituted one such group. Their numerical strength is more than 90 lakhs, constituting 53 per cent of all workers in the organized sector. One of their segments (central government non-departmental commercial enterprises) has 21 lakh workers whose economic and political interests are linked by virtue of their facing a common employer. Their wages and benefits are determined by the bargaining which takes place between the government, generally at the highest level, and the apex trade unions. The bargaining process is indeed a great unifier of fragmented trade unions of public enterprises. In this sense, trade union activity at the national level is virtually dominated by the public sector unions. As a matter of fact, a Joint Action Front consisting of all non-congress trade unison organized a 75-day strike in 1981 in Bangalore which involved 125,000 workers one the issue of 'linkage clause', whereby concessions granted to workers in one public enterprise are claimed by those in others as well. Centralised decision-making obviously enhances the power of trade unions in the public sector. Managers do not have the authority to deal with the collective demands of workers, which are regarded as policy matters. Therefore, the former buy peace by appeasing labour. These conditions have created a 'labour aristocracy' n 'high wage is lands' with much greater job security as compared to the workers in the private sector. The public sector workers not only earn more, but their real income has also increased at an annual rate of 5 per cent since 1975. Moreover, they get cheap accommodation, medial care and schooling for children in new townships especially constructed for public enterprises.

Given the job security, automatic promotion and attractive educational and health services of the public sector, its workers have a strong interest in preserving, if not strengthening, their privileged positions. As one of the prime beneficiaries of the system they obviously resist any erosion or deterioration in the role of the public sector.

The budgetary responsibilities of a modern government are vast and grave, for budget, to quote the often quoted Gladstone, goes "to the root of prosperity of individuals, the relations of classes, and the strength of kingdom." In the budget-making are projected the financial policy of the government, the aspirations and anxieties of its several organs. The budgetary responsibilities, strictly speaking, are not the exclusive concern of one particular ministry, however powerful it may be. All the ministries come into the picture at various stages and in varying capacities. The Indian financial codes enjoin upon the Union Executive the responsibilities for the preparation of budget estimates. The word 'budget' to be sure, does not figure at all in the Constitution of India. Article 112 of the Constitution refers to the laying of an 'Annual Financial Statement,' which is a statement of the estimated receipts and expenditure of the Government of India for the ensuing financial year. The Statement consists of three statements: (A) Statement of Revenue, (B) Statement of Expenditure, and (C) an overall Statement (Deficit or Surplus of Statements A and B; and contains other receipts from loans, Post Office Savings Banks, and National Savings Certificates. Previously, the Demands for Grants were presented to Parliament in consolidated volumes for all Ministries. From the year 1959-60, the Demands are being presented in separate volumes for individual Ministries.

There are four parts of a Demand. Part I shows the Service for which the Demand is intended and the total gross amount. Part II shows the summary of the various items of expenditure arranged under primary units of appropriation and the Ministry on whose behalf the expenditures are to be accounted. Part III gives the details of the lump sum amounts shown in Part II. Part IV is only a footnote under the Demand. As the amounts shown in Parts I, II and III, are for gross expenditure, the recoveries from other governments, *ad hoc* funds, etc., and from interdepartmental adjustments under the Demand are not brought out in the main Demand. These are shown in Part IV for the information of Parliament. But the recoveries are adjusted in accounts in reduction of expenditure. For voting purposes, gross amounts are necessary as this amount has to be taken out first from the consolidated fund for expenditure with the approval of Parliament.

Government accounts are divided into four main divisions: (1) Revenue, (2) Capital, (3) Debt, and (4) Remittance. The estimates of expenditure are divided into two parts, of which the first shows the Standing Charges, and the second part shows the Fresh Charges.

Part II of the "Introductory Note" to the "Explanatory Memorandum on the Budget of the Central Government for 1961-62" gives details of the changes introduced in accounting and budgetary structure with effect 'from the financial year 1962-63. The majo rchanges mentioned are as follows: (1) As constitutionally, there can be no direct Demand on revenue, the nomenclature of the section "Direct Demands on Revenue" (which include at present major heads concerning expenditure on collection of taxes, duties and other principal sources of Government revenues) is being changed to "Collection of Taxes, Duties and other Principal Revenue." The nomenclature of the corresponding section on the receipt side is also being changed from "Principal Heads of Revenue," (2) As the payment of States' share of Union Excise Duties is essentially a transfer of revenue from the Union to the States, these payments and receipts are adjusted under separate major heads in Section "L—Contributions and Miscellaneous Adjustments" instead as till recently under the head "2—Union Excise Duties" in the accounts of the Central Government and under "II – Union Excise Duties" in the States' section of the accounts. Duties and taxes, such as, Terminal Taxes, Entertainment Taxes, Taxes on Vehicles, etc., which are collected by the Central and State Governments and net proceeds are paid to the local bodies are, like the States' share of Union Excise Duties, also adjusted in the accounts of both Centrel and State Governments under a new major head in Section "L—Contributions and Miscellaneous Adjustments." (3) All non-statutory grants from Union to the States, being not final expenditures but merely transfer of resources from the Centre to the States, are adjusted under the major head "XLIX—Grants-in-aid from Central Government" in the State accounts and as payment under the major head "61—Grants-in-aid to the State Governments" in the Central accounts. (4) Provision for all grants to States is included in a composite demand in 1962-63 under the control of the Ministry of Finance. In the new demand the grants are shown under separate sub-heads according to the subjects to which they relate and portions there-of placed at the disposal of the administrative ministries concerned. Similarly, a separate composite demand for grants to State, debitable to Capital, is introduced in 1962-63. (5) By far the major portion of the expenditure recorded under the group head "Civil Administration" is essentially not on civil administration, but represents social and developmental services. In order, therefore to draw a clear distinction between the two categories, the group head is spilt up into two separate sections, namely, (i) Administrative Services, and (ii) Social and Development Services. The expenditure on Community Development Projects, National Extension Service and Local Development Works, which was hitherto recorded in Section "Extraordinary Items", is transferred to the new section "Social and Developmental Services." (6) The entire expenditure on labour and employment is from 1962-63 onwards, booked under a separate new major head "46—Labour and Employment," instead as until recently under the major heads "47—Miscellaneous Departments" and "57—Miscellaneous."

It may be mentioned that there is no single budget for the entire country; States have their own budgets, the Constitution being federal. Even at the Union level, there are two budgets—(i) the General Budget, and (ii) the Railway Budget. The Railway Budget was separated from the General Budget in 1921. The advantage of this arrangement is, first, that a business approach to the railway policy is facilitated, and, secondly, the railways, after paying a fixed annual contribution to the general revenue of the country, can keep their profits for their own development.

The Ministry of Finance, dealing with the financial business of the Government, has overall responsibility for framing the budget. The Finance Minister is the steward of the nation's purse. It is his paramount duty that the national finances are conducted prudently and efficiently. The Finance Ministry, responsible for raising necessary revenues for the State, must have a predominant voice in determining the amount, and, in some degree, the character of the expenditure. The Financial Rules of the Union Government confer the financial powers upon the Ministry of Finance. This arrangement has been envisaged under Article 77 (3) of the Indian Constitution, which authorised the Union President to make rules for conducting the business of the Union Government. The Finance Ministry is responsible for the preparation of the Annual Financial Statement (*i.e.,* the Budget), for piloting it through Parliament, for supervising its execution by the various departments, for collection of revenue, for giving financial control generally. This position the Finance Ministry did not always enjoy. Its control over other Ministries/Departments grew only gradually—it was, to be sure, resented in the beginning by other members of the Governor-General's Council on the ground of departmental autonomy and prestige. The gradual development of popular control over government and of parliamentary Government strengthened the position of the Finance Department. The Montford Reforms of 1919 provided for financial control by the Finance Department over other Departments. The constitution of the Public Accounts Committee of the Legislature and the appointment of Comptroller and Auditor-General to scrutinise and audit the accounts of the Departments went in the direction of enchancing the power and prestige of the Finance Department.

In the preparation of budget estimates for the ensuing financial year in India—the financial year commences on April 1, and ends on March 31—four different organs are involved—(i) the Finance Ministry, (ii) the administrative Ministries, (iii) the Planning Commission, and (iv) the Comptroller and Auditor-General.

The Finance Ministry has the overall responsibility for the framing of the budget, but it is the administrative ministries which have the detailed knowledge of administrative requirements. For incorporating the plan priorities in the Budget, the Finance Ministry has to be in close touch with the Planning commission. Also, the Comptroller and Auditor-General comes into the picture since it is he who makes available the accounting skills—so necessary for the preparation of the estimates.

The work in connection with the preparation of the budget estimates begins 6 to 8 months before the commencement of the next financial year. The initiative comes from the Finance Ministry which despatches a circular to the various administrative Ministries and departments, asking them to start preparing estimates of expenditure. The general rule is that he who spends the money must also prepare estimates for it. The 'skeleton forms' are supplied wherein the estimates and the other requisite information have to be filled in. the administrative Ministries, in turn, pass on these printed forms to the disbursing officers, *i.e.*, the heads of offices (*e.g.*, Deputy Commissioners in districts). Each form contains columns for—

(a) actuals of the previous year;
(b) sanctioned estimates for the current year;
(c) revised estimates for the current year;
(d) budget estimates of the next year; and
(e) actuals of the current year available at the time of preparation of he estimates and actuals for the corresponding period of the previous year.

The estimates of the coming year are made on the basis of–

(a) the revised estimates on the current year;
(b) the 12 months' actuals of the last and previous years;
(c) any recognisable regularity in past year's figures ; and
(d) any special circumstances causing variations.

The estimates prepared by the disbursing officers are sent to the head of the department in two parts. Part I relates to revenue and standing charges. Part II is further subdivided into two categories. In the first category figure those items which are continuing from year to year. The second category relates to entirely fresh items.

These estimates are sent to the head of department, who

consolidates them for the whole department after such review and revision as may be considered necessary. The estimates from the various departments are, then, sent to the administrative Ministry where again they are subjected to a scrutiny in the light of its general policy. The estimates are, then, passed on to the Budget Division of the Ministry of Finance, by the administrative Ministry sometime in the middle of November.

The searchlight of the Budget Division in the Finance Ministry is turned to these estimates sent by the administrative Ministry. Its scrutiny is, to be sure, different in character from that of the latter (the administrative Ministry). It does not go into the policy of the expenditure—this is, in the main, the responsibility of the administrative Ministry itself. It is mainly concerned with economy and has to keep the demands of the several administrative Departments/ Ministries within the funds available to the Government. Its scrutiny is from the financial point of view, *i.e.,* of economy and availability of funds. In carrying out this function, the Finance Ministry does not behave as an expert on the numerous proposals involving expenditure. It "possesses a traditional expertise in criticism and cross examination, born of long *experience* but continuously brought up to date. Subject to that, its attitude is somewhat that of the Intelligent layman;" it asks such questions as:

> "Is the proposed expenditure really necessary?
> If so, How have we so long done without it? Why now?
> What is done elsewhere?
> What will it cost and where from is the money to come?
> Who will go short as a consequence of it?
> Are new developments likely to render it necessary?"

It may be mentioned here that this exacting scrutiny is applied only to the proposals for new expenditure. For, the rule is that no proposals for new or increased expenditure, for any department, can be incorporated in the budget without the concurrence of the Ministry of Finance. The administrative Ministries should not get more funds than they really need in face of the limited resources available with the Government.

As the position stands, the Finance Ministry passes the demands of the several administrative Ministries, calls for the justification of expenditure, and fixes a net figure for each Ministry. It may be borne in mind that neither the Finance Ministry nor the Finance Minister is an autocract in these matters. The imperative demands of the Five Year Plan, the policy decisions of the Cabinet, the current conditions in the country—all these must find a reflection in the budget and, to the degree, restrict the Finance Minister's say. The Finance Ministry closely looks into all proposals that impose a new, or an increased, charge on the Government.

New charges are of two classes—(i) grants for purchases, constructions, etc., and (ii) grants for establishment. Big purchases or constructions, like the atomic energy reactor in Bombay, are undertaken with the concurrence of the Cabinet. Evidently, the Finance Ministry's control in regard to inclusion of such charges in the budget may appear to be somewhat restricted. But it watches closely the establishment proposals involving extra expenditure. In case the Minister in charge of a spending department finds the Finance Ministry's 'No' unpalatable, he may take the matter to the Cabinet, whose decision binds all individual members. If the member feels strongly over the matter and cannot reconcile himself to the decision of the Cabinet, the may sever his association with the government by resigning. Any way, the Finance Minister's position in the Cabinet is a peculiarly strong one; the Cabinet must give special weight to his views, at any rate when the expenditure at stake is of a significant dimension. A former Finance Minister's pronouncement, albeit in a different context, that " a Finance Minister can function adequately only from a position of strength and not from one a of weakness," is a pointer in this direction.

Why is the Finance Ministry endowed with such control over the estimate of the spending ministries? Two reasons may be given for this. In the first place, the Finance Ministry is not itself a spending ministry and can, therefore, act as the disinterested guardian of the tax-payers' interests. In the second place, this Ministry has to find out ways and means to meet the proposed expenditure; logically, thus, it must have a say in determining whether it should be incurred or not. To quote the words of the Haldane Committee, "... if he the Finance Minister) is to be held responsible for filling the reservoir and maintaining a certain depth of water in it, he must also be in a position to regulate the outflow." The Finance Ministry's predominant position *vis-à-vis* the spending ministries has, of late, come in for criticism on a number of grounds. It is useful to note the following observation made by Appleby:

> "Under the present system, 'schemes' or projects of various kinds are presented to the Finance Ministry throughout the year, some for early clearance and apportionment of funds, some as a hostage to later budgets. These schemes are usually not much more than policy ideas, they are almost never actual administrative and expenditure projections ready for serious consideration as such. Their shortcomings are the primary occasion for most of the delay and confusion now rather erroneously charged against the Finance Ministry. As time for making the budget is approached, all these schemes on file are examined, some are selected, and these, in addition to normal 'establishment' expenditures, become the budget of a particular Ministry. All schemes remaining in the file have been approved in principle. Those not actually included in the budget remain in the file, and may be activated in any subsequent year or at any time within a year. Years after they were first submitted and approved in principle, some one or another may suddenly be activated, although by that time the original rough estimates of cost and even important elements in the scheme, may be wholly outmoded.
>
> "This whole system requires the agencies to submit many schemes they have little hope of being able to put into action. It establishes a pattern of poor cost estimates and poor budgeting which, in turn, are justifications for detailed financial intervention.
>
> "There is another element in the picture that deserves much

attention. The Ministers, knowing that Finance will reduce their requests, are given to loose and extravagant estimates of cost. They are given positive encouragement to do this. When a particular Ministry submits a tightly estimated project, Finance has complained: "You put us in a difficult position by making it so hard for us to reduce your figures." Actually a tight and sound estimate should be encouraged in everyway possible, and endorsed by quick and unmodified approval. Conversely, the loose estimate should be over-penalised. The primary responsibility of Finance should be to encourage and to stimulate good budgeting in the agencies, and its whole review should be based on sampling analysis which constitutes a search for poor budgeting; if the sample analysis which constitutes a search for poor budgeting; if the sample reveals good budgeting, the request should be given maximum approval."

Enactment of the Budget

It is a cardinal principle that no taxation can be levied and no expenditure incurred, without the prior approval of Parliament. The journey of the Budget, or the 'Annual Financial Statement,' through Parliament, is the vital part of the process. In Parliament, it goes through the following five stages:

1. Presentation to the Legislature;
2. General Discussion;
3. Voting of Demand for Grants;
4. Consideration and passing of the Appropriation Bill; and
5. Consideration and passing of the Taxation proposals, that is, the Finance Bill.

Besides the General Budget ('the Annual Financial Statement'), there is also, the Railway Budget, separated from the former as early as 1921. Same procedures govern both the budgets. The Railway Budget is regularised by Rule 134 of the Rules of Procedure and Conduct of Business in Parliament, which makes provision for the submission of budget in two or more parts, each Part to be dealt with in the same manner as if it were a budget. The Railway Budget precedes the General Budget.

The powers of Parliament in respect to the enactment of the Budget are enshrined in the Constitution itself. The relevant Articles are 112 to 117 of the Constitution. The following provisions in this respect may be worth noting:

1. No demand for a grant shall be made except on the recommendation of the President.

2. No proposal relating to expenditure can be brought without the recommendation of the President.

3. Parliament cannot increase a tax though it is empowered to reduce or abolish it.

4. 'Charged' expenditure upon the Consolidated Fund of India shall not be submitted to the vote of Parliament, though it is subject to discussion.

5. Parliament cannot amend the Appropriation Bill in a way as to have the effect of varying the amount, or altering the destination, of any grant or of varying the amount of any 'charged' expenditure.

6. Powers of the Rajya Sabha are quite restricted in financial matters. Voting of demands for grants is the exclusive privilege of the Lok Sabha. In the passing of the Finance Bill as well, the Rajya Sabha has severely limited powers in that it must give its concurrence, with or without any recommendation, within fourteen days. The Lok Sabha may accept or reject any or all of these recommendations. The Finance Bill, however, does not go again to the Upper House; it is submitted to the President for assent. For the first time, in 1977, the Rajya Sabha made some changes in the Finance Bill. But the Lok Sabha reasserted its supremacy by rejecting these changes and adopting the Finance Bill in its original form.

The Budget—'a statement of the estimated receipts and expenditures of the Government of India for the financial year—distinguishes the estimates of expenditure *charged upon* the Consolidated Fund of India from those *made from* the Consolidated Fund of India. The 'charged' expenditure includes the salaries and allowances of certain high officials, debt charges, certain pensions, sums required to satisfy any judgment, decree or award of any court or arbitral tribunals, etc. This part of the total (*i.e.*, the charged expenditure) is not subject to the vote of Parliament, though it can be discussed. The underlying idea of keeping away the salaries and allowances of the President, Judges of the Supreme Court, Speaker, Deputy Speaker, Chairman and Deputy Chairman of the Upper House of Parliament, Comptroller and Auditor-General of India, from the influence of the vote is to reinforce their independence and remove them from the sphere of party politics. Debt charges, certain pensions, sums required to satisfy any judgment, etc., of a court of arbitral tribunal are, inevitably, of fixed nature, and can, accordingly, suffer no reduction or alteration.

Similarly, the Constitution lays down that the estimates of expenditure embodied in the budget shall distinguish expenditure on revenue account from other expenditures. The excess of the revenue receipts over the expenditure on revenue account is the surplus, or deficit is the resultant of the expenditure on revenue account minus the revenue receipts.

The Finance Minister presents the budget to the Lok Sabha on the last working-day of February. This he does with a speech known as the Budget speech. The budget is laid before the Rajya Sabha at the end of the Budget speech in the Lower House.

A discussion does not immediately follow the presentation of the budget. This occasion comes after a few days when a general discussion of the budget takes place. At this stage, which usually lasts for two or three days, the Lok Sabha discusses the budget as a whole on any question of principle involved therein. Details of the budget are, however, not discussed. There is no voting, nor are cut motions allowed. General discussion of the budget is a hang-over of the past when Indian legislature could just air its grievances without any right of voting. Under the new dispensation, it serves some purposes—the members have an opportunity to discuss revenue estimates, the ways and means programmes of the government, and, what is perhaps the most important purpose, the 'charged' expenditure. To the Government, this stage provides a foretaste of the feelings of the House on budget proposals for taxes as well as expenditure. At the end of the debate, the Finance Minister makes a general reply, rebutting, as is to be expected, the various charges made by the members.

The third stage is the voting of demands for grants, the demands being presented ministry-wise. Voting is restricted to the votable parts of the expenditure: the 'charged' expenditure is not submitted to vote. Further, voting the estimates of expenditure is the exclusive privilege of the Lok Sabha. The Upper House does not share this privilege.

The General Budget is divided into 109 demands, 103 for civil expenditure and 6 for defence expenditure. The Railway Budget contains 32 demands. Each demand is subject to a vote, and runs in the following form: "That a sum not exceeding...be granted to the President to defray the charge which will come in course of payment during the year ending 31st March, 19.... In respect of .... (the subject of vote is stated here)." The demand is introduced by the Minister in charge of the subject, with a speech, which is "largely political, very seldom financial." This is the state of active discussions and members bring the department and the government under the fire of criticism. The discussion is sparked off by moving cut motions; the idea behind these is that members specify the precise points on which they wish to concentrate discussion. Cut motions are of three kinds—(i) disapproval policy cut, (ii) economy cut, and (iii) token cut. The principal merit of these cut motions lies in exposing and publicising the lapses of administration which otherwise might go undetected in a vast administration like ours. The cut motion is, of course, defeated because of the majority behind the Cabinet.

Twenty-six days have been fixed for the voting of demands in India. During this period Lok Sabha has to pass all the demands. The Speaker, in consultation with the leader of the House, fixes a time-limit for each demand as well as for the entire expenditure part of the budget. A demand is subjected to vote as soon as the time-limit fixed for it, is reached. Likewise, on the last day fixed for the voting of demands, all the remaining demands are subjected to vote, though the House might not have discussed them. In England, too, a similar state of affairs prevails, as is made to by Hilton Young: "Between a third and a half of total expenditure for the year is often voted in an hour or so, without any sort or kind of debate or criticism. A more unsatisfactory state of affairs could hardly be imagined. It reduces the whole laborious process of the control of expenditure by the House to something of a farce."

It is pertinent to repeat here that no demand for a grant shall be made except on the recommendation of the President, and, further, the Lok Sabha shall have power to assent, or to refuse to assent, to any demand, or to assent to any demand subject to a reduction of the amount specified herein. This means that the honourable members can only reduce or reject the proposed items of expenditure. In practice, they may not do even this because of the majority behind the Cabinet. Cut motions are, accordingly, symbolic, they just provide the honourable members with a stick with which to 'beat' the government. A criticism of the government is the main plank of the discussion, at the end of which the Minister in-charge of the subject makes a general reply to the criticism rebutting the charges and assuring the removal of the grievances pointed out by the members. At the end, the demand is put to vote. A demand becomes a grant after it has been duly voted.

A somewhat longer discussion of several demands for grants has been possible since the introduction of a *vote on account.* The financial year begins on April 1, but Parliament continues discussing the budget even after the inauguration of the new financial year. Will not, therefore, the new year open without any financial provisions for it? It is precisely this contingency which the device of the *vote on account* wards off. *A vote on account* is an advance grant made by Parliament in respect of the estimated expenditure for a part of the ensuing financial year, pending the regular passage of the budget.

After all the demands for grants relating to tall the ministries have been passed by the Lok Sabha, the Appropriation Bill embodying all the voted demands as well as the Consolidated Fund Charges is introduced in the Lok Sabha. The passage of this Bill is necessary to legalise the demands as voted and to authorise the withdrawal of money from the Consolidated Fund of India. The Constitution lays down: "...no money shall be withdrawn from the Consolidated Fund of India except under appropriation made by law." The Bill undergoes the procedure that attends to any other bill. No amendment, however, can be made to the Bill, as all the grants embodied in it have already been voted; the 'charged' expenditure is never put to vote. Yet, this stage provides another opportunity for further discussion. While explaining the scope of discussion on an Appropriation Bill, the Speaker of the Lok Sabha stated: "... the Appropriation Bill may, in a sense, be said to be a formal legislation to give a statutory form to the decisions of the House in respect of the various Demands of Grants both on account of the General Budget and the Railway Budget. Though the Bills are, thus, formal ones they are yet important as a further opportunity which they give...of making suggestions and comments on the activities of Government in respect of the various heads under which the moneys are being authorised to be drawn from the Consolidated Fund," After its passage in the Lok Sabha, it is forwarded to the Rajya Sabha. Being a money bill the latter cannot amend or reject it; it returns the Bill with its recommendations within fourteen days. The Lower House may accept or reject any or all of these recommendations. It is, then, sent to the president for assent, which is given as a matter of course.

Parliamentary authorisation of expenditure does not complete the process. Ways and means must be provided to meet the expenditure And for this, recourse has to be made to taxation.

Article 263 of the Indian Constitution lays down that no tax shall be levied or collected except by authority of law. Since Parliament is the law-making body, it is this august body, which must give consent to the taxation proposals of the government. Some of the taxes are permanent and their rates are fixed by the Government under the provisions of the Acts governing them. Others are to be authorized annually by the legislature—the examples being income-tax, customs, etc. It is necessary that the taxes derived from annual and temporary acts should, as P.K. Wattal observes, "bear a substantial proportion to the total revenue and not be nominal or insignificant in character, so that the Government may, by economising on superfluities, avoid recourse to Parliament." This arrangement places the Government under the obligation to annually appear before Parliament to give an account of its stewardship. On closer scrutiny, therefore, this arrangement is intrinsic to the democratic form of Government.

All the taxation proposals of the Government for the ensuing financial year are incorporated in a bill, known as the Finance Bill. Being a money bill, it follows the procedure governing the former. A proposal to increase a tax or introduce a new tax cannot be introduced except on the recommendation of the President. Further, unlike the Appropriation Bill, amendments to decrease or reject a tax may be moved; and are sometimes even accepted by the Government. The Parliament, thus, enjoys comparatively greater freedom in reducing taxes proposed by the Government. Thus, in 1951, Parliament succeeded in slicing down taxation to the tune of Rs. 5 crores. After the passage of the Finance Bill in the Lok Sabha, it is sent to the Rajya Sabha for its concurrence. The latter has to return the Bill with its recommendations within fourteen days. The Lower House may accept or reject any or all of the recommendations. In any case, it is sent to the President for his assent; after the assent it becomes the law of the land.

It must be here pointed out that under the federal set-up, as we have in India, the Parliament (and the Union Government) possesses a prescribed sphere within which to levy taxes. The principal items of revenue in the Union list are as follows:

(1) Railways.

(2) Posts and telegraphs, telephones, wireless, broadcasting and other like forms of communication.

(3) Property of the Union and the revenue therefore, but as regards property situated in a State, specified in Part A, or part B of the First Schedule, subject to legislation by the State, save in so far as Parliament by law otherwise provides.

(4) Public debt of the Union.

(5) Currency, coinage and legal tender; foreign exchange.

(6) Foreign loans.

(7) Reserve Bank of India.

(8) Post Office Savings Bank.

(9) Lotteries organised by the Government of India or the Government of a State.

(10) Taxes on income other than agricultural income.

(11) Duties of customs including export duties.

(12) Duties of excise on tobacco and other goods manufactured or produced in India except—

(a) opium, Indian hemp and other narcotic drugs and narcotics, but including medicinal and toilet preparations containing alcohol or any substance included in sub-paragraph

(b) of this entry.

(13) Corporation tax.

(14) Taxes on the capital value of the assets, exclusive of agricultural land of individuals and companies; taxes on the capital of companies.

(15) Estate duty in respect of property other than agricultural land.

(16) Terminal taxes on goods or passengers, carried by railways, sea or air; taxes on railway fares and freights.

(17) Taxes other than stamp duties on transaction in stock exchanges and future markets.

(18) Rates of stamp duty in respect of bills of exchange, cheques, promissory notes, bills of landing, letters of credit, policies of insurance, transfer of shares, debentures, proxies and receipts.

(19) Taxes on the sale or purchases of newspapers and on advertisement published therein.

(20) Fees in respect of any of the matters in the Union List, but not including fess taken in any court.

Under the Constitution such stamp duties and duties of excise on medicinal and toilet preparations as are mentioned in the Union List shall be levied by the Government of India, but shall be collected—

(i) in the case where such duties are leviable within any State specified in Part C of the First Schedule, by the Government of India, and

(ii) in other cases, by the State within which such duties are respectively leviable.

Taxes levied and collected by the Union but assigned to the States:

The following duties and taxes shall be levied and collected by the Government of India, but the net proceeds in any financial year of such duties or tax (except the proceeds attributable to State specified in part C of the First Schedule) shall be distributed among those States in accordance with which such principles of distribution as may be formulated by Parliament by law—

(i) duties in respect of succession to other than agricultural land;

(ii) estate duty in respect of property other than agricultural land;

(iii) terminal taxes on goods or passengers carried by railway, sea or air;

(iv) taxes on railway fares and freights;

(v) taxes other than stamp duties on transactions in stock exchanges and markets;

(vi) taxes on the sale or purchase of newspapers and on advertisements published therein.

We have so far discussed the enactment of the budget. It may be recalled that the budget embodies ordinary annual estimates, both of receipts and expenditures. It is likely that, under special or extra-ordinary circumstances, these estimates may not hold good. To meet these circumstances, provision has been made for the following kinds of grants; (i) vote on account, (ii) vote on credit, (iii) exceptional grant, (iv) excess grant, (v) token grant, and (vi) supplementary grant.

Vote on account has already been discussed. The Lok Sabha can grant vote on credit to meet an expenditure whose amount of details cannot be precisely stated an account of the magnitude or the indefinite character of the service (for example, war). It is thus, a provision has been made for the vote on credit in article 116(b), though this device has not so far been used in India. The Lok Sabha can make an exceptional grant which forms no part of the current service of any financial year.

Excess grant is voted after the Financial year. In India, there is no scheme of centralised payment as in Britain. Since the disbursing authorities are spread all over the country, it is obviously not possible to keep the expenditure within the limit set up by Parliament. Excess money is sometimes spent. Such expenditure is regularized by obtaining an excess grant from Parliament. All such demands for excess grants need first be approved by the Public Accounts Committee before submission to the Lok Sabha. Thus, eleven demands for excess grants in respect of the General Budget for 1958-59 were voted in 1961. Similarly, three demands for excess grants in respect of the Railway Budget for 1958-59 were passed in 1961.

Token grant must not be confused with token vote which is a device of taking parliamentary approval for a self-financing scheme. When funds to meet the proposed expenditure on a new service can be made available by re-appropriation, a demand for a token amount (say, Rs. 10) is put to vote, and funds may be made available on Parliament's approval of the demand. This is known as token grant.

When framing the budget, the Government cannot anticipate, and accordingly incorporate, all of its requirements at the beginning of the financial year. Sometimes, the original estimates for the service are found insufficient in the course of the implementation of the approve scheme. Additional funds are also required to finance a new scheme not envisaged in the budget. Consequently, supplementary budgets incorporating such additional estimates for expenditure are introduced in Parliament during the course of the year. The procedure prescribed for the original budget is followed in the case of supplementary budgets also.

The device of supplementary grants has been profusely used in India. In 1948-49, for example, the supplementary grants totalled Rs. 118 crores as against the original budget of Rs. 245 crores. After Two months of the passing of the Railway Budget for the year 1959-1960, the Railway Minister approached Parliament for supplementary grant for the Railways. In 1973, too, the Central Government presented a supplementary budget. It need be pointed out that the system of supplementary demands not only weakens parliamentary control over public expenditure, but also amounts to a breach of contract between the "Government and the Parliament." Durell rightly point out: "it is a sound principle, that one, and only one estimate of national expenditure should be laid before the Parliament during each session; for to render parliamentary control effectual it is necessary that the House of Commons should have the money transactions of the year presented to it in one mass an in one account." Recourse to the supplementary grants should be made only sparingly.

The Finance Ministry's control over the spending Ministries does not cease with the presentation of the budget to Parliament. Its control is continuous, operating both before and after parliamentary approval of the estimates. At the time of the framing of budget estimates, the Finance Ministry's check is very broad. Hence, a more detailed control by it is necessary before any money is actually spent. The Parliament makes the grants to the Government as a whole (technically to be president) and not to individual Ministries. The Finance Ministry, as the agency responsible for managing the finances of the Government, need, therefore, be convinced about the desirability and prudence of the proposed expenditure before it lets the administrative Ministry involved to proceed with it. True, the concurrence of the Finance Ministry is not required for the normal existing expenditure, which is taken as a matter of routine. But new expenditure must have the prior approval of the Finance Ministry. This implies that the latter's concurrence with proposal for expenditure over new schemes is only tentative at the preparatory stage of the budget. "The Budget Division of the Ministry of Finance," explains the Estimates Committee, in its Ninth Report, 1953-54, "receives the various proposals from the Ministries in one lumpsum during one or two months towards the close of the financial year. Consequently, the Budget Division does not have sufficient time to examine the proposals in greater detail and to scrutinize each and every item carefully. The practice has, therefore, been that the Budget Division applies broad checks and determines certain gross amounts for the various schemes without committing itself or the Ministry of Finance to their spending during the next financial year. The system is that whatever has been included in the estimates is merely with a view to get the vote of the House thereon and does not entitle the administrative Ministry to incur expenditure unless a detailed expenditure sanction has been issued by the Ministry of Finance."

Taking the sanction from the Ministry of Finance before embarking upon new expenditure served well the imperialist

Government in India, primarily interested in law and order and defence. This explains why the delegation of financial powers to administrative Ministries and subordinate authorities was so limited in scope. This arrangement, however, ill-suited to an expanding Government wedded to the concept of the Welfare State and rapid comprehensive, socio-economic development; constrained Paul Appleby to regard that the need for the delegation of powers was the worst shortcoming of Indian administration. Considering the crying need for wider delegations to administrative Ministries and subordinate authorities, the Government of India Promulgated "Delegation of powers, Rules, 1959," in December 1958. Subject to certain general limitations wide Financial powers have been devolved upon the administrative Ministries. Full powers have been granted for appropriations and reappropriations provided that the expenditure lies within the scope of the grant. The departments of the Central Government can sanction expenditure on any scheme involving an outlay of Rs. 50 lakhs. The departments are empowered to enter into contracts to make purchases up to Rs. 25 lakhs or, for proprietary articles, up to Rs. 5 lakhs. The administrative Ministries' power to create permanent and temporary posts and to incur contingent and miscellaneous expenditure have been considerably enhanced. As stated earlier, these delegations are subject to certain general limitations, such as:

(i) Public revenues are to be spent on legitimate objects;

(ii) Subordinate authority can sanction expenditure in those cases in which it is authorised;

(iii) Any expenditure which involves the introduction of a new principle or practice likely to lead to increased expenditure in future must be referred to the Finance Ministry; and

(iv) The power to sanction of subordinate authority is subject to any special or general instruction which the delegating authority may issues.

As a part of this scheme of delegation of powers, each

administrative Ministry has now a Financial Branch consisting of the Financial Adviser, Deputy Financial Adviser or Assistant Financial adviser. This staff is solely concerned with the financial and budgetary work and is associated with the formulation of proposals to be included in the budget. This staff must be consulted in all financial matters involving the exercise of the powers now delegated or matters requiring reference to the Ministry of Finance. It also helps the Ministry in the control of expenditure against appropriation . It has been provided that all cases in which the advice of the Financial Adviser of the Ministry is not accepted have to be referred to the Secretary of the Ministry for orders and the case has to be presented to the Minister, if the Secretary too differs from the advice. These Financial Advisers work under the control of the Secretary of the department. Now, the departmental Secretary has the informed and constructive criticism flowing from within his Ministry from person well-grounded in financial knowledge and familiar with the difficulties of administrative phase of the operating Ministry. It must be noted that the delegating authority's responsibility does not suffer a diminution with the delegation; rather, it increases as it has to frame adequate rules of observation, and also to undertake review from time to time.

In a bid to further streamline the administrative machinery the Government of India, has, since August 1961, devolved greater responsibility for financial management both on the administrative Ministries and executive agencies. The scheme includes, (i) formulating of a programme for incentive pre-budget scrutiny between the Ministry of Finance and the administrative Ministry necessitating the preparation of budget estimates earlier that usual in cases in which actuals of the last year are not an important consideration; (ii) further liberalisation of financial powers to the Ministries in order to avoid references to the Finance Ministry in the post-budget period except on vital matters; and (iii) the exercise of control of important financial aspects by the Finance Ministry through adequate reporting system and test checks.

Scheme of Integrated Financial Advisers

In 1976, the scheme of integrated Financial Advisers was

introduced in all the ministries in the Central Government. In pursuance of this scheme, Integrated Financial Advisers of the rank of joint secretary or additional secretary have been appointed in the administrative ministries. A Financial Adviser is responsible both to the administrative ministry in which he is posted as well as to the Ministry of Finance. Wider financial powers have simultaneously been delegated to the administrative ministries as part of the scheme of financial reform. The Financial Adviser assists in budget formulation, scrutiny of projects and programmes by the Ministry of Finance. He is also associated with post-budget vigilance to ensure that there are neither considerable short-falls in expenditure nor unforeseen excesses. There is now a close association of Integrated Financial Adviser with the formulation and implementation of all proposals involving expenditure. The Integrated Financial Adviser is also responsible for the preparation of the Ministry's performance budget and the monitoring of progress of various schemes against the budget.

In matters involving any departures from the prevalent budgeting and accounting procedures, consultation with the budget division of the Department of the Economic Affairs (Ministry of Finance) continues to be obligatory. Similarly, respect of the formulation of the concerned ministry's development plans, the Plan Finance Division of the Department of Expenditure is required to be consulted.

Many changes were made in the financial administration of the Central Government in 1976. Since then, the Secretary of a Ministry is the chief accounting authority, and it is he who has to sign the appropriation accounts and ensure preparation of financial accounts of his ministry. The Integrated Financial Adviser, assisted by the circle and pay officers of the ministry, is made responsible, among other things, for keeping entitlement, loan and provident fund accounts. He arranges for the pre-check and payment of all bills by cheques. Maintenance of records relating to payment, reconciliation with banks and final compilation of accounts, etc., is now the responsibility of the ministry, not of the Auditor-

General. For the efficient implementation of these financial reforms, a senior officer who has the necessary expertise and knowledge of the civil accounting system and its rules is appointed in each ministry.

Under the new accounting dispensation, the field formations or offices of the different ministries are organised into suitable circles depending upon the nature and volume of work involved. Each circle has one or two more pay officers who are to pre-check all claims and make payments through cheques or demand drafts. They would compile monthly accounts and send them to the Integrated Financial Adviser of the respective ministry. Each ministry has an internal audit cell and although it is organisationally a part of the office of the Integrated Financial Adviser, it is directly under the Secretary of the ministry. The account circles constitute the forward base of the internal audit cells, each ministry, in consultation with the Auditor-General, determines the manner in which its accounts are to be maintained and furnished to the Comptroller and Auditor-General. The ministries also evolve suitable procedures to facilitate the linking of accounts with performance budgeting and performance appraisal.

The Finance Ministry's predominant position manifests itself in other ways as well as the post-budgetary stage. It watches the progress of expenditure in the spending departments through monthly expenditure statements, periodic reports from them, and cautioning them when necessary. Also, it sees that the unspent balances are surrendered by the spending Ministries as early as possible before the close of the financial year. Above all, it gives financial advice and guidance to the spending Ministries generally.

The Finance Ministry's control over expenditure at the execution stage of the budget has come in for a great deal of adverse criticism. The remedy lies in the Administrative Ministries preparing fully detailed schemes at the very outset so that Finance Ministry may give its sanction to them at an early date bringing to minimum the post budgetary checking and control. As Sir Edward Bridges has pointed out in his Stamp Memorial Lectures,

1950, the real function of the Finance Ministry today is to ensure that money is spent in the best way to achieve certain declared objectives, *i.e.*, to ensure the judicious harnessing of resources. Significant is also the following observation of the Planning Commission:

> "A plan of economic development necessarily postulates substantial increase in public expenditure. The importance of securing economy and sound financial control which is already generally recognized is, therefore, further emphasised by the needs of national planning. The objects of financial control are to ensure, (1) that no wastage of resources occurs, (2) that public money is not misapplied, and (3) that for the money spent adequate results are obtained. Within the administration the responsibility for ensuring that these conditions are observed rests equally upon the administrative authorities and upon finance departments, although necessarily, the indent latter have special duties to discharge. There is need always for close co-operation at each level between the financial and the administrative authorities so that, if any difficulties are encountered, they can be removed through personal consultation at an early stage in the formulation of a proposal and before commitments are entered into. Financial procedures, which, on the one hand, secure adequate control and, on the other, avoid too great an interference in carrying out their own programems, are essential to the efficient execution of the Five Year Plan."

But total elimination of such control is not consistent with the financial accountability of the Government to Parliament.

Trade Unions

AT its 33rd session in 1986, AITUC officials denounced the new policy of denigrating the public sector as dangerous, because it (public sector) 'has been responsible for building a strong industrial base in the core sector leading to self-reliance' and 'plays an objectively progressive role' by creating employment opportunities, promoting regional development, building a self-reliant economy and keeping the multinations at bay. Other trade unions, such as CITU,-criticized the policy of economic liberalization more vociferously, attributing it to the weakness rather than the strength of the government. CITU members regarded the scuttling of the public sector as not only bad for workers, but also counter-productive for the Indian capitalist class in the long run since it would further subjugate the country to international capital. Leaving economic development to market forces would gear industrial development to the needs of international capital rather than to those of the Indian people. To express their concern all trade unions, excluding INTUC, organized a convention in October 1986 to oppose the policy of liberalization. On 21 January 1987, 21 lakh workers of the public sector struck work, not for pushing any economic demands but as a political gesture to 'Save Public Sector, Save National Economy.' Another group that opposed the NEP was the left intellectuals. They apprehended as sharp inflow of foreign capital that would undermine the country's autonomy. The World Bank estimated at that time that the seventh Plan would call for a doubling of the gross capital inflow from $17.5 billion to $34.5 billon during the plan period. Since the concessional aid had dried up India was expected to enter into commercial loan commitments of the order of $4.5 billion a year during the plan. The policy of import liberalization was expected to worsen eh position. Under the circumstances, growing external debt was the topmost concern of the participants of seminar organized by the West Bengal government in 1985.

Public sector workers and the leftists were antagonized by the NEP for obvious reasons. But even a section of the ruling party and some industrialists disliked the rabid criticism of the public sector. A cabinet minister, K.K. Tewari called it 'debunking of the Nehru Model.' In May 1985 the Congress Working committee defended the public sector as 'the sheet anchor of India' progress the national instrument for rapid industrialization and for the spread of modern technology into the remotest areas of the country.' And even the PM, who initially endorsed Sathe's vitroic attack on the public sector, spoke up in its defence following the strike of workers. He said, 'The public sector is not an albatross round the people's neck, but an engine of growth and a catalyst of change,' Later at an international conference of public sector executives, he reiterated that 'it is because we invested in the public sector that we have this strength to-day' to question the adverse GATT regulations.

The combined opposition by the public sector workers and left politicians stalemated the NEP by the end of 1986. With regard to fiscal policy the government resorted to pragmatic adjustment and fine turning within the liberalized framework. In the budget of 1987 custom duties on all imports of machinery and capital goods were raised to 85 per cent, the hike for power projects and fertilizers being milder—35 per cent and 15 per cent respectively; profitable zero tax companies were subjected to 30 per cent minimum tax and excise duties were also enhanced.

Foreign Trade

Nevertheless, the process of liberalization continued. Foreign trade was further deregulated with the announcement of three year policy. Despite the deepening deficit in the balance of payments, the OGLlist was enlarged and the import of capital goods was further relaxed. In June 1998 the industries requiring licencing for MRTP/FERA companies from seventy-seven to twenty–six. They were exempt from the licencing requirement if they were established industries is specified backward areas and the investment was less than Rs 50 crores; and in those cases where they set up their units at specified distances outside twenty-one cities, as long as the investment was less than Rs 15 crores. In the following month sixty-nine single product MRTP companies were allowed to diversity (broadband) themselves

Some public enterprises were also integrated with the private sector through the back door. In the field of oil refining. Tata Chemicals collaborated with the Indian Oil Corporation to jointly buildand manage a Rs 1,500 crores oil refinery at Karnal while Indian Rayons of Birlas negotiated tie up with Hindustan petroleum Cooperation to construct and run a Rs 1,200 crores refinery at

Mangalore. This was ostensibly done to overcome resource crunch. In 1988 six of the country's largest sector units entered into a minority equity arrangement with a consultancy firm of non-resident Indians based in the US, seemingly for the purposes of technological mordernisation. There were also moves towards the privatization. In 1988 a sick public sector unit, scooter India, was sold off to Bajaj Auto limited; but it seemed like and isolated case.

Thus, despite resistance from trade union and leftists, the public sector was attenuated. Fresh expansion, in the sense of setting up new plants, was foreclosed; the growth of existing units was circumscribed by the availability of internal sources and the quantum of borrowings from the capital market; some companies were integrated with the private sector and a firm was even privatized. In any case, all units were henceforth supposed to emulate the management practices of the private sector. Several public enterprises in fact intensified their in housetraining programmes, where experts from management institutes motivated their middle level managers to adopt 'successful' management practices. While the distinction between the public and private sectors seemed fudged for all practical purposes, full scale privatization was preempted by the resistance of pro-public sector sections such as the organized technocracy and labour aristocracy, backed ideologically by the sizeable, vocal left in the mass media, academia and politics.

The decline of the public sector was accompanied by the growing presence of international capital.

Foreign collaborations jumped from 752 in 1964, itself a record, to 1,024 in 1985 and then tapered off at 957 in 1986 and 853 in 1987, rising again to 926 in 1988. A detailed analysis reveals that thee collaborations continued to increase in seven areas, namely, engineering, consultancy, drugs and pharmaceuticals, food processing, medical and surgical equipments, paper and paper products and information industries. The number of collaborations in these sectors, which apparently benefited from the policy of liberalized import of technology, doubled in three years. Segments in which foreign collaborations sharply increased with the policy announcement buy declined after a year comprised machinery, chemicals, transportation, telecommunications, metal products, textiles, leather and scientific and office equipment. In the remaining industrial areas foreign collaborations declined after the policy announcement. The major collaborators were the USA, West Germany, the UK, Japan and Italy. While the number of collaborations with all these countries shot up in 1985, in the case of Italy and Japan the increase was sustained in 1986 as well. In term of value of foreign investment, the USA not only topped the list, but its rate of investment, the USA not only topped the list, but its rate of investment (approvals) was also sustained up to 19990. West Germany, Italy and Japan stepped up their investment in 1985 and then became cautious.

The economic relations between India and the United States qualitatively improved following, NEP. In three high technology categories—electronics, computers and telecommunications equipment—American exports to India increased by 47 per cent, from $149 million in 1985 to $220 million in 1986. These of course were the very areas in which American multinationals had a keen interest in expanding their business. Their importance to American companies is indicated by the Goldfield Telecommunications Mission, which estimated the Indian telecommunications market at $6-10 billion during the Seventh Plan period. The world telecommunications market was put at $55 billion, of which the US share was about $25 billion.

Emphasising the importance of the changes that took place as a result of the NEP, American ambassador John Gunther dean in a meeting with FICCI on 9 October 1987 said: American corporations have recognized the new business climate in India created by promulgation of more liberal policies and the signing of the Memorandum of Undertaking on transfer of Technology. The US business community has responded with investment. In the past two years Americans invested more in Indian than they had in the entire previous decade.

Major US companies—many on the leading edge of technology—have entered into many on the leading edge of technology—have entered into collaboration with Indian institutions. The names f these companies have come to be synonymous with the economic dynamism of today's American economy: firms such as Allen-Bradley , Allied Signal, Du Pont, Foxboro, Honeywell, Molex, NCR, Prim Computer, United Technologies, Westinghouse and Xerox. Those are only a few among many.

There are 61 new projects in agriculture alone. Cooperation in space missions presents simultaneously some of our greatest hopes and achievements. The INSAT 1 series of communications satellites, which are American-built to Indian specification, are perhaps the leading example. INSAT IB, which plays a key role in you country's communications, was launched from an American space shuttle. Its backup and successor, INSAT 1C, would have followed the same path into space but for our Challenger tragedy. Despite that setback, we are once again on the road to an important venture. An American firm is now building the advanced Indian-designed INSAT 1D. When it is ready, it will be carried aloft on the first commercial launch of an American Delta rocket.

The United States has provided a supercomputer for monsoon research, which is among the most closely held in the entire range of US high technology. In May 1985 telephone traffic between the United States and India has grown from 700 calls per day to 2,700—far exceeding India's telephone communication with any other country. At officials level we have seen a virtual parade of high-level visits and consultations between representatives of out two countries. Perhaps the most remarkable of these exchanges have come in the areas of a security and defense.

Previously, defence cooperation consisted primarily of a small base of officer exchanges and training programmes. It was only after 1985, and especially after the 1986 visit of Secretary Weinberger, that real progress came. After considerable exploration, the United states approved the sale of an advanced jet fighter engine, the same one used in our top line F-18 Hornet, for use in the development of India's light combat aircraft. We agreed on a 'mission area' approach, under which other component technologies for this project have been approved. Just last month a license was issued so India could acquire a very powerful IBM 3090 computer with appropriate software for use in the design and manufacture of the aircraft a new gas turbine engine for Indian destroyers and specialized radars for other uses. Defense technology teams from India have been given access to some of our most advanced and most sensitive defense production facilities. Where they have seen items of interest, we have opened discussions to see what can be cleared for transfer to India.

These programmes obviously represent only a small corner in the overall picture of the Indian defense establishment. More people are engaged in the process, from cabinet ministers to students and more resources, both public and private, are involved. Thee developments in the space of just two years clearly indicated the extent of India's business relations with the US. They had indeed entered a new phase of growth. Even in the area of defence, where the Soviets had a well-developed niche, the US made a successful bid, shedding tits reservations dating back to the Himalayan war. The black of rapport in this area was decisively terminated in 1986 with enthusiastic tie-ups. Thus, the NEP resulted in (a) arresting the growth of the public sector and (b) integration the national industrial sector, especially its advanced segments, with foreign industries.

Such countries, therefore, have a greater responsibility in controlling damage caused to the environment by the use of such pollution-causing materials. Some of the important measures being considered for this purpose are increased use of renewable and clean sources of energy, less use of fossil fuels. Organic farming, measures to reduce global warming and global limits on carbon emission. Many international agreements have been signed among countries; some of them are the agreement on Environment and agreement on Climate Change and Global Warming.

3

Theory of International Economy

Economically developed country, people earn a higher income and all the requirements and facilities needed are available to them. Even when some of the goods are not produced within that country, it has the capability to purchase and to import from other countries. Generally, economic development of a country is measured on the basis of its national income and per capita income. National income is defined as the total value of all the goods and services produced within a country plus income coming from abroad. When the total national income is divided by the total population, it is called per capital income. Both these concepts are described in terms of money. Every country tries to raise its national income and per capital income with the available resources. For achieving a higher level of economic development, these two are essential requirements, but may not be sufficient. People have to be ensured a regular and higher income provided with basic amenities like food, clothing shelter, health and education. Thus, economic development can be defined as long term increase in per capital income along with improvement in quality of life.

The World is undergoing structural adaptation, reason being that the World Economy is continuing to grow slowly. Despite the success in reducing inflation, almost everywhere, expectations of faster growth have not been fulfilled. Since, the economic recovery that started in 1993, in no year has World output growth exceeded 3% per annum so far. The prospects of the same are for a continuation of this slow growth in the years to come also. A certain pattern of growth may be absorved in the Developing World since 1990, where growth has averaged 4.85% including China, and 3.9% if China is excluded. Much of this growth has been due to East Asia, where expansion has been both fast and stable.

International economics has for its field of study and practice the traffic in goods, services, gifts, capital and the precious metals as the ownership of these item changes from the residents of one country to these of another. It describes and analyses this traffic, as well as the laws, institutions and practices under which it operates. It draws inferences, develops tendencies and laws that condition the manner in which International transactions take place.

The principles and theories of International economics not only are consistent with the general body of economic theory, but are often a special application of these more general laws. International economics has a long and interesting history and arrived at its present state of development after a long journey of many years by trial and error method. The pattern of International economic relations has seldom remained stable for a long period, country after country has risen to importance in the field of International Trade.

Adam Smith in his book entitled "An Inquiry into the Nature and Causes of the Wealth of Nations", quoted that "What is prudence in the conduct of every private family, can scarce be folly in that of a great kingdom. If a foreign country can supply us with a commodity cheapter than we ourselves can make it, better buy it, than to produce it. Thus, Adam Smith in the late 1700's, characterised the advantages of individual and international specialisation.

The fundamental argument for international specialisa-tion and exchange of goods and services rests on a theory popularised by David Ricardo (1772-1823). His analysis, later on is being called the principle of "Comparative costs", marked an advance ever Smith's for Ricardo reasoned that it might be advantageous for a nations to import an item even if it could be produced internally at a lower cost. Much of today's international economic theory represents either a modification or a refinement of the early principle.

The development of the principle of comparative advantage was furthered by John E. Cairnes (1832-1875). One of the problems where he directed his attention was the theory of value in domestic and international trade. Then, much of the success in modernising the foundations of international economic theory is attributed to Alfred Marshall (1892-1924). His meet famous work, *Principles of Economics,* represented an endeavour to improve upon and to synthesise the cost theories of the Classical School and utility theories of the Austrian or Psychological School. It is generally recognised that capital is a balancing item. While Sir Arthur Satler pointed out in 1880-1913 that Income on investment should be treated as a balancing item.

Further, modification of the principle of Comparative costs was provided by F.W. Taussing (1859-1940). He concluded that despite the unrealistic assumptions, their treatment of trade theory was approximately correct. Gottfried Haborler also endeavoured to improve the theory of trade by important shift in assumptions and analysis. Despite various efforts to bring the principle of comparative advantage class to reality, it remained subject to persistent criticism. One of the more constructive critics was Bortil Ohlin, who, in following an approach employed by Hockacher, introduced the mutual interdependence theory (1933). Ohlin's mutual interdependence theory received widespread acceptance. It not only provides and adequate and realistic explanation for the causes of trade but it is also a complete theory in the sense that all relevant variables are embodied in it.

Where the foreign demand for a country's exports is inelastic lower prices do not necessarily mean increased exports and a larger volume of money in circulation,but could result in lower exports and a smaller volume of money in circulation. Where balance of payments adjustments are not automatically made by changes in exchange rates or prices, there is a possibility that they will be so adjusted by means of changes in interests rates or income. Few International Economist are of the view that the reduction of nationalism and the abolition of all barriers to International Trade would place nations and all factors of production, wherever they are located, into competition with one another, with the result that there would be a levelling of the economies of all countries.

The arguments in favour of protection is based on keeping the money at home, to reduce unemployment, for equalisation of production costs, infant industry argument, cheap foreign labour, National security, diversification, etc.

Custom Simplification

The customs tariff is one of several obstacles which importers of foreign goods into the domestic country must meet. As the executive branch sought to reduce tariffs through the application of the Reciprocal Trade Agreements, the complexity of customs regulations, tariff rates, procedures, classifications, and valuations become increasingly apparent. These regulations constitute a sort of "invisible tariff" which effectively serve to confound exporters and importers alike and to impade the importation of goods into the other countries.

The Kennedy Round was 6th in the series of Trade negotiations. The GATT sponsored Kennedy Round which was one of the more important of the several negotiating sessions which have been undertaken. The completion of the negotiations in itself reflects a continued willingness on the part of most of the major trading nations to work toward the liberalisation of World Trade, particularly in industrial commodities.

Development of Underdeveloped Areas

A growing awareness of their relative poverty has stirred the people in the underdeveloped areas to an impatient clamer for material improvement. The desire of many countries in for greater economic development. By a simple definition, countries are classified as "Underdeveloped" previously and now "developing countries" if the per capita income of their inhabitants is low relative to other countries.

A more extended definition suggest that although developing countries presently have relatively low-incomes, they do contain potential natural or human resources for a marked increase in income. Such resources are not being fully or efficiently utilised but await the introduction of complementary resources or structured changes within the productive system. One of the common traits of the developing areas is low per capita income. Their poor economic status is reflected in other standards, including low-calorie diets, literacy rates, and expectancy of life. Another characteristic, developing countries are predominantly primary-goods producers, with agriculture, mining, and petroleum representing the major industries. An additional characteristic closely related to the foregoing is the dependence of such countries on one or two types of export items, usually raw materials of foodstuffs, as the source of foreign exchange earnings.

John Stuart Mill noted the impact of International trade on social attitudes and behaviour and suggested that greater importance may be given to the direct gains associated with international specialisation and exchange. It is generally agreed that foreign trade performed the role of an "Engine of Growth". If gain would not have been possible, there would be no basis for an exchange of commodities among nations. Specialisation and trade enable countries to use their resources at a comparative advantage; and the gain they derive is reflected in the differential between internal cost ratios and external terms of trade. According to the mutual inter-dependence theory, which focusses attention on the basic cause of commerce between areas, trade makes it possible for the industry to adapt to the local condition of production. Trade contributes to a greater volume of production and, further more, and in this process each trading region reaps some gain. Exports is a leading sector and moreover exports should be capable enough to finance imports. Exports are useful not because they serve to atimulate investment and income, but rather because they put off deflationary measures which otherwise would be instituted because of a deterioration in the balance of payments situation.

We know that the study of International Economics is the

oldest branch of the discipline. The first acceptable data for the Gross National Product (GDP) date from the 1930s, while the Foreign Trade Data can be traced back to Medieval times. Ancient times saw not only extensive trade but also problems of currency and exchange. International Economic traditionally has dealt with the differences among Nations—both the 'Natural' and those "Created' by the states with their various regulations.

No doubt, the effects of Regional and Cultural differences form part of the International Economics, they are often not as important owing to the effects of different acts of rules and regulations. Further, national laws also tend to isolate each nation from its neighbours, making a considerable difference in the way trade is conducted within a country and between countries. Moreover trade helps in efficient global allocation of resources.

International migration on a large scale is impracticable, but nations can improve their economic situations by exchanging goods and services. The central concept of the International trade theory has been of the "Comparative Advantage" of a trading nation.

We know that the Classical Economist were the champions of the cause of free trade. But during the great depression of 1930s the World saw how weak, it was, and how far away the Classical argument was away from the realities of everyday life. Trade in the modern World has became more and an exchange of industrial products among the rich countries. The exports of developing countries are still mainly consisted of raw materials and basic commodities with the slight opening for their manufactured exports increasingly threatened by a variety of factors tending to become more and more restrictive. Moreover, there was not a significant change in the trade policies of Developed Countries and the problems of Developing Countries were further aggravated as their trade failed to keep pace, on the other hand, richer countries recorded further increase in their Gross National Product and benefits of their affluence failed to penetrate the large number of developing countries. In 1964, the United Nations Conference on Trade and Development (UNCTAD) was established in December,

1964. Prior to this, International Trade problems were being considered primarily within the framework of GATT (1948).

The main purpose behind establishing the UNCTAD was to solve the problems of World Trade and Developments arising from the dissatisfactory working of the GATT. The idea of GSP emerged in the Second UNCTAD at Delhi in 1968 and the whole scheme of Generalised System of Preferences (GSP) was finalised in October, 1970. European Economic Community (EEC) was the first to implement the GSP in July, 1971. GSP in a significant departure from the trade pattern based in Most Favoured Nations clause and the principle of reciprocity. GSP was aimed at to bring about a better balançe between the lending trading countries and their weak partners i.e. developing countries.

It is very important to bear in mind that the GSP markets are essentially "Buyers Markets" wherein suppliers from all over the World compets. The buyers, therefore, expect prompt and regular supplies strictly as per the approved samples, so as not to upset the commitments to their own customers. Only few countries could get the benefits during the period of more than a 26 years of its operation. Moreover, GSP is not a panacea for all the trade and development problems faced by the Developing Countries.

Thus, the old paradigm of comparative advantage vested for these countries having labour-intensive products and techniques alongwith the specific natural resources derived and soil-based products. Arthur Lewis postulated that Developing Countries having comparative advantage in labour-intensive products and in labour-intensive techniques, made possible because of unlimited surplus labour. But now, with modern technology and mobility of finance and capital these countries can obtain, and are obtaining comparative advantage in capital intensive and technology intensive products and services.

A significant development in 1996, 1997 and on the basis of estimated and expected figures for the year 1998, it has been observed that their is a slowdown in the World Trade. While, the

World merchandise exports had grown at rates 3 to 4 times than that of World output in the previous 3 years upto 1997, the differences were much smaller and a tendency which can be expected to continue in the coming years, as the initial effects of widespread trade liberalisation and globalisation, particularly in Developing Countries, taper, off. This recent slowdown in World Trade has also been associated with a weakening of Commodity Prices. After two years of sustained increases, many non-oil commodity prices had began to decline in 1996 and 1997, mainly those of interest to Developing Countries. Increased Flexibility of the initiative of certain conditions of determining country eligibility, as well as promptness in implementation, are the real ground realities for ensuring a lasting and rapid solution to the "debt crisis" of not only Africa but also in other Regions.

The United States recovered by investment, which has brought about a significant increase in productivity, particularly in manufacturing goods. Japan could reap the benefits of its fiscal packages, growing at 3.5% in 1996 and of the same level during 1997 after a prolonged recession phase. This has been greatly owing to the depreciation of yen against the dollar. Now, the performance of the Japanese economy will mainly depend on reduction in budget deficit and increasing exports.

It is expected that if monetary policy is tightened in the United States of America, its affects may not be limited to widening the global deflationary gap. Alongwith this, if upward pressure on the dollar is kept, the effect might multiply, rather than to reduce, trade imbalances.

New Paradigms in International Economics

The big recent paradigm of the World Economy is the existence of unleasing of Market forces. The deregulation of domestic markets and their opening up to international competition have become universal features. The "invisible hand" of, Adam Smith, new operates globally and with fewer counter-failing pressures. Many International Economists are optimistic about the prospects for faster growth and for convergence of incomes and living standards which greater global competition will bring.

Presently with globalisation, capital, technology and enterprise have become mobile factors of production. Further, within the groups of countries formation of a labour block has also become a mobile agent Moreover, skilled and technical labour is more mobile than ordinary/unskilled labour among the different countries. Further, multinational companies are making the services of land more and more mobile. Thus, with free mobility of factors of production, International Economics theory is undergoing a tremendous change. From Table 9.1 the trend of exports as percentage to GDP in the International Economy may be seen as under:-

However, there is also another big paradigm in the International Economy i.e. widening income gaps. Since, the early 1980s the World Economy has been characterised by rising inequalities and slow growth. Income gaps between the North and South have further widened. In 1965, the average per capita income of the G 7 countries as was 20 times that of the World's poorest seven countries, now it is more than 39 times as much. No doubt, some of the developing countries are growing faster than Industrial countries, but nevertheless not fast enough too narrow the absolute per capita income gap.

Further, growing wage inequality between skilled and unskilled workers, gaining of capital in comparison with the labour, rapid expansion of Public and Private Debt, Agricultural price liberalisation have not boosted the income of farmers are such problems, which are going to become global day by day.

Most of the recent accounts of the flying geese paradigm paint a harmoninous picture in which East Asian development is presented almost in entirely cooperative terms, while the potentially conflictual and competitive aspects of this process are virtually ignored. The new trading regime under the WTO has reduced the scope for general forms of tariff protection, many trade related subsidies and performance standards and the tax enforcement of intellectual property rights. The Uruguay Round has clearly opened up new export opportunities for developing countries and improved their security of market acccess. Further, the agreement on Subsidies and countervailing measures defines "subsidies" for the first time.

tightous the discipline on subsidies, and extends them to all W.T.O. member countries.

The WTO seems to have taken a cautious step towards correcting some of the anomalies in the multilateral trading system adversely affecting the interests of the developing countries. In its meeting held in May, 1998 at Geneva, acknoledged the fact that the three-year old WTO regime has not helped the poor countries in stepping up their exports. The same has also been confirmed by the studies conducted by the United Nations and other Institutions/countries. More significantly, the liberalisation of trade in goods has proceeded very slowly in these sections of the International Economy where the developing countries, rightly emphasised the need for amendments in the Uruguay Round agreements in the services sector, agriculture and trade-related intellectual property rights. Now, a large proportion of liquidity growth stems from the Financial Intermediation of Private Banking Institutions, as surplus funds flow-into the International Credit Markets and ultimately are lent onward to countries who are in deficits in balance of payments.

The largest part of the deficits has been financed by running-up foreign debts rather than by bringing down foreign reserves i.e. Liability Financing rather thank "Asset Financing" of imbalances.

The successful completion of the Uruguay Round in 1883 represented the most extensive multilateral trade agreement in the history of International Economics. Where after seven years of negotiations GATT's 117members reached at consensus on many contentious issues, including for the first time services, trade related investment measures, and intellectual property rights. The Round had barely drawn to a close, however, when consideration began about the agenda for future multilateral negatiations. This Round of negotiations was precedent for setting in linking trade policy, as a compliance mechanism, to non-trade objectives through the intellectual property decisions, and will continue as a competitive policy, with labour standards and trade and environmental improvements.

In the traditional approach, tariffs were to be reduced, but by and large, nations were left free to pursue domestic policies with regard to competition (anti-trust), environment, and labour standards. The deregulation of domestic markets and their spending up to International competition have become a universal paradigm. Hence, International Trade remained still a political act, whether it takes under a system of free trade or protection, of state trading or private enterprise, of most-favoured nation clause, or of discriminatory treatments.

The liberalisation and globalisation of the World Financial Markets has raised a new class to power i.e. of these who trade in global currency and Bend Markets. With this, the old Webbhy song befits very well:-

> "The Banks are made of Marble
> with a guard at every door,
> And the Vaults are filled with Silver,
> That the Workers struggled for".

Competition is the basic aim of leading World Countries. Therefore, in international dealing, there is a scope of freedom and competition. Exchange settlements and new trade embargees are also a International Institutional phenomena. Hence, in a changing and expanding scenario of International trade, which deals in foreign market, it is very essential to keep a vigilant vision on every business movement, because in present days scenario, business more of loss, however, in an indigenous or global market, is a tough task rather challenging than the previous time. The major forms of International Business consists of exporting, licensing by joint ventures, manufacturing in a Foreign country, management contracts and consultancy services.

The following aspects of the International Economy deserve special consideration:-

— To re-negotiate the debts of developing countries.

— To redefine the terms of trade and to assure greater access to Developed Market economies.

— To further improve the decision-making process of the IMF, IBRD and WTO.

— To attain the United Nations, Official Development Assistance targets.

— Indexation of the Primary Commodities' prices with those of Manufacturing goods.

— To consider to create a Common Fund to help to stabilise commodities Prices of such products.

New International Economic Order

The present International economic order; Aid, trade and economic development; the struggle for the New International Economic Order; sovereignty over natural resources and crisis in energy resources.

The present international economic order was evolved over a period of four decades of so, since the termination of the Second World War. The present order, in essence, is radically different from the order that obtained during the earlier period.

The present international economic order has, without any doubt, brought about unprecedented growth of technology, manufactures and agricultural product have been witnessed over the past few decades. However, unwittingly, the present order has also thrown in some challenges which need be faced boldly, and if necessary even by giving a new shape to the system.

First, of all the present order is characterized by the creation and widening of the gap between the rich and the poor states; the gap can be seen in the form of large differences in the per capita income of poor and rich nations—on an average the per capital income of poor countries is hardly 1/50 of that obtaining in an industrially advanced country. Not only this gap has come to subsist, and projections for future provide that the gap may indeed widen.

Secondly, the present system is not essentially based on free enterprise and free markets, because it is guided and manipulated in these respects. In actual practice in place of open and expanding trade we see a tariff system with low tariffs for raw materials and high tariff for industrial products. This had blocked the Industrialisation of the poor countries. The flow of capital and the credit system is also dominated by United States, European countries and the oil producing countries. There is no free flow of technology and the system of regulating the ownership of patents, which restricts the use of those patents to rich countries.

Finally, the notion of readily available raw materials is also virtually non-existent because we are confronted with the threat of scarcity.

Thus, we find that the present international economic system is not as free as it often claimed. The present system is largely guided and manipulated for the benefit of rich countries. If we are genuinely interested in finding a solution to the problem of an equitable division of property, of scarcity of natural resources and of depollution of the environment, the only solution lies in the New International Economic Order.

The Less developed Countries (LDCs) have been making persistent demands for introducing fundamental reforms in the economic, commercial and financial relationships between themselves and the developed countries. The call for New International Economic Order is based on the assumption that the prevalent international order perpetuates and aggravates international inequalities and that new relationship of interdependence should replace the older patterns of dependence and unequal exchange. It is argued by the advocates of New International Economic Order that the rich developed countries and that it is in their self interest to encourage the promotion of growth and development of the poor countries in order to expand their markets.

The less developed countries hold the view that the Developed Countries must recognize the growing power of the commodity producers as evident from the success of Organisation of Petroleum Exporting Countries (OPEC) in raising oil prices, and accept that the locus of power has inclined in their favour.

The spirit of the New International Economic Order is envisaged in the Charter of Economic Rights and Duties of States adopted by the UN's 27th General session on December 12, 1974, asserting its main objectives:

"The achievement of more rational and equitable international economic relations and the encouragement of structural changes in the world economy, the creation of conditions which permit the further expansion of trade and intensification of economic cooperation among all nations; the strengthening of the economic independence of developing countries, the establishment and promotion of international economic relations taking into account the agreed differences in development of the developing countries and their specific needs."

The New International Economic Order embodies exhaustive and ambitious purpose. The main objective is no less than the creation of a new structure of economic relationships, warranting fundamental changes in a large number of related field—commodity trade, market access and preference, aid flows, the activities of multinational corporations, the international monetary system, the restructuring of international institutions, the transfer of technology, etc.

Goals and Means

New International Economic Order deals both with goals and means. The goals which are rather more evident from all the UN conferences held on this issue, lay emphasis on the desire for a more just distribution of world economic resources among the countries—rich as well as poor.

In the wake of the oil crisis in 1973, the OPEC countries with a little below 300 million people have been able to raise their incomes sharply. The rest of the poor countries with about five times people have rather been placed in more precarious position. The oil crisis helped only a handful of countries—some of whom were already rich—whereas the vast majority lost by it. The poor remain poor. The "25 poorest countries" are mentioned in world forums but no practical action has so far been initiated to help thee nations. Besides the need of making NIEO's benefit available to the poorest states has not been given serious though. The developed countries are putting up firm resistance against it. Another reason is that the less developed countries have already suffered so much at the hands of Super Power that these states now stand inflexibly on the principle of sovereignty and do not allow any foreign countries or the UN to interfere in their internal affairs.

Mini-Income Target: The New International economic Order sets forth another goal to create a material minimal standard of living, a mini-income for those who are facing harsh economic realities. Its purpose is to persuade the rich countries to bring reforms in the international economy. As owing to various reasons, the principle of sovereignty will play a decisive role in relation to UN also in the near future, such a goal should practically imply that the rich countries accepted such reforms within NIO which would be instrumental in creating a mini-income for the poorest countries and that their aid for development would be channeled to poorest countries and in particular to those countries which carry out a conscious policy of leveling and justice inside their own borders.

Parts and the whole : there are three parts of entity embodying the NIEO The first is to the extent to which the developing countries can force the rich countries to a more just distribution of world income than the one we have today. For instance, the price policy of the OPEC cartel, which in one stroke was able to redistribute about a couple of per cents of world income from the rich to the oil producing countries. Several raw material countries are dreaming about how by acting in the similar manner, they could form the cartels also for other raw materials and force the developed countries to pay many a times higher than that the importers pay now.

The second factor is that of morality that the rich should share their wealth with less developed countries.

The third and most important motive behind the NIEO is of

a materiality more concrete future. It emphasizes that it is in the common interest of developing and industrial countries alike to elaborate an NIEO; for example, both sides can have a common interest in the reduction in the fluctuation of prices of raw materials and therefore accept certain stabilization agreements; the governments in rich countries could come to find that it would be in the interest of the large consumer groups to import cheaper goods from the developing countries, although it could hit some home industries and its workers whose problems would have to be solved in another way—through labour market policies.

These three parts –the threat, the morals, and the common interests, can said to be the main parts in the entity called NIEO. However, the entity is greater than and different from the parts of comprising it.

The Means or the Instrument of Economic Policy

The means for realizing the NIEO are basically instruments of economic policies which can be mutually devised by the developed countries and less developed countries. The NIEO can be realized through international trade. The LDCs want better financial possibilities to develop their economies. They want to have a greater inflow of one of the most dynamic development factors—science and technology—and at the same time these countries opt for exercising control over its composition. The developing countries aspire for acquiring help as well as industrialization and development in agricultural sector. Besides, these countries want a greater formal as well as real power in the decisive institutions which govern the international economic development, especially the entire UN system. The prominent means through which NIEO can be realized are explained below:

Foreign Trade: The major demands of the LDCs in respect of foreign trade are they want higher prices on their export goods, some sort of guarantee of a similar development for export and import prices and better possibilities for facilitating admission to the markets of the rich countries.

The case of export cartel of the OPEC countries, with a four fold doubling of the oil prices, has provided an impetus to the developing countries. It has motivated the raw materials exporting countries to search out the possibilities of crating other cartels for raw materials between the developing countries or if this does not work out, at least some sort of international raw material agreements which should provide the developed countries good prices and ability in their countries.

There are possibilities that effective cartels might perhaps be formed in the bauxite or copper production on the model of oil cartels. But it is doubtful if cartel method would be successful. The case of oil export is different. Even prior to the oil crisis, the oil export from the oil producing countries was about 50 percent larger than the sum of the five next most important export commodities of the less developed countries—copper, coffee, sugar, cotton and natural rubber. Currently, the oil export from the developing countries is almost exceeding the sum of all other exports from them. Another factor disfavouring cartel system is that it redistributes the profits from trade in an unsystematic manner. This system helps only rich countries whereas the countries like India and Bangladesh are losers. Moreover, developing countries are not the only countries which export raw materials. The United States, the Soviet Union and a host of other developed countries are more benefited from cartel system than the developing countries.

There are proposals to create raw material agreements between the rich and developing countries. The past experience reflects the unsuccessful misled of such attempts. Both rich and poor countries share a common interest in a certain stability in price development and perhaps some practical results can be worked out in this direction. The expectations that such stabilisation agreements at the same time should envisage a price policy which severely redistributes gains from rich to poor countries, cannot be particularly high. The endeavours to relate important and export price development for the less developed countries with the help of indexing appear to be too complicated to yield quicker results.

Better recourse for the developing countries is to open their own markets in the developed countries for exporting their products.

The developed countries can provide protection to the interest of less developed countries. Mutually agreed norms can be worked out with a view to distribute the burden justly.

Development Aid: It is widely argued that the rich countries should contribute one per cent of their total production to the developing countries. The poor countries should share the development expertise of the rich countries. Development aid is a powerful means to realize the objectives of NIEO quicker and sooner.

Another way through which developed countries can help the LDCs is the writing-off of old debts or putting a moratorium over it. The poor countries which are mostly indebted too, should in this way get an extra assistance, which would be valuable. This type of measure can easily be carried through politically n the rich countries than development and to the same tune.

Science and Technology: the developing countries require and in their scientific and technological development, technical assistance provides gains and savings which can further be invested in economic development. However, scientific and technological now-how is precisely not under the direct control of the states but under the control of multinational enterprises. These transnational corporations do not use science and technology in the interest of developing countries but more in their monopolistic interests A study conducted by the UNCTAD reveals that of all patents in the world, about six percent are owned by the less developed countries. Other about 84 per cent is owned by the multinational corporations operating in the developing countries. And of these only 5 percent is used in production. The transnational enterprises are there to thwart the efforts of others from starting production of the goods patented that is a protection against competition. In reality, the patents of the multinational corporations effectively discourage all indigenous national efforts in the developing countries to develop their productivity with the help of modern technology.

The Soviet Union and Japan have made considerable development by copying and imitating foreign techniques. For realizing the objectives of the NIEO, it is necessary that developing countries should scrap the present patent system and work out norms authorizing the developing countries with rights to produce any technique which they are capable of producing. It ha to be ensured that such a system of rules is not exploited by the Multinational Corporations.

Industry and Agriculture: Much has been said in the domain of industry and agriculture in the international forums. No new special proposals have come forward in regard to the NIEO. It is well known that developing countries want to raise their degree of industrialization. The process of industrialization can not be had in isolation. The process entails the involvement of industrialized countries. It is not clear how far these industrialized countries are willing to help and cooperate with the developing countries. The developing countries which share seven per cent of industrial production during the recent session of the General Assembly of the UN, wanted to establish a principle that they (developing countries) should be entitled to "a larger percentual share of world industrial production." This demand of developing countries was strongly opposed by the representatives of the European Community and Japan. Developed countries were willing to accept only that the developing countries are entitled to a "larger industrial production."

Agriculture is another realm where developed countries are reluctant to cooperate with the developing countries. The United States has the greatest export surplus which can be used for help in starvation or disaster. This can perhaps help in feeding the millions in the poorest countries. But inside the United States, there are lobbies which hold the view that food assistance to developing countries helps in augmenting population "uncontrollably," that America cannot alone finance the food deficit of the developing countries. A section in America is of view that the Soviet Union can purchase the whole surplus and that food can be used as a weapon like oil. However, the developed countries can afford to share their food surplus with the poor countries.

Share in Decision-making: The New York Times. In a leading article in May 1975 about how to save UNO, wrote, "The reason why the UN General Assembly. But in General Assembly nor real decisions are taken. It adopts only resolutions and principles which cannot force others to act on it. However, the powerful bodies where decisions are taken and can be enforced are the Security Council of the UN, the World Bank and other important economic organisations. The developing countries have little or no power in these important world bodies. These are dominated by the developed countries. It is because of this reason that the resolutions inside the UN system often get a progressive and in relation to the problems of the developing countries very positive form whereas the positive actions continue not to be taken or to be minimal. The gap between words and action widens.

NIEO—The Basis

A new International Economic Order (NIEO) is the only alternative that can go a long way in securing an equitable partnership between the rich and the poor nations. The issue of securing NIEO can be legitimately described as the most vital issue of contemporary international relations. The first two decades after the Second World War were dominated by the decolonisation movement, and these witnessed the rise of a number of sovereign independent states in Asia and Africa. These new states, being motivated by a strong desire for development and full participation in international relations, started working for securing their due rights and roles in international relations. However, the abject poverty, scarcity of resources and under development that characterised their people made it difficult for them to secure the desired objectives. Their dependence upon the developed and rich countries, particularly for their economic needs, forced them to live with the domination of the international system by the rich and powerful states. The rich countries came up with several instruments like foreign aid, Multinational Corporations, IMF, SDR etc., which were apparently designed to help the poor countries but which were in reality the instruments for perpetuating their neo-colonialist control over their former colonies. The new states found themselves in a situation in which despite the sovereign independent statuses, they found themselves dependent upon the rich for meeting even their primary needs. Their dependence was exploited by the developed countries for influencing their economies and policies. The international economic system was and continues to be exploited by thee rich states to their own advantage and the net result came in the form of a big gap between the rich and the poor. Inequalities and imbalances in international economy and trade that came to be developed as a result of the protectionist and neo-colonial policies of the developed nations, created a situation in which the poor underdeveloped countries found themselves being squeezed into being economic dependencies and satellites of the developed countries. The international economic system became more partial and exploitative. The energy crisis of 70s and several other harmful developments, made the underdeveloped countries totally dissatisfied with the prevailing system. They started making efforts towards the securing of their rights vis-à-vis the developed states. The existence of several international movements like NAM, Afro-Asian Solidarity Movement, Third World Unity ad consolidation drive etc, provided them with the opportunity to share their problems and thoughts. The net result came in the form of the demand for restructuring of the international economic system—the creation of a new international economic order, with a view to make it equitable and jut, and to end the existing system which was partial in favouring the interests of the developed countries, and which was giving little help to the third world countries towards the securing of their goals of development. The demand for NIEO has, however, failed to carry much conviction with the developed countries. They are in no mood to accept the demand as its acceptance is bound to end their existing superior position and role in internal relations. Their opposition to the demand has come in the form of consolidation of their collective economic power as well as in the form of consolidation of their collective economic power as well as in the form o attempts to delay or evade the conduct of global negotiations over the issue. The commitment and determination of the Third World countries to secure NIEO versus the attempt of the developed countries to torpedo the demand have together made the issue of NIEO a burning issue of contemporary international relations.

Since early 1970s the issue of New International Economic Order has been the frontal issue in international relations involving the developing countries or the third world on the one side and the developed countries or the first Two Worlds on the otherwise. The former regards the restructuring of the existing international economic order as the only way to get out of their present problems of poverty, scarcity, economic problems, imbalances and under—development. By this step alone can the existing era of neo-colonialism can be ended and Third World countries can become really freed politically as well as economically. As against this, the developed countries appear in no mood of accepting a total change of existing economic order as it is bound to involve a decrease in their role in international relations and a burden on their economies. They advocate that the existing system, through several reforms and well planned and executed steps, alone can secure the desired changes in international economic system. They regard the existing economic institutions and instruments of international economy as the best available means for securing development of the Third World countries. They, therefore, oppose the demand for the total restructuring of international economic order—i.e. the demand for NIEO.

This difference of approach between the developed and under developing countries has made the issue NIEO as the most vital issue in the relations between them. Since early 1970's the debate on a NIEO has opened a new chapter in international elations. It can be legitimately described as one of the key issues of contemporary international relations.

Infact, the qualitative change in the nature of International Politics form a subject studying power and security in international relations to a subject studying the issues of "development," "welfare," "economic order among nations" has appeared because of the continuing debate on NIEO. Presently, socio-economic issues and the struggle and assertiveness by the underdeveloped countries form a vital core of international relations.

What is NIEO: NIEO constitutes a framework for eliminating the existing era of international economic system which, with all its features. is mostly catering to the needs and interests of the developed countries to the detriment of the underdeveloped, the third World. It stands for making the international system fairer, just and equable by adopting a code of conduct for the developed countries and by accepting the due rights of the underdeveloped countries. It is regarded as the only way to end the existing neo-colonial control that the developed countries are continuing to exercise over the newly emerged sovereign independent nations which constitute the Third World, it stands for arresting the widening gap between the "spectacularly growing developed countries" and the "lagging behind developing countries." It seeks to end the existing imbalance and inequalities in the economic relations between the underdeveloped and the developed worlds. It seeks to end the existing monopolistic control of the developed countries over international trade, economy technological know—how and international economic institutions.

In simple words, New International Economic Order constitutes a frame—work for ending the existing anarchy in international economic system which is being utilized by a small number of developed countries for their own advantage and for maintain their neo-colonial control over the underdeveloped countries. It stands for eliminating the exiting imbalances and inequalities by restructuring the existing international economic system and institutions. It seeks to secure an equitable and fairer distribution of world income and resources as can enable both the developed words and the Third World to develop side by side.

Need for NIEO: The emergence of a stron demand for a New Intrnational EconomciOrder has bene largely due to the sharp and big changes in the international system of the post-war period. Initially,the weakened position of Europe, the rise of two super powers, the emergence of cold war, the rise of strong anti-imperialist and anti-colonialist movement, the emergence of a rapid process of decolonisation etc., wer eresponsible for changing fast the politicalmap of the world and the contents of relations among nations. Later on, the rise of new consciousness among the newly emerged countries of Asia, Africa and Latin America, the constitutions created by the lététente between the two-superpowers, the example of economic recovery secured by European countries, the rise of local leviathans like India and Brazil, the change form confrontation to limited confrontation in the relations between USA and USSR and a host of other factors were responsible for bringing into focus the economic dimension of international relations. The commitment of the new states—the Third World, to secure socio-economic development and to play their due role in international relations further brought a big change in international relation.

In early 1970s, international relations came to be dominated by economic issues. Around this time a new kind of configuration emerged in international relations. It undermined the ideological overtones of the cold war era and brought into focus economic issues of development and underdevelopment. The conflict between socialist East and Capitalist West came to be over stepped by the conflict between the excolonial underdeveloped poor 'have-nots' of the Southern Hemisphere-The Third World, on the one hand, and the economically developed and technologically advanced haves of the Northern Hemisphere—the two developed worlds. As a result, new economic consciousness and the conflict between the developed and the underdeveloped countries in international relations together found a manifestation in the form of North-South controversy over the issue of a new international economic order.

Factors that have Influenced the Demand for NIEO

The emergence of the demand for NIEO has been largely due to the following factors:

The Big North South Gap: a yawning economic gap exists between the developed and the lowly developed countries. The North with nearly 30% of world population controls more than 70% of world's income and wealth. The South has to satisfy the needs of more than 70% of world population with the help of less than 30% of resources. The per capital income of the two dozen industrialized countries is between $ 3000 to $ 6000, where as that of 125 developing countries is about $ 100. IN THE WORDS OF Jan tinberger, "We have today about 2/3rd of mankind living on less than 30 cents a day. We have today a situation where there are about one billion illiterate people around the world. Although the world has both the means and technology to spread the education. We have nearly 70% of the children in the Third World suffering from malnutrition, although the world has the means to feed them. We have mal-distribution of worlds resources on the scale where the industrialized countries are consuming world's resources on a scale about 20 times more than the resources than the poor countries. We have a situation where in the third World, millions of people toil under a burning sun from morning till dusk for miserable reward and premature death without discovering the reason why?" The wide gap between the North and the South seriously limits the scope of economic relations and trade between them. The affluence of the developed compared with the poverty, scarcity and under development that prevail in the lowly developed countries makes the international system imbalanced. While the outbreak of a big famine in Ethiopia and several other African states reflects the poverty of the South, the star was programmes and the continued arms race highlights the richness of the North. The South as such stands totally dissatisfied with the existing economic system.

Ever Widening Gap. The big economic and development gap that exists between the North and the South has been increasing at an alarming rate. The developed are becoming richer and the underdeveloped are becoming poorer, particularly after 1970s. By virtue of being technologically advanced and industrially developed, the countries of the North are strengthening their control over international trade and income. Both UNCTAD and GATT have virtually failed to prevent the widening gap between the rich and the poor. The record of UNCTAD clearly shows that the efforts of the developing countries to attain self-sustained growth have not received adequate support. The pattern of international trade continues to favour the developed countries. The energy crisis, the falling exports, the stiff competition in world market, the monopolistic role of the Multinational corporations, the inadequacy of Bretten Wood in the Contemporary times, the inadequate and limited foreign aid to the developing countries etc., have all combined to perpetuate and increase the gap between the North and the South.

"A combination of the persistent monetary crisis, exacerbated by inflationary trends and balanced of payment problems, continued deterioration in terms of trade and aid, prevalent draught conditions and above all the recent energy crisis have brought to the fore the array of grave economic social problems for the third world. The stark realities of economic conditions in the Third World are too grim to be ignored." The gap between the per capital incomes of the rich nations and the poor nations is widening. For example, the share of the developing nations in world trade declined from 21.8% in 1960 to 17.6% in 1970. Though the report for 1984 appears encouraging yet the continuance of the trend towards a decline in the world trade share of the Third World continues to be there. The transfer of resources to the Third World is continuously declining while their external debt has been continuously declining while their external debt has been continuously increasing rather multiplying. The increase the oil import bill of the developing countries has further hit hard their economies. This ever-widening gap has been a source big dissatisfaction for the Third World countries and they regard NIEO as the only way out.

Increased Global Interdependence but Continued Low Role of the South: Despite the big gap that exists between the developed and the under developed countries, the global interdependence has increased in our times. Both the developed and the under developed world today find themselves increasingly dependent upon each other. In the words of Edward L. More. "Evidence for the existence of a high level of interdependence in certain areas of the international system abounds. The recent global problem in respect of energy resources, the frequent currency crisis after 1967, and the suspicious raised for Soviet and American intentions in the Strategic Arms Limitation Talks bear testimony to the fact that international, and even predominantly domestic events have an increasingly deeper impact on a growing number of political systems throughout the world.". The developed countries find themselves dependent upon the under developed countries for the purchase of raw materials and for the sale of manufactured goods. The economic prosperity of the rich stands linked up with the purchasing power of the poor. The under developed also continue to depend upon the developed countries mainly for: (i) securing economic, technological and industrial aid; (ii) selling their commodities; and (iii) securing access to advanced technology.

However, due to the big and ever-increasing gap that exits between the North and the South, the global interdependence continues to be exploited by the former for strengthening their economic conditions. The hope that the developed countries would come for the with international actions augmenting the transfer of resources and liberalisation of trade, has proved to be wrong. In actual practice the developed countries have failed to appreciate properly, the importance of interdependence and have continued to pursue their desire objectives in the global international trade and economy without much regard to the perceptions and needs of the developing countries. Backed by three powerful weapons—technological, political and military power, the developed countries have maintained successfully their control and superior role in international economic order. This has been a source of grave dissatisfaction for the underdeveloped countries. 'The concept of interdependence existed the prospects of increased and active participation of the developing countries in international decision-making, however, much to their disappointment, they find themselves playing a secondary role in the ear of neocolonialism. 'The underdeveloped countries now fully realize the partial nature of the existing economic system and hence advocate a new economic order.

Neo-colonial Control of the north over South: Despite the fact of global interdependence and the sovereign equal status of all the members of international community, the underdeveloped countries find themselves living in an era of neo-colonialism in which the developed countries continue to control their economics and policies. The dawn of independence and the resulting sovereign status has made them free only politically, economically and in actual practice they continue to be dependent upon the development countries. Being poor and under developed with abject poverty and scarcity of essential goods as their "assets," they find themselves helplessly dependent upon the developed for securing aid and help for meeting their primary needs and desires. They are very sore of the situation because they feel, and quite rightly so, that their present position is the result of the exploitation that they suffered during the past several centuries of their existence under the yoke of western imperialism. Their former colonial masters are the present day rich and developed nations. These could develop only because of their ability and success in exploiting the wealth and resources of their colonies. Even now they continue to exercise a neo-colonial control over the economies and policies of the developing countries. "The essence of neo-colonialism,' observes *N. Nkrumah*, "is that the state which is subject to it is, n theory, independent and has all the outward trapping of international sovereignty, in reality its economic system and thus its internal policy is directed from outside. "Though several subtle devices like foreign aid, military help, alliance, partnership, interventions, multinational corporations international economic policies etc., the developed countries are in a position to maintain and increase tneir control over existing international economic order and the economies and policies of the developing countries. The attempts of the developing countries to get rid of neo-colonialism have found manifestation in their demand for a new international economic order.

Excessive and One-sided exploitation of World Income and resources by the developed Countries: Another fact of the relations between developed and under developed countries is the continued disproportionately large exploitation of world resources and in come by the former. Under multifarious disguises the stronger and rich countries are successful in maintaining the appropriation of world resources to the detriment of poor and weak countries. Being technologically and industrially advanced and economically affluent, the developed countries continue to have virtual control over the raw material markets, what partically amounts to a monopoly over manufactured products and capital equipment. They have been able to proceed at will infixing the prices of the raw materials that they take from the developing countries. Consequently, they are in a position to drain the resources and income of the Third World, and put unhealthy pressure on the poor countries. For example on 8th May 1990, the IMF at its meeting adopted a US sponsored proposal which sought to link the 50% increase in its quota with the provision for the suspension of a member of failure to repay its areas. It was a device to get legalized pressure tactics. That is why it was described by the Indian Foreign Minister as unfair and draconian.

The control of international economic institutions and world economy further strengthen the hold of the developed over the developing countries. By virtue of their dominant position the developed minority finds it easy and expedient to determine at will the allocation of world resources in tune with their desired objectives. The will to gain and cling to their position of dominance over world resources has been the guiding principle of the behaviour of the developed countries." This has been a source of much disappointment for the developing countries. They want to end this domination of the developed countries by securing a fairer and just new international economic order.

The inglorious and He economic Role of the Multinational Corporations: Through a large and extensive between of transnational/ multinational corporations, the developed countries have been exercising an unhealthy and undesirable control over the economics and policies of the developing countries. MNCs are owned by the developed countries and these function as their extra-governmental arms for extending their control over markets, economies and policies of the developing countries. A large number of industries in the developing countries are owned by these MNCs. Many international patents are controlled by them. They have a monopolistic control over advanced technology. There are about 5000 gain MNCs of seven countries U.S.A., U.K., France, FRG, Italy, Japan and Canada which are controlling more than 50% of the world production. These corporations virtually control the natural resources and raw materials that are found in abundance in the under-developed countries. By virtue of their monopolistic position, the MNCs make huge profits through their ministries and centres in the developing countries. Even a country like India, which is definitely more developed than other developing countries, continues to suffered economic exploitation at the hands of several MNCs.

The MNCS Have created and are still creating several barriers aimed at checking the "access to markets" and "access to advance technology" efforts of the developing countries. These corporations have the ability to check the rate of economic growth and development and to mould the way of industrial and economic development in the under-developed countries in a way as is deemed ideal to the interests of the MNCs. The barriers to entry created by the MNCS can hardly be countered by the developing countries through any negotiations. Here the developing countries are most vulnerable. "Their exports, be it of manufactured commodities or of primary products, are under the dominant influence of the operation of Trans-national Corporations. Nearly 40% of the world trade is intra-firm trade. The developing countries often find it very difficult to get their due share in world trade because of the monopolistic role of the MNCs." The MNCs have a formidable control over the international trade and these have effected deep peneterations into the economies of the developing countries. The developing countries are sick of the situation and they advocate an end to MNC menace in international economic trade and industrial relations. For this purpose they demand a new international economic order.

The Failure of the Bretten "Voods: The underdeveloped countries have now fully realized the inherent-weaknesses and absolute partial and harmful nature and working of the existing international economic systems. The recurrent monetary crisis which have come to characterize the prevailing international economic system, the failure GATT and UNCTAD, the difficulties in the way of securing and using "special drawing rights," the teaming large payments defects and increased external indebtedness of the under-developed countries, reflects and increased external indebtedness of the under-developed countries, reflects fully the failure of the Breten Woods and the existing international trade system. In fact, in almost everyway existing international system is proving to be a big failure for the countries of the Third World. It is in no meaning for way helping these countries to secure the desired goal of "development." The Third World, therefore, demands a restructuring of international economic system in such a way as shall ensure fair and jut distribution of world income, resources and trade among all the countries. This demand has got christianied as the issue of New International Economic order, and its stands for a new economic system capable of securing the development economic, technological and industrial, or the under-developed side by side with the developed.

All these factors have combined to make the Third World countries rally around the demand for NIEO as they consider it a the way to end their neo-colonial existence in the contemporary era of international relations.

Major Themes and Issues of New international Economic Order

The concept of the New International Economic Order involves several these and issue which the underdeveloped countries desire to settle through global negotiations, more particularly through a North—south dialogue. The following are the major theme of the concept of NIEO:

Restructuring of world Economic relations. The first theme of NIEO is the urgent need for restructuring the world economic relations on a just and reasonable basis. The existing economic relations are characterized by the developing countries as "anachronistic and irrelevant". Realizing the non-viable nature of the existing economic order, the developing countries advocate a new economic order based on equality, interdependence mutual benefit and support for the rights of all nations to work for securing progress, development and a chance for a fair share in world wealth and income.

Institution a changes. In the jargon of contemporary international relations, two institutional changes are deemed essential for safeguarding the rights and securing the needs of the under-developed vis-à-vis the developed countries. First relates to the restructuring of the existing rules and regulations governing the international economic relations, and second relates to the formation of new institutions and systems of cooperation among nations. Presently, the rules governing international economic and trade retains as well as the international institutions responsible for realizing an enforcing these rules and regulations are such, as favour the interests and needs of the developed countries. The World Bank, the IMF, the conventions governing "Intellectual property" (patents, copyright etc.) and other economic institutions stand dominated by the developed countries. GATT is more conducive to the interests of the rich and developed countries. As such NIEO seeks to restructure these rules and institutions wit a view to make these useful for all without any bias or discrimination.

End of Protectionism in International Economy and Trade the concept of NIEO stands for eliminating the existing system of protectionist trade and policies which is destined by the developed countries to safeguard their interests in international economy and trade. By several protectionist trade and economic in international economy and trade. By several protectionist trade and economic policies the developed countries are in a position to impose discriminatory limits on exports to other countries and to make the world trade highly competitive—to the direct and big disadvantage for the developing countries. Discriminatory limits on exports and imports, even against the GATT rules, are frequently made and pressed into use by the developed countries. The past record of international trade bears test into myth this charge. Australia, Canada, France, the United Kingdom, the United States and Sweden have imposed new quotas and so called 'orderly marketing arrangement on the developing countries exports of footwear. A new protocol of the Multi-Fibre arrangement, covering the period through 1981, the permitted imposition of more severe restrictions on clothing and textile. Under it, the EM reduced 1978 quotas for three countries beneath the actual 1976 levels and severely limited the growth of quotas of other countries, including many that are only beginning to export these exports. Analysing the bad effects of such protectionist policies and trade, on the economies and international trade of the developing countries. A President of the World Bank. Mr. Mcnamara in one of his speeches observed, "the net effect of all these restrictive measures will be to limit the growth of developing countries' export f clothing and textile on only 5% per annum over the next few years compared to some 16% per annum in the period of 1967-76. The European Community and United States have introduced special protective measures regarding steel, which pose serious difficulties for those developing countries now emerging as exporters. UK has imposed quotas on television set from the developing countries and similar action has been threatened in the United States and elsewhere." Such protectionist trade and policies have been a source of a big strain and loss for the developing countries Their import bills have boomed while their exports have tended to be stagnant. The need is to end protectionism in trade and economy, and this is a vital theme of NIEO.

Transfer of Capital Resources. Another theme of NIEO is the actual transfer of capital resources along with the knowledge to put them to beneficial use in order to enable the underdeveloped countries not only to produce more for themselves but also to produce more for export to other countries. These transfers can take place either through private investment or economic aid channeled through official agencies both bilateral and multilateral. Cancellation of outstanding debts of the Third World countries and the grant of 0.7% of G.N.P. international as developmental aid to the developing countries can solve the capital needs of the entire Third World.

Transfer of Technology. Technology plays a key role in economic development. The inability of the developing countries to register a higher economic growth rate and development is largely due to the low-level of technology that is at their disposal. The recourse to advanced technology is vitally necessary for increased and efficient productivity. Its contribution, along with other factor's of production, is always substantial for all round development. For securing advance technology the developing countries find themselves dependent upon the development countries. The later, through international patents and protective policies and measures have a virtual monopoly over advanced technological know-how and expertise. They are not prepared to transfer it to the developing countries without getting favorable commitments and several desired trade and economic agreements. Often their terms are not reasonable from the developing countries' point of view. Through NIEO, the Third World wants to systematize and facilitate the transfer of advanced technology from the developed to the developing countries.

Control over the Growing Menace of Multinational Corporations. Presently, several multinational corporations (MNCs) are playing a big role in the spheres of international economy, trade technology and industrial production. They are controlling almost all the international patents in respect of advanced technological know-how. These are the instruments of the developed countries for maintaining their control over international economy and trade as well as for directing and controlling the economies and policies of the third World countries the developing countries are often forced by the developed countries to import the required technology through the expansion of cooperation with the MNCs which are held to be the mot important channel for the transfer of capital technology and managerial expertise. However, this exercise involves high costs and heavy burdens for the developing countries. MNCs charge very high fees for the supply of advanced technology. With poor economic resources and poverty writ large, the developing countries find it very difficult, to purchase the technology from the MNCs. The fear of MNCs' interference with their domestic markets, economies, social and cultural values and decision-making further prevents them to deal with MNCs. The role of MNCs in international economy has been negative and damaging as it has been a source of maintaining and increasing the gap between developed and developing countries. These have always acted as instruments of neo-colonialism of the rich over the poor countries. These have often played a dirty role in securing the overthrow elected governments in many developing countries. Dr. B.N. Merhrish, in his article; "India and the NIEO', has well summarized the Menace of MNCs in international relations: "The strategies of MNCs and their responses to governmental and international policies are such that instead of increases to governmental and international policies are such that instead of increase in their share of benefit, the host countries lose some of the benefits stemming from the activities of multinational corporations. "Multinational Corporations are know to have applied diplomatic pressure to secure more favourable terms. They are a syn bol of the 'international oligopoly." They have been trying to sabotage the development strategy formulated by the United Nations and refuse to meet the needs of the developing countries." Indeed, the role of MNCs in international economic and political relations has been unhealthy and harmful. The developing countries want an end to the menace of MNCs and for this advocate the formulations of a code of conduct for these corporations as a part of a new international economic order. "An essential ingredient in the new international economic order is, " writes Paul A. Tharp, "a set of policies to curb the monopolistic practices of the multinational corporations, especially trade."

Recognition and Protection of the Interest of the Commodity Producers. In this era of global interdependence, the commodity producers—mostly the developing countries, are playing almost as important a role as is being played by the industrialized and advanced countries. However, the existing international economic order gives only marginal importance to the commodity producers. The lack of rules for safeguarding their interests make the developing countries live at the mercy of the developed countries. The dependence of the developing countries for the export of their commodities, the cut-throat unchecked open competition in international markets and protectionism in trade policies of the developed countries, together combine to make the lot of the Third world very poor and unfruitful. The developing countries want an international code of rules for protecting their trade interests. International agreements to raise and stabilize the prices of raw material products exported by developing countries have been a prominent theme in the new economic order." The success of the producer cartels in oil and bauxite has stimulated interest in similar programmes for copper, tin, nickel, and primary products (Jute etc.) in general.'

A Greater and Fixed Share in International Exports and a total Revision of the Brettonwoods System. Another important theme of the New economic order is the securing of improved access to export markets in rich countries. The existing system unduly favours the rich *vis-a-is* the poor. In the presence of big economic and industrial gap between the developed and the developing countries. GATT and UNCTAD and failed to produce the desired effect and change in internal economic and trade system. Unregulated and open competition between the developed and the underdeveloped countries has proved to be a highly damaging aspect of international trade relations as it has always favoured the developed to the disadvantage of the underdeveloped. The Third world countries demands a definite fixed share in all international exports and tariff preferences in their favour as part of a new economic order. They argue that greater export sales facilitated by tariff preferences for developing countries and an end to shameful non-tariff barriers in some more developed countries would have a number of beneficial effects. With greater foreign exchange earnings, the developing countries could import the larger volume of capital goods and raw materials necessary to sustain more rapid growth of output, income and employment and thereby move towards development. The need is to end the existing terms of international economic relations and trade which are unfavourable to the Third World countries. GATT and UNCTAD have virtually outlived their existence and so is the case of the entire Brettonwoods System. Bretton woods has failed to create new truly global economic institutions for coordinating international economic relations. It has tended to favour he rich to the disadvantage f the poor. GATT has not been fully successful to secure greater trade liberalization. Open competition among the developed and the developing countries has proved to be a barrier to the growth of the Third World. IMF has nearly failed to meet the developmental loan requirements of the third world. International economic institutions have come to be dominated by the rich and advanced countries. The Brettewoods has Failed to be adequately responsive to the needs of the developing countries. The need, therefore, is to replace it by a new economic system. The third World demands a new system with a new set of priorities, principles procedures. And definite rules for governing contemporary international economic relations. The whole exercise should ensure the fulfillment of developmental needs of the developing countries as a part of total restructuring of international economic order on principles of equitable and just distribution of world income, resources and wealth among all the nations

Self-Reliance, Finally, a major theme of NIEO is self-reliance. The developing countries aspire to move from underdevelopment to development. They want to be self-reliant—capable of satisfying the needs of their populations. This alone can ensure their effective and equal participations in international relations. The developing countries are fully aware that this objective can be achieved only by their own determination and efforts. However, they are also conscious of their present dependence upon the developed. For overcoming it, they want a new international economic order with a view to eliminate the existing partial and rich dominated international economic systems.

Mini-Income targets. The NIEO involves a demand for creating a material minimal standard of living, a mini income for those who are facing harsh economic realities. The developed and rich countries should accept and introduced such reforms in the international system as can lead to fixed mini incomes for the poor and developing countries. This can go a long way to help the poor countries in their struggles to withstand he current economic hardships. Henry Kissinger, a former US Secretary of State, has rightly remarked that "International cooperation must be directed to the problems of creating a secure basic economic security for all and this challenge is above ideologies and block politics. No international order can be considered must if cooperation with the aim to raise the poorest of the world to a decent standard of living is one of its basic principles."

Conclusion. All these themes and issues together constitute the warp and woof of the concept of New international Economic

Order. The developing countries are demanding: (i) a restructuring of the existing economic order; (ii) total recasting of the Brettenwoods System; (iii) an increased and definite share in world trade; (iv) writing off the old debts; (v) grant of international developmental aid; (vi) transfer of advanced technology by the developed countries; (vii) increased help for the development of agriculture and industry; and (viii) a due share in international decision-making. Fr achieving this, the Third World countries want a comprehensive North-South dialogue. They are also trying to develop through the promotion of South-South Cooperation for mutual development. The July 1985 conference of the ministers of the 'Group of 77' countries agreed to work out a mutual General scheme for tariff Preferences (GSTP) for the Third World countries. This is expected to facilitate and increase import—export relations among the developing countries. The luck-warm and almost evasive attitude of the developed countries ahs forced the Third World to go in for South-South Cooperation. The issue of NIEO has come to be a big controversial issue, rather the biggest issue in the relations between the two Developed Worlds and the Third World.

Emergence and Struggle of the Concept of NIEO

The evolution of the concept of New International Economic Order can be traced from mid-70s, more particularly from 1 May, 1974, because on this day, the sixth special session of he UN General Assembly adopted a "Declaration on the establishment of New International economic Order" and there after several steps were initiated towards its achievement. Before 11974, NIEO was almost a theoretical and rhetorical phrase, after this Declaration it came t be practical action. The declaration proposed to replace the existing inequitable economic system as based upon the Bretton Woods proposals by a new intrnational economic sysem based upon the concept of equitable distribution of world income and resources. The new system was "TO CORRECT INEQualitIES anD REDREss existing injustices nd ensure steady and speedy economic devlopment, peace and justice for present and future generations," and "to restore socialjustice in the world which has disappeared over decades of capitalism, imperisalism and the monopoly of technical talent."

The adoption of this declaration by the UNO ws the result of consistent and persistent efforts of the tird World. The Afro-Asian Conference in Bendung (1955). Non-aligned conferences in Belgrade (1961) Cairo (1964), Lusaka (1970) and Algeria (1973) played an important role in strengthening international public opinion in favour of NIEO. In1974, the UN General Assembly took up the discussion of raw material and development as it was recommended by the Algiers non-alignment summit. The sixth special session of UN General Assembly (9 April to 2 May, 1974) adopted the declaration for the establishment of NIEO. By this time, the western attitude under western a change. Moving away from skepticism and indifference toword cooperation, governments began to show a growing readiness to seek the road to political stability and economic prosperity in a more rational way through negotiations. The raw material producing countries has also come of age. Politically, they were able to defend their sovereign rights, economically they seemed equipped to purse their national aspirations and internationally they appeared to be committed to seek cooperation.

The Principles adopted by the U.N. Sixth Special session. The Declaration adopted by the Sixth special Session of the UN Assembly included the principles mentioned below:

(i) Full permanent sovereignty of every state over its natural resources and all economic activities including the right to nationalize or transfer its ownership to its nationals.

(ii) Right of all states and people to restitution and full compensation for the exploration and depletion of and damages to the natural resources and all other resource under foreign occupation or alien or colonial domination or apartheid.

(iii) Regulation and supervision of the activities of transnational corporations.

(iv) Just and equitable relationship between the prices of raw materials, primary products, manufactured and semi-manufactured goods exported by developed countries.

(v) Development aid without strings and flow of real resources to developing countries.

(vi) Transfer of science and technology to developing countries and improvement of their indigenous technology.

(vii) The need for all states to put an end to the waste of natural resources.

(viii) Facilitating the role of producer's associations in the sustained growth of economy and accelerating the development of developing countries.

Guidelines for Securing the above Principles. The resolution on NIEO laid down several guidelines with respect to the securing of these principles:

(i) fundamental problems of raw materials and prime commodities related to trade and development.

(ii) International monetary system.

(iii) Industrialization.

(iv) Transfer of technology.

(v) Regulation and control over the activities of transnational corporations.

(vi) Charter of Economic Rights and Duties.

(vii) Assistance in the exercise of permanent sovereignty of states over natural resources. Strengthening the role of the UN system in the field of international economic cooperation.

Seventh special Session of U.N. General assembly. The General assembly Seventh special session on Development and International economic Co-operation in September 1975 served as a turning point in the North-South dialogue because of the realism displayed by both the third World and the West in their negotiations. Sympathetic cooperation between the "group of 77' and the West, resulted in a compromise resolution which, when implemented, will prove to be a long a awaited milestone in the path of the Third Word's progress.

The Provisions of the 1975 Resolution. The basic provisions of the resolution read:

(i) The expansion and diversification of trade, improvement of productivity, and the increase of export earnings of the developing countries.

(ii) The attainment of stable, remunerative and equitable prices for exported raw materials.

(iii) The reduction or removal of tariff and non-tariff barriers affecting the exports of the developing countries.

(iv) An increase in the volume and improvement of their term of development assistance.

(v) The attainment of the official development assistance target of 0.7 percent GNP of all donor countries by the end of this decade.

(vi) An increase in he developing countries access on favourable terms to world capital market.

(vii) The relief of debt burdens of the most seriously affected countries

(viii) Increasing international contact and surveillence over the creation and equitable distribution of world liquidity.

(ix) Facilitating the process of industrialization in the developing world.

Lima Conference 1975. At the Lima conference of the Foreign Ministers of the Non-aligned nations, a convention establishing solidarity fund for economic and social development was approved. This fund was to be financed principally through voluntary contributions, and Kuwait offered to make an initial contribution of one billion dollars. It was further decided at this conference to establish a special fund financing buffer stocks of raw materials and primary products exported by the developing countries.

Parts Dialogue 1975. For analysing and improving the relations between the developed and developing nations, a conference was held in Paris in December 1975. Twenty-eight developing and developed nations attended this conference and discussed issue of international economic cooperations, and to initiate an intensified dialogue. The participates agreed to establish an international secretariat and 4 commissions: (i) Energy: (ii) Raw Materials; (iii) Development; and (iv) Financial Affairs. The developing countries were successful in persuading the developed countries to accept that there was a firm link between the problem of energy and the problem of development. However, nothing concrete could emerge on the issue of NIEO.

Colombo Summit of the Non-aligned. At the Colombo summit of the nonaliged nations (1976) it was agreed. (1) to mutually assist each other to reach an annual target of 4% in food and agricultural production in the next 10 years, (2) to initiate a plan of mutual cooperation to diminish their dependence on multi-national pharmaceutical companies, (3) to create a "Third World Bank's, (4) to explore ways and means of breaking communication barriers that separate these countries, and (5) to set-up a news agency pool to diminish their dependence on Western news agencies.

UN General Assembly Special Session 1980. Acting on the demand made by the Third world countries, the U.N. general Assembly met on 25 August 1980 in a special session for discussion the economic relations between the two developed worlds and the Third World. In this session, he third World countries demanded increased aid, cancellation of their more than $360 billion debts, more free trade and guaranteed prices for raw-material. However, their demands produced little impact on the developed countries and consequently, the session failed to produce and tangible result except that in initiated the process for opening nine months of global negotiations, beginning from January 1981, which were designed to secure more frutful and equitable trade and economic relations between the developed and the developing countries. However, these negotiations also failed to make any real headway.

Cancun Summit 1981. Leaders of 14 developing and 8 industrialized nations met in Cancun, Mexico, on October 22-23, 1981, to discuss the progress of North-south negotiation in the United Nations and other forums, It was described as an International Meeting on Cooperation and development.

Invitations were sent out to 23 Nations of whom only the Soviet Union failed to respond. The Soviet Union described it as "dialogue of the deaf" which could serve only to exemplify the differences between the developing and industrialized nations. Cuba, despite being the current chairman of the NAM, was not invited to the summit, since it was felt by the 11 co-sponsors that Cuban participation would precipitte the withdrawal of the United States.

The Cancun summit began on October 21, with President Lopez Portillo and M. Pierre Trudeau as co-chairmen. In his speech, President Lopez Portillo observed that international financial and trade institutions such as the IMF, the World Bank and the GATT had "depend resentment and frustration', since they tended to come" mere sounding boards" for the countries which dominated the voting.

U.S. President Reagan, while addressing he summit on he first day confirmed that the United States was prepared to take part in the global negotiations provided that the following conditions were met: (i) that global negotiations should be oriented towards specific areas; (ii) that they should not seek to create new international institutions, but should recognize the "competence, functions and powers" of existing international agencies; (iii) that they should be aimed at achieving greater international economic growth; and (iv) that they should be held in a cooperative atmosphere "rather than one in which views became polarized and chances for agreement are needlessly sacrified." Among other representatives of industrialized countries, President Mittrrand, Mr. Trudeau and Mr

Falldin, all expressed support for the launching of global negotiations at the United Nations.

At the end of the meeting, Britain the U.S.A. and Western Germany maintained their view that negotiations on restructuring the world economy should take place in the relevant international agencies, while the other 19 leaders favoured placing ultimate authority over global negotiations in the United Nations. According to the summary of the proceedings issued by the two co chairman (no official communique was issued). The heads of the state and government confirmed "a consensus to launch global negotiations on a basis to be mutually agreed in circumstances offering the prospect of meaningful progress." However, no agreed target date for their commencement was specified. This summit virtually failed to arrive at an agreed decision regarding future course of North-South-South economic relations.

December 1981 Resolution and its Failure. In early December 1981, the representatives of the developing countries at the United Nations, drafted a resolution for the General Assembly proposing North-South negotiations on restructuring the international economy. However, because of the U.S. objections on the plea that it posed a threat to the independence of established economic institutions like World Ban and the IMF, the resolution was not taken up for discussion. Since the failure of this resolution no major resolution move have been made for securing North-South dialogue over NIEO.

South-South meet at New Delhi, 1982. With a view to secure increased economic and trade cooperation among the developing countries, as well as for securing coordination in their policies over the issue of the approach to be pursued within the Group of77 (Now nearly 120 developing countries). The meeting too place on February 22-24, 1982 and was attended by the representatives of 44 developing countries. Rs. Indira Gandhi in her opining speech expressed concern over what she described as "visible deterioration in the global economy since the Cancum summit", and she was especially critical of "protectionism in industrialised countries" which she said had "victimized the developing world".

"Developing countries should close their ranks to withstand pressure from affluent nations."

The South-south cooperation conference agreed to concentrate upon the following points for further considerations; (i) The formulation of programmes for agricultural self-reliance and food self-sufficiency: (ii) the creation of a world Bank "energy affiliate"; and (iii) the creation of a multi-lateral financing facility for joint ventures and technical cooperation among developing countries. On the last subject, an expert group was to be convened under Indian chairmanship to report back to the Group of 77.

The conference concluded with unanimous acceptance of the importance of cooperation for collective self-reliance, and with a renewed call for efforts to reach an agreement on the launching of North-South global economic negotiations.

South-South cooperation GSTP July 1985. The idea of Global System of Trade Preference (GSTP) was mooted first in 1982 and took shape at the two UNCTAD meetings in 1984 which did the spadework. This idea was mooted for securing increased trade cooperation and relations among the developing countries.

The two day ministerial level meeting of the developing countries was help on 25-26, 1985 to consider GSTP as means for promoting South-South cooperation. The then Union commerce Minister of India, Mr. V.P. Singh presided over the meeting with was inaugurated by Prime Minister Rajiv Gandhi. In his speech, the Prime Minister called upon the developing countries to work or collective self-reliance through boosting their trade. More than 70 countries which deliberated for two day on way of making south-South cooperation meaningful and mature agreed that the negotiating committed (for GSTP) should consider across the board tariff reduction of up to ten percent in addition to a product-by-product approach. The GSTP declaration also unidentified sectors for particular social-economic importance for the developing countries such as processed tropical products, non-textile measures. Another important decision of meeting was to take up periodic reviews at political levels for monitoring and evaluation of the progress relating to GSTP, and that the next such meeting will be help in Brazil.

The Delhi meeting made a decisive breakthrough by approving to have a workable counterpart to the rich nations concept of the Global Scheme of Preferences. According to the time-table chalked out at the meeting, agreement incorporating ground rules were to be completed by October 31, 1985. The techniques and modalities were to be worked out by December 31, 1985. The techniques and modalities were to be worked out b December 31, 1985. The techniques and modalities were to be worked out by December 31, 1985, and a negotiating plan was to be drawn up by February 28, 1986. The first round of talks (negotiating plan was to be drawn up by February 28, 1986. the first round of talks (negotiations) was to begin not later than May 1, 1986. This tie-bound schedule was made to secure definite progress towards GSTP among the developing countries. In actual practice, however, no results were achieved. Talks were held but no agreement was made.

With title hope for an early north-south dialogue/agreement over NIEO, the promotion at South-south cooperation constitutes the best way for the developing countries to develop. South-South cooperation constitutes a good step towards a defacto NIEO. NAM< group of 77 and the third World countries in all conferences have been trying hard to secure a North-south dilogue on NIEO, but their efforts have not yet been successful. As an alternative, a programme for South-South cooperation is gradually emerging. The third World countries regard it as their best. NAM has taken a lead in this direction. The Eighth NAM summit decided to hold a full fledged conference of the nonaligned Foreign Ministers on sough-south cooperation. June 1987 Non-aligned Foreign Ministers Conference on South-south Cooperation. The pyongyang Conference, The first conference of Non-aligned Foreign Ministers on South-South cooperation was held on 12 and 13 June, 1987 at Pyonyang. It gave a call to give new impetus to cooperation among the non-aligned and other developing countries and adopt a new approach to make such cooperation among the non-aligned and other developing countries and adopt a new approach to make such cooperation more dynamic. The ministers while adopting the Pyongyang declaration, listed a number of measures to develop and strengthen economic independence of these countries which would build collective self-reliance and increase their bargaining power in negotiations with the North.

Reaffirming the unwavering commitment of all non-aligned countries to economic cooperation among themselves, the declaration noted that the current world economic crisis and the economic policy of some rich nations had a negative impact on the economies of countries of the south. Referring to the indebtedness of developing countries, the declaration called for a political dialogue between the developed and the Third World Countries to resolve the problem up paid debts.

Reiterating its demand for an international conference on money an finance for development at the earliest, the declaration expressed concern at the continuous decline incommodity prices and regretted that certain developed countries did not show the required political will to remove trade imbalance at the Ist Uruguay meeting.

An action plan, incorporated in the declaration, called for measures for economic cooperation at the national, regional and international levels to promote South-south cooperation.

The plansaid competent professonal consultancy organisaiotn savailable in developingcountires must eb tappedina better way to implemnt various acton oriented programmes.

It called forpayments and eclerign house arrangementsto support expansion of trade amogndeveloping countries under the global system of trade preferences.

Tehadoptionof the Pyongyang declaration and the planof a ctonadopted by this conference of 101 delegations from NAM counries could go a long way towards increasing and expanding cooperation among th edeveloping countries in carrying forward the struggle for the NIEO. The Pyongyang Declarations gave a call for a political North South dialogue on the debt crisis—

though a reitertion of earlier such appeals from other forums—came not a minute too soon. The Third World countries among themselves carry a debt burden of well over a trillion dollars and its repayment is running into great difficulties. Some African countries have to set apart as much as 40 to 60 percent of their annual export earning for debt servicing. Such indeed is the seriousness of the debt crisis that the rate of IMF loan disbursements has not fallen to less than the then money it gets back from the debtor nations and the much flaunted baker Plant has also failed to defuse the debt bomb. Unless urgent political talks are held between the North and the South to resolve this crisis, it could lead to a major economic disaster.

Commenting upon the Pyongyang Declaration, the Tribune in one of its editionals rightly observed, "The declaration ha rightly stressed the inter-relationship between peace, disarmament and development because much of the Third World debt burden has been caused by avoidable purchase of weaponary from the developed countries. The high rate of obsolescence of sophisticated weaponry makes it imperative for them to go on allocating higher amounts for weapons purchases just to maintain what could be called the balance of terror in the world. A global disarmament arrangement is, thus, a necessary con commitment of a new international economic order. To the extent the deliberations at Pynyang helped to expand mutual cooperation among the Third World countries and encourage South-south trade and economic cooperation to reduce their dependence on the rich countries by building up a regime of collective self-reliance, they will be planning a major role in saving the world from the gravest economic disaster it has faced since 1929."

Meetings of South-South Commission. The second meeting of South-South Commission for betterment of third world countries was held at Kual Lumpur March 1988. In it the Malayasian PM Mr. Mahathir Mohammed urged the member states to formulate a multipronged strategy to combat the economic problems in developing countries brought on by statement in the implementation of the NIEO. The meeting, the first of its kind, dedicated itself to focus on issues of South-South co-operation for self-reliance and South-North relations. The commission which was presided over by former Tanzanian president Julius Nyerere was entrusted with the task of analyzing and commenting on the evolving global environment as was being influenced by recent political, economic and technological changes in the North.

Till Today (1990) the South Commission has held in all, seven sessions but its meetings have resulted into no concrete results.

The continued Neo-colonial control of the North over the economies and policies of the South, the protectionist politics adopted by the industrialized countries against the import of processed and unprocessed commodities from the Third World countries, the steep fall in their population, growth rate and the resultant slow-down in the growth of the inelastic demand for essential commodities, the persistent fall in the commodity prices very the past few years and the steady development of a rapid global movement toward an "international service and information economy" the changes in Eastern Europe containing the possibility of diversion of Foreign Aid from developed to the Eastern European states, have all made an imperative to usher in an era of South-South Cooperation for the sheer survival of the Third World countries." North is not agreeing in favour of NIEO. The South has only one alternative development through South-south cooperation.

Meeting of G-15. With a view to encourage and lead the drive for South-South cooperation, a three day summit meeting of the groups of 15 (G-15) Third world countries were held at Kuala Lumpur on 1 June 1990. It was designed to act as an 'action group' for the south. The leaders of G-15 made it clear that the Action group was to be an elitist group of a rival competitor to South-South cooperation; Group of 77 and NAM movements. They described its role as a catalyst group intended to invigorate action towards increased and mature South-South cooperation.

The joint communiqué issued after the G-15 meeting listed several agreements among the 15 developing countries for increasing

South-South cooperation and for adopting an agreed stand at the Uruguay Round of trade talk under GATT. The communiqué declared "We affirm our commitment to a balanced and successful conclusion of the Uruguay Round of Multilateral trade Negotiations which takes into account the concerns and needs of the developing countries. We shall closely consult each other and coordinate our efforts towards this end." "It gave a cal for increased South – South cooperation, North-south cooperation, end of buyers conference, and immediate steps for securing GSTP among Third World countries," GSTP (Global System of trade Preferences) among the Third World countries was accepted as a necessary and valuable vehicle for promoting trade and closer economic cooperation among them. It gave a call that the second round of negotiations be launched under GSTP as soon as possible.

Among other things, the group agreed on about a dozen projects for South—south cooperation, with three of them ready to be started off immediately. The other projects requiring more details would be worked on further, with the countries proposing them being responsible for the follow-up further, with the countries proposing them being responsible for the follow-up actions.

The co-operation projects include a trade financing facility, to start on a bilateral basis first among any two countries through guarantees of the respective central banks, while exports would meet and consult further on how this type of payment arrangements and guarantees could be multlatralised. The other two projects are the establishment of a South Investment. Trade and Technology data Exchange Centre, and of a Business and Investment Forum for the South.

The G-15 communique also covered a number of critical issues (including finance, debt, trade, technology and environment).

In terms of action, the leaders agreed that financial experts from their countries should met and discuss the external debt problem with a view to formulating common approaches.

In the area of trade, and ongoing Uruguay Round. they

agreed to "Closely consult each other and co-ordinate our efforts" to achieve a balanced and successful outcome of Uruguay Round which would take into account "the concerns and needs of the developing countries."

In the area of technology, they underscored the importance of improving the access to as well as diffusion and utilization of new technologies in the south and the need of any regime on intellectual property to effectively promote technological development in the Third world and its access t high technologies. They also agreed to "initiate a significant programme of cooperation in science and technology to enhance the development of the south."

In other areas of joint action the G-15 agreed on consulting the G-24 (The Third World Ground IMF. World Bank institution at Washington) regarding modalities for assisting Third World countries in their dealings with the multilateral financial institutions and in advising Third Word countries on possible effects of the condition imposed by institutions for taking their loans.

G-15 leaders also agreed to holo their summit meeting on an annual basis (The next to be held in 1991—perhaps in June—in Caraces, Venezuela); on the setting up of a teering Committee on the three Foreign Ministers (from Malaysia, Venezuela and Senegal) for coordinating the work of G-15 until the next summit, and on some institutional support. For the last objective, the Steering Committee was given the mandate to decide on the size and location of small group of permanent staff to assist it.

With these agreements and a general understanding to act as catalyst or an Action group of securing South-South cooperation and for affecting North-south relations in a desired way, the G-15 meeting covered a good ground. However, its actual success can be determined by is future role and success with GATT and in resolving other issues of South-South and North-south relations.

Meanwhile the relations between the North and South, i.e., between the developed and the developing countries, continue to be what these have been since 1970s. The North is continuing it control over international economic system as well as over the economies and policies of the Third world countries.

At the beginning of 1990s, which promises to be a decade of even greater challenges,.there are greater prospects of a 'replay" of the adverse factors such as dwindling of financial flows, trade protection and abnormal interest rates. Growth prospects of the major industrial nations are not rated high, at lest in the initial years the decade. There are serious concerns about the trade and economic groupings of powerful nations like the single European Community Market by 1993, US-Canada free trade zone, and other groupings that could follow especially in the event of the failure of the Uruguay round of trade negotiations at the end of 1990.

Experts in global economy have cautioned that the international environment might not be markedly better in the 1990s and the Third World might not regain the growth momentum of the 1950s and 1060s. In regard to resource flows from developed nations, greater attention is now being focused on eastern Europe which is undergoing a total transformation, both political and economic. The reconstruction and adjustments of these countries, shifting their centralized planning to market orientations, could not only be a long drawn out process but also involved the import of massive capital from western nations.

Already there is a competition for saving from richer countries and the surpluses of countries like Japan and Germany. The latter would divert much of its resources to the economy of Germany, while Japanese surpluses will continue to flow, at lest in the first half of the decade, to the UNITED States as well as to the countries of east and South-east Asia, that is, mainly the relatively better off developing countries in the category of new industrializing economies (NIEs).

Overall, the global prospects are hardly conducive for the developing countries to continue to adhere to the dependence syndrome. NAM Economic Committee 1992

The NAM Economic committee (1992) Chaired by Indonesian President Suharto has called for democratization of international relations both in economic and political sectors.

The Economic Committee, did not is cuss that Indonesian proposal to establish a committee to deal with the huge debt of the non-aligned countries. The global issues covered related to international economic-co-operation and environment. It has been agreed that conservation of the environment be linked to the eradication of poverty, especially in developing countries.

It has been noted that the successful outcome of the Uruguay round of multilateral trade negotiations though still uncertain, is a matter of great importance to the developing countries. The principal concern remains the roll back of protectionist measure. The pressure from the industrially advanced countries on issues, such as intellectual property rights must be resisted.

The Committee has strongly urged the producer and consumer countries to make every effort to revive commodity agreements which have lapsed for all products except rubber, because such agreement are not only in the interests of producers, but of consumers as well. It has also urged the signatories to the common fund in the framework of the Integrated programme of commodities to revive the schemes and to make them fully operational. The proposals for the convening of an international conference on commodities with a view to reviewing the principal activity of the common fund was supported.

The committee underlined the need to forge a new, global consensus and commitment to strengthen international economic co-operation for development. It was convinced that international economic cooperation for development can only be fruitful if it is not perceived in terms of demands on the side of the developing countries and charity on the side of the developed ones.

Dakar Summit of the Group-15, 1992

From the joint communiqué adopted at the Dakar (Senegal) Summit, two issues relating to the dialogue with the G-7 stand out. The first in the problem of external debt faced by the third world and the second, international trade, with special emphasis on trade in commodities. The G-15 has identified the areas of trade it is trade in primary commodities, which continues to be of vital importance to them. The present situation is characterized by a continuing fluctuation of prices and a long-term trend which has resulted in historically low level of prices of primary commodities. The factors responsible for this are, structural adjustment programmes, debt servicing and the substitution of primary commodities with synthetics. Apart form commodities the trade regime in textile an clothing has remained discriminatory and restrictive. There I a need of liberalization in textiles trade and to fully restore the application of the normal rules of free and non-discriminatory trade in the area.

On the issue of the external debt of developing countries, it is asking for lower debt servicing rations, which can be achieved through an increase in the flow of finance, including concessional finance for development. It has asked for an increase in real terms of resources available under the Tenth Replenishment of he International Development association, additional financial flows under the Structural Adjustment Facility for medium-term concessional flows to low income countries, as strengthening of the capital base of the World Bank and the regional development banks and generous flows from the fourth Replenishment of the International Fund for Agricultural Development.

G-15 has launched a few special projects of them, India is the coordination for The South Investment, Trade and Technology data Exchange centre, which was approved at te first g-15 summit in Kuala Lumpure is already operational. The SIT TDEC data base currently contains over 7,000 documents detailing mainly trade related information.

Greater global interdependence and prolonged economic recession in the North underline the need for South to look to itself to accelerate development and growth. Areas identified for South-South cooperation include the projection bilateral payments arrangements, on population and family planning, self-propelling growth schemes, technical personnel training development of non metallic mineral raw materials, environment mining, river and watershed recovery project.

Dunkel Draft

GATT is a multilateral body that lays down a common code of conduct in international trade and acts as a forum for negotiations and consultations to overcome trade problem and reduce trade barriers. So far seven rounds have been completed and 8th round (Urugnay Round) is under progress.

The Uruguay Round started in 1986. It has a two part agenda relating to trade in goods and negotiations relating to trade in sources.

During 1990, the progress of negotiations were impeded by serious disagreements, particularly in the following area; (a) the alleged abuse of "anti-dumping" measures to protect the importing country's domestic industry, in contravention of GATT rules, (b) Agricultural trade, (c) Progressive dissoluton of multifiber agreement. Talks finally collapsed in Dec. 1990 de to EEC's firm and UN compromising stand on agricultural subsidies. Negotiations again resumed in Feb. 1991.

To break this deadlock M Arthur Dunkel present a draft on Dec. 20, 1991 which contains the substance of discussion of all hitherto disputed points of agenda and required the members to accept it or reject it. There are main three areas which require attention.

First, the draft on Trade related Aspects of Intellectual Property Rights (TIPS) related to the awarding of both product and process patents for all categories of inventions, including areas like drugs and pharmaceuticals. This means, for instance India's existing patent laws need to be changed and it is likely that many existing technological development projects would be abandoned. Article 27 (3) of the TRIPS agreement stipulates that patent should be given micro organism, which will mean to patent life. It will have far reaching consequences on the developing countries.

The second area is agriculture, where the draft seeks to grant of product and process patents to all bio-technological innovations ir :luding micro organism, all non-biological and micro-biological process for the production of plant and animals. Thus, the proposal would act as a barrier to the modernization of agriculture in the developing countries since the local seed companies and formers would be debarred from multiplying seeds and selling them to other farmers. Under new provisions, the MNCs will have very little compulsion to transfer new technology to the developing countries enterprise.

The third areas is Trade Related Investment Measures (TRIMS) which suggests that developing countries should lift all restrictions on foreign investment. The draft permits foreign firms to refuse granting patent rights and increase to them the access of import of goods. It will mean much worse term for technical collaboration and will lead to reimposition of technological dependency in critical areas. The country would be prohibited from placing any obligations on foreign investors relating to export promotion, use of local component and raw materials and technological transfer requirements.

The Dunkel draft has grave implications for the economic sovereignty and well being of the people in the developing countries the main concern in the areas, related to TRIPS, TRIMS and GATS, textiles and agriculture, has been ignored. By bringing all into GATT, the draft has gone beyond the *Puntadel Este* Declaration in promoting the interest of the developed countries.

Instead of self-reliance and indigenous development it opens the way for the unlimited control by MNCs of the economies of the Third world. It reverse the developing countries demand of the 'new international economic order." Moreover, the draft rather than satisfying the needs of the people in the Third World, will impose heavier burden of external debt and debt servicing. The destruction o local technology and small companies and weakening of the country's industrial muscle, will increase misery and unemployment.

The developing countries cannot surrender their right to use the instrument of subsidies. to promote particular agricultural crop. The Dunkel draft will obstruct the modernization and spread the new technology to the various sections of the farmers in the developing countries.

The successful completion of the Uruguay Round is crucial for the victor o the principle of multilateratlism in International trade and help in facilitating the developing countries demand of the' new international economic order.

Genesis of the New International Economic Order

Evidence of Persistent Inequities

1970s were also marked by a major challenge by Third World nations against an international economic order that they believed to be strongly stacked against their economic interest. Although we have identified and analyzed the fundamental areas of content in our chapters on international trade, private investment, and foreign assistance, it is useful to reiterate the impressive and growing evidence that demonstrates how poor nations are being disadvantaged by existing global market structures.

First, there is the substantial imbalance in the distribution of international monetary reserves. Although third World nations contained over 70% of the world's population, they received less than 4% of the international reserves of $131 billon during the first a half of the 1970s. Because rich nations control the creation and distribution of these reserves (e.g., through their own monetary expansion and through their effective control over actions of the IMF). They have the power to manipulate these international financial assets to their own benefit.

Second, rich nations benefit disproportionately in the distribution of the value added to the products traded between themselves and the poor nations. Unlike the developed countries. Third world nations receive back only as mall fraction of the final price obtained from international purchases of their products. The reason is simple: LDCs are often too weak and powerless to exercise any substantial control over the processing, shipping, and marketing of their primary products. Often they themselves must purchase back at substantially marked-up, prices the final products processed from their own raw materials.

Third, in order to protect and perpetuate profits and jobs in uncompetitive and declining sectors of their economies, rice nations typically resort to tariff and non-tariff protection of inefficient domestic industries while restricting immigration to maintain high wages. Thus, their rhetoric in support of the "free" working of the international market mechanism belies the reality of their market management and control. Third world countries contented, therefore, that any genuine competitive successes they may realize from international trade become nullified by the restrictive commercial policies of increasingly protectionist industrial nations.

Fourth, most of the contracts, leases, and concessions that the multinational corporations have negotiated in the past with the developing countries have unfairly benefited the MNCs at the expense of the host country. Thus LDC host governments contend that because of royalty payments, tax concessions.

In addition to political and philosophical writings an important precursor of international organisation has been the practice of multinational conferences, which has paralleled the growth of the nation-state system since the Peace of Westphalia (1648). In the closing phases of the bloody and destructive Thirty years' war (1618-48), assemblies of victorious and vanquished nation-states met for over tree years at Osnabruck and Munser (in the German Province of Westphalia)) in what came to be referred to as the First European Congress. The result of the war and the protracted negotiations was the establishment of the first international balance-of-power system. The balance-of-power concept has sine provided the political framework of the international system-except during the time of Louis XIV, Napoleon Bonaparte, and Adolf Hitler.

Major conferences have been convened in every century since the Westphalia conference. Together with the gradual codification of international law. These conferences. have contributed to the structuring and restructuring of Europe. The Peace of UTERECHT (17130, which ended the War of the Spanish Succession, reaffirmed the principle of balance of power as the only keep to peace. Then came the French Revolution (1989), which marked the birth of modern (mass supported) nationalist movements. Among other principles, the French revolutionaries advocated nonintervention in the affairs of other countries, the renunciation of wars of conquest, and national self-determination in the form of plebiscites. Following Napoleon's imperial adventures, which were considered by some as an attempt to universalize the ideals of the French Revolution, the victorious anti-napolenoic coalition met at the great congress of Vienna (1815). There, it structured the nineteenth-century balance-of-power system and contributed to the exiting body f international law. Among other rules, the Congress established categories of diplomatic envoys, general principles for the navigation of international rivers, and provisions for the suppression of the slave trade.

The Monroe Doctrine (1823) of the United States was an early, if toothless, proclamation of regional independence against external (i.e., European) intervention and manipulation. The Peace of Paris (1856), following the Crimean war, reaffirmed the principle of national self-determination and applied it to the disputed provinces of Wallachia and Moldavia. In the declaration of Paris in 1856, laws of war and rights of neutral were identified. This year marked the take-off joint of international law. The Brussels Congress (1874) resulted in a code of land warfare approved b fifteen nation-states. The Berlin Conference (1884-1885) continued earlier attempts to abolish the solve trade. It also sought to split the pie represented by European colonization of the Third World (which was then referred to contemptuously by the Europeans as *terra riullius*- "no man's land"), so as not to disrupt the stability of the balance-of-power system.

Simultaneously, public international unions such as the International telegraphic Union (1865), the Universal Postal Union (1857) the Rhine River commission (1804, and the Danube river Commission (1857) become permanent international institutions.

Their subdivision—bureaus, councils, and conferences—served as institutional prototypes for the League of Nations and the United Nations. Beyond this, the public international unions contributed to the development of international administrative law in the so-called functional (that is, technical, economic, and social) areas.

With the Hague Conference (1899 and 1907), an important threshold was crossed on the way to international institutionalization. These conferences, which were meant to occur every seven years, were convened in time of peace and enjoyed the nearly universal participation of the then-recognized nation-states. Unlike the great-power conferences of the nineteenth century, the Hague conference had been designed to achieve settlements immediately after war and crises, the hague conference were preventive and regulatory in nature. Moreover, the great power conferences had been the work of the few and powerful. In contrast the Hague conferences exhibited the ligitimization process that only full participation—of small as well as great powers—can bring about. The 1899 Hague conference produced major regulatory instruments, such as the convention for the pacific settlement of disputes (which established the permanent Court of Arbitration), the convention on laws and customs of land warfare, and the convention on laws of naval warfare. The 1907 Hague conference updated the 1899 conventions and produced ten more conventions on neutrality and land and sea warfare.

It is Claude, a well-known scholar of international organisation, has effectively summarized the ancestors of international organisations in terms of what he views as three "major streams of development" in the nineteenth century. In the Concert of Europe system and the ad hoc great-power conferences that followed, Claude sees the precursor of the United Nations Security Council. The Concert of Europe was the product of a consensus among great powers that only the could define the grand security questions and the tolerable limits within which the balance-of-power system could shift.

The Higue Conferences have been portrayed by Claude as

the precursors of the United Nations General. assembly. The egalitrarian concept of "one nation, one vote" was clearly reflected in the hauge movement. Resolutions adopted by majority vote (rather than unanimously) gradually become an acceptable rule of international organization. The occurrence of the Hague Conferences reflected the decision of the participating governments to limit their sovereignty voluntarily in order to aid in the development of rules of international law designed to minimize conflict in the international system and to maximize cooperation and conciliation.

The third and perhaps the most influential stream of development was the creation and expansion o public international unions, such as the universal Postal Union and the Rhine and Danube river commissions. These unions were designed to carryout economic and social activities analogues to those of specialized agencies of the United Nations, such as the International Monetary Fund (IMF), the International civil Aviation Organisations (ICAO), the Food and Agriculture Organisation (FAO), and the Inter-governmental Maritime consultative Organisation (IMCO). A major contribution of these early public international unions was that their structure (conference, council, and secretariat) was subsequently adopted by the most advanced international organizations. The public international unions stand for the process of functional cooperation. Functional activities, which are understood to be technical, scientific, and economic—in short, Non political—activities, are presumably easier to organise than political activities. The incentives of collective functional projects are strong and their success in mutually profitable. Notion states have sown less reluctance to limit their sovereignty in functional than in political sphere of activity.

4

Towards Globalisation and Liberalisation

Introduction

Some of the things that we use in our day-to-day life. Whether they are necessities like food, clothing, furniture, electrical goods, medicine or other items of comfort or entertainment, many of these goods come to us through a network of global proportions. The raw material might have been extracted in one country; the knowledge on processing this war material might have been with some other country; it might have been actually processed in another place; and the money to produce it might have come from altogether different country. People in different parts of the world are inter-linked their interdependence is not only limited to production or distribution of goods. They are influenced by each other in spheres like education, art and literature as well. This kind of interaction of nations and peoples through trade, investment, travel, popular culture, and other forms is a trend towards globalisation.

In the process of globalisaiton, countries become interdependent and the distance between people gets shortened. One country depends on the other for its development. Japan, for example, one of the important players in cotton textile industry, depends on raw cotton produced in India and other countries. India's cashewnut industry, a pioneer in the international cashewnut market, depends on production of raw cashew in the African countries. We all know the extent to which information technology industries of the USA depend on talented engineers from India and other developing countries. Globalisaiton includes movement of not only goods and money but also of people.

Early Globalisation

Globalisaiton is not something new, from around 200 BC to AD 1000, the most significant example of interaction and long-distance trade was happened through silk Route. The silk route stretched nearly 6,000 km across central and south-west Asia, linking China to India, western Asia, and the Mediterranean. Along the Silk Route, goods, people, and ideas travelled thousands of kilometres between China, India, and Europe. Extensive interaction between peoples, by travelling over vat distances took place across Asia between A.D. 1000 and A.d. 1500. During this period the maritime system on the Indian Ocean also gained importance. The oceanic routes between South-east Asia and the Middle East greatly expanded. It is not only goods and pole who travelled across the world but also the technology. Indian, during this period, was to only the seat of learning and spiritually, but also the centre of wealth. It was called a Golden Bird, and it attracted traders and travellers from other parts of the world. It was during the Mongol rule in china that many Chinese inventions such as gunpowder, printing, the blast furnace, silk machinery, paper money and playing cards found their way to Europe. In fat, these trade relations sowed the seeds of modern globalisaiton. Today's globalisation has been characterised by 'brain drain', or exodus of talented people from the East to the west. The world in the 14th century witnessed the same phenomenon; but, the flow moved the other way, from west to East.

In the early forms of globalisaiton, the textiles of India, the spices of Indonesia and East Africa, the gold and tin of Malaya, the batik and carpets of Java, the gold of Zimbabwe, and the silks porcelain and tea of China made their way to Europe. The eagerness of he Europeans to find their sources in the East Sparked the European age of Exploration. Thus, today's globalisaiton under the auspices of the west is possible mainly because of the framework established by the Indians, the Arabs and the Chinese in the past.

Towards Modern Globalisation

Technological innovations have played an important role in the process of globalisajton. Another factor contributing to this is the establishment of international institutions such as the United Nations Organization, World Bank and World Trade Organization. Moreover, the opening up of markets for private companies outside their home country and consumerism set the trends towards the spread of globalisaiton to various parts of the world. The globalisaiton gives thrust to two areas: (a) liberalisation and (b) privatisation. Liberalisation means relation of government regulations relating to various activities in industrial and service sectors and encouragement of foreign companies to set up businesses and production units within the domestic area. Though privation , private sector companies are allowed to produce goods and services, which were not allowed in the past. It also includes the sale of the assets of the public sector companies to private sector companies. The modern form of globalisaiton had started since the Second World War, but it has attracted more attention during the last 20 years. The modern globalisaiton is mainly centred around developed countries. These countries deplete a major part of natural resources all around the world. People of these countries account for 20 per cent of the world population but consumer more than 80 per cent of the earth's natural resources. They control most of the latest technology. Developing countries are depending on these countries for technology, money expertise and arms. Globalisaiton allows multinational companies rather than the governments play a key role in man countries They possess resources, technology and support of governments for their activities. Many multinational companies relocate their factories from one country to another country. In this process, information technology enables them to break down their production and distribution activities and go around the world

Globalisation has become a deeply controversial issue. While most governments and main steam political parties are anxious to position themselves to take advantage of the benefits of the new globalized economy, an antiglobalization movement has emerged, most strongly in developed states but also, to some extent, in developing ones. In some respects, divisions over globalisation have replaced more traditional lift-right divisions, based upon the ideological struggle between capitalism and socialism. There is, nevertheless, a sense in which the proversus anti-globalisation debate is nothing more than a reworking of the older and more familiar ideological divide. This is because the interconnectedness that lies at the heart of globalisation is, as yet, in variably linked to the extension of market exchange and commercial practices. Globalisation thus has a pronounced neoliberal or free-market ideological character. Capitalism, in short, remains the issue. Supporters of globalization, some times called globalists, usually argue that capitalism tends towards general prosperity and widening opportunities, in which case global capitalism will allow these benefits to be enjoyed by more people n more countries. Opponents of globalisation, on the other hand, tend to associate capitalism within equality and exploitation, in which case global capitalism will simply generate new forms of misery and injustice. In one important respect, however, the globalisation debate is new: it is conducted within a post socialist framework that no longer recognizes that there are viable alternatives to market structures and capitalist organizations, rather than between global capitalism and any qualitatively different alternative.

Theories of Globalisation

A first set of debates is between believers and skeptics over whether globalisation is actually happening and, by extension, about the forces that are driving it. The believers, who include both supporters and opponents of the process, argue that globalization draws attention to t profound, even revolutionary, set of economic cultural technological and political shifts that have intensified since the 1980s. Chief amongst these are much higher levels of world trade and, in particular, a dramatic increase in financial and currency transactions; the advent of new information and communication technologies that provide instant access to images and messages across he globe; and the emergence of global commodities that are available almost anywhere in the world. In its most extreme version, hyper globalism, this view subscribes to a form of technological determinism that suggests that new, globalised cultural and economic patterns became inevitable once technology such as computerized financial trading satellite communications, mobile phones and the Internet became widely available. Nevertheless, there is evidence of a slowdown in the pace of globalisation since the 1990s, which has been further strengthened by the impact of the events of September 11, 2201 on, for instance, the global economy and interstate security measures.

On the other hand, the sceptcs, often subscribing to a traditional or 'old' left analysis of capitalism, argue either that there is little that is new about globalisation or that its impact as been exaggerated for political reasons. Karl Marx now reborn as a theorist of globalisation rather than a proponent of class struggle, drew attention to the international character of capitalist organization as early as that mid-nineteenth century. J.A. Hobson 1858-1940) and V.I. Lenin each highlighted intrinsic links between capitalism and imperialism in the early twentieth century. Moreover, despite the undoubted growth in world trade from the late nineteenth century onwards, the skeptics point out that the overwhelming bulk of economic activity still takes place within, not across, national boundaries. National economies, in other words, are not as irrelevant as globalisation theorists usually suggest. From this perspective, globalisation is often seen less as a revolutionary economic or technological force and more as an ideological device used by politicians and theorists who support neoliberal economics and wish to advance corporate interest (Hirst and Thompson, 1999). The globalisation thesis has two major advantages in this respect. First, it portrays certain tendencies—namely, the shift towards labour flexibility and weaker trade unions, controls on public spending and particularly welfare budgets, and a scaling-down of business regulation—as inevitable and therefore irresistible. Second, it suggest that such shifts are part of an impersonal process, and not one linked to an agent, such as a big business, hose interest might be seen to drive, and be served by, globalizing tendencies.

Despite intensifying interest in the phenomenon of globalisation since the 1980s the term is still used to refer, variously to a process, a policy, a marketing strategy, a predicament or even an ideology. The problem with globalisation is that it is not so much an 'it' as a 'them': it is not a single process but a complex of processes, sometimes overlapping and interlocking processes but also, at times, contradictory and oppositional ones. It is difficult there fore to reduce globalisation to a single theme, Perhaps the best attempt to o this was in Kenichi Ohmae's (1989) idea of 'borderless world'. This not only refers to the tendency of traditional political borders, based on national and state boundaries, to become permeable; it also implies that divisions between people previously separated by time and space have become less significant and are sometimes entirely irrelevant. Scholter (2000) therefore argued that globalisation is linked to the growth of 'supra territorial' relations between people, a reconfiguration of social space in which territory matters less because an increasing range of connections have a 'transworld' or 'transborder' character. For instance, huge flows of electronic money now surge around the world at the flick of a computer switch, ensuring that currency and other financial markets react almost immediately to economic events anywhere in the world. Similarly, cable and statellite technology allow telephone messages and television programmes to be transmitted around the world almost instantaneously. Globalisation is the emergence of a complex web of interconnectedness that means that our lives are increasingly shaped by events that occur, and decisions that are made, at a great distance from us. The central feature of globalisation is therefore that geographical distance is of declining relevance, and that territorial boundaries, such as those between nation states, are becoming less significant. By no means, however, does globalisation imply that 'the local' and 'the national' are subordinate to "the global'. Rather, it highlights the deepening as well as the broadening of the political process, in the sense that local, national and global events (or perhaps local, regional, nations international and global events) constantly interact.

The interconnectedness that globalisation has sawned is multidimensional. The popular image of globalisation is that it is a top-down process, the establishment of a single global system that imprints itself on all parts of the world. In this view, globalisation is linked to homogenization as cultural, social, economic and political diversity are destroyed in a world in which we all watch the same television programmes, buy the same commodities, eat the same food, support the same sports starts and follow the antics of the same celebrative. Nevertheless, globalisation often goes hand in hand with localization, regionalisation and multiculturalism. This occurs for a variety of reasons. In the first place, the declining capacity of the nation-state to organize economic and political life in a meaningful way allows power to be sucked downwards as well as squeezed upwards. Thus, as allegiances based on the nation and political national is made, they are often replaced by ones linked to local community or region, or religious and ethnic identify. Religious fundamentalism can, for instance, be seen as a response to globalisation. Second, the fear or threat of homogenization, especially when it is perceived as a form of imperialism, provokes cultural an political resistance. This can lead to a resurgence of interest in declining language and minority cultures as well as to a backlash against globalisation, most obviously through the emergence of new 'anti-capitalist' and anti-free-trade social movements. Third, rather than simply bringing about a global monoculture, globalisation has in some ways fashioned more complex patterns of social and cultural diversity in developing and developed states alike. In developing states western consumer goods and images have been absorbed into more traditional cultural practices through a process of indigenization. Developed states, also, have not escaped the wider impact of cultural exchange, being, in return for Coca-Cola, McDonald's and MTV, increasingly influenced by non-western religions, medicines and therapeutic practices, and art, music and literature.

Distinctive forms of economic, cultural and political globalisation can also be identified, Economic globalisation is reflected in the idea that no national economy is now an island:

all economies have to a greater or leaser extent, been absorbed into an interlocking global economy. The OECD (1995) thus defined globalisation as 'a shift from a world distinct national economies to a global economy in which production is internationalised and finanicial capital flows freely and instantly between countries. The collapse of communism gave powerful imetus to economic globalisation in that it paved the way for the absorption into the globalcapitalist system of the last significant block of states that had remained outside it. Economic globalisation, for that matter also helped to precipitate the collapse of communism in that lower trade barriers, an end to exchange controls and freer movement of investment capital from the 1980sonwards had helped to whiden the economic gap between the capitalist West and an economically stagnant communist East. One of the key implications of economic globalisation is the reduced capacity of national governments to manage their economies and, in particular, to resist their restructuring along free market lines.

Cultural globalisation is the process whereby information, commodities and images that have been produced in one part of the world enter into a global flow that tends to 'flattern out' cultural differences between nations, regions and individuals by the growth of transactional companies and the emergence of global commodities, cultural globalisation is also fuelled b the so-called information revolution, the spread of satellite communication, telecommunications networks, information technology and the Interest, and global media corporations. However, as pointed out earlier, culture both serves and constrains the forces of globalisation. In addition to the ubiquity of Hollywood movies. Nike running shoes and Starbucks coffee houses, selling goods across the world requires a sensitivity to indigenous cultures and social practices.

Political globalisation is evident in the growing importance of international organiations. These are organizations that are transnational in that they exercise jurisdiction not within a single state, but within an international area comprising several states. Most such organisations have emerged in the post-1945 period: examples include the United Nations, NATO, the European Economic

Community and its various successors, the EC and the EU, the World Ban, the International Monetary Fund (IMF), the Organization for Economi: Cooperation and Development (OECD) and the World Trade Organisation (WTO). When they conform to the principles of intergovernmentatlism international organisations provide a mechanism that enables states-at least in theory, to take concerted action without acrificing national sovereignty. Supranational bodies, on the other hand, are able to impose their will on nation-states. The inter-state emphasis of political globalisation sets it apart form the rival conceptions of economic and cultural globalistion, which highlight the role of non-state and market-based actors. Moreover, insofar as it reflects an idealist commitment to internationalism and some form of world government, political globalisation lags markedly behind economic and cultural globalisation. Whereas a global state remains a very instant prospect, global civil society, based on the active of transactional corporations, nongovernmental organisations (NGOs) and international pressure groups, have become very much a reality.

The idea of a 'North-South divide' was popularized through the work of the so called Brandit Reports; north-South. A Programme for Survival (1980) and Common Crisis: North-South Coöperation for World Recovery (1983). Although the division of the world into a 'North' ad a "south' is based on the tendency for industrial development to be concentrated in the northern he misphere, and for poverty and disadvantage to be concentrated in the southern hemisphere (apart from Australasia), the terms are essentially conceptual rather than geographical. The concept of the North South divide draw attention to the way in which aid, third-world debt and the practices of MNCs help to perpetuate structural inequalities between the high age, high-investment industrialized North and the low-wage, low-investment, predominantly rural South. The Brandt Reports also highlighted in interdependence of the North and the South, Emphasizing that the long-term prosperity of the North is dependent on the development of the South.

The most intense debate about globalisation nevertheless concerns its implications for equality and poverty. Critics of globalisation have drawn attention to the emergence of new and deeply entrenched patterns of inequality; globalisation is thus a game of winners and losers. The winners are invariably identified as multinational corporations and industrially advanced states generally, but particularly the United States; the losers, in contrast, are in the developing world, where wages are low, regulation is weak or non-extent, and where production is increasingly orientated around global markets rather than domestic needs. Whereas the US and European economies grew strongly in the 1980s and 1990s on the basis of globalisation and technological advance, absolute living standards fell in the poorest parts of the world, notably in sub-Saharan Africa, where 40 per cent of people live below the poverty lie. Wallerstein (1984), drawing on the Marxist view of capitalism as essentially exploitative, highlighted the structural condition of uneven political and economic development that led to growing inequality between 'core' and 'peripheral' parts of the economic world-system. Global tensions have come to be seen less in terms of East versus west and more in terms of a North-South divide.

Globalists, however, point out that the rich may have got richer but the poor are now also, in most cases, less poor. From the perspective of liberal pluralism, the emergence f a global economy is to be welcomed because free trade allows each country to specialize in the production of those goods and services that it is best suited to produce. This leads to international specialization and mutual benefits. For instance, the transfer of production from developed to developing states benefits the former because production costs, an therefore prices, are kept low, but also benefits the latter because wage levels tend to rise, albeit from a low base, which will stimulate the domestic economy and foster enterprise. In this view, the only parts of the world that fail to benefit from globalisation are those that remain outside it.

Globalisation has also been criticized because of its tendency towards risk, uncertainly and instability. Globalists certainly acknowledge the dynamism that is inherent in any competitive market order, but, following the principles of classical economics, point out that market tend towards log-term equilibrium, supply eventually coming into line with demand. In this view, the uncertainty and insecurity that are associated with the emergence of a global economy are likely to decline as more stable patterns of economic activity take shape. Nevertheless, globalisation has been associated with increased risk and uncertainty in at least three deeper ways. In the first place, economic decision-making is increasingly influenced by global financial markets that are inherently unstable. This is because much of their activity is speculative, and they are driven by short-term economic considerations. The fate of companies, industries, national economies and even regions of the world is therefore subject to the whims of financial markets. The financial crisis in Mexico in 1995 and the Asian financial crisis of 1997-99 may only be early indications of a crisis-prone and more unpredictable world economy. George Soros (1998) argued that such crises threatened the open society, and can be prevented only by far greater regulation, aimed at bringing speculative financial flows under control.

A second form of uncertainty is summed up in Ulrich Beck's (19920 idea of a 'risk society'. A risk society is one that is characterized by rising individualism and an associated weakening of tradition, community and established institutions. Uncertainty, in this respect, goes beyond an increase in the pace and reduction in the predictability of economic and social change, in that it has a personal, even psychic dimension: when all fixed points are undermined, people's basic values even sense of identity are called into question. As Marx put it in the Communist Manifesto ([1848] 1967), 'All that is solid melts into air'. A third form of instability is the alleged tendency of globalisation towards environmental crisis and destruction. Eco-socialists explain this by reference to capitalism's blind concern with profit and its insensitivity towards ecological issues. Radical ecologists, for their part, believe that globalisation is merely an extension of indisutrailism, and economic system that is characterised by large-scale production, the accumulation of capital and relentless growth. By spreading materialism and entrenching absolute fait in science and technology, industrialism undermines human values and deadens ecological sensibilities. Reformist ecologists call for global environmental protection. However, as the faltering process of implementing the 1997 Koto Protocol on climate change demonstrates, concerted state action in this area is difficult to achieve because of the economic sacrifices involved.

The most significant political debate associated with globalisation concerns its impact on democracy. Supporters of globalisation argued that it is a major factor underpinning the trend towards demoncratisation. In its most optimistic version, advanced by Fukuyama (1989, 1992), this view suggests that globalisation will lead to the end of history', in that the extension of market capitalism will lead to a universal acceptance of liberal democratic principles and structures. Economic freedom is inevitably associated with political freedom, because the complex and diverse pressures unleashed by market economies can be contained only within open and democratic societies. Globalisation can nevertheless be seen to have undermined democracy in two important ways. First, it has concentrated economic power, and therefore, political power, in the hands of multinational corporations (MNCs). Thee are business organisations that produce output in more than one state. MNCs now dominate mot of the world's markets. Notable examples include General Motors, Ford, Esso, Shell, BP, MCDonald's, AT&T, and the News Corporation, General Motors, to take jut one instance, has an annual revenge that is almost equal to the combined GDP of Ireland. New Zealand, Uruguay, Sri Lanka, Kenya, Nambia, Nicaragua and Chad. Such economic and financial power is also allied to the ability to manipulate consumer tastes and entrench materialist values through the development of brands (Klein, 2000). However, it is the capacity of MNCs to relocate capital and production elsewhere in the world that gives them a decisive advantage over national governments and enables them, effectively, to escape democratic control. Developing-world states are particularly vulnerable in this respect, as they provide MNCs with source of cheap labour and low production costs without being able to oblige them to make long-term investments or shift decision-making power form the 'home' country to the 'host' one.

Second, democracy is threatened by the fact that the page of economic globalisation far outstrips that of political gobalisation. Whereas economic activity increasingly pays little attention to national borders, politics continues to operate largely within them, the international organisations that do exist being too weak to call global capitalism to account. This has led to calls for a cosmopolitan conception of democracy Held, 1995). The extension of democratic forms and processes across territorial borders would require not merely the strengthening of organisations such as the European Union and the United Nations, but also the reduction of democratic deficits from which these bodies currently suffer. Moreover, the institutions of global economic governance such as the IMF, the World Bank, the OECD and the G7, need to develop some independence from the interests of MNCs and give greater attention to issues such as human rights, economic justice and environmental protection.

Towards Globalisation and Liberalisation

Trade union resistance held back the government in 1988 and in the following year the National front government made attempts, albeit abortive, to alter the path of development. Moreover, government revenues depended heavily on import taxes, so that the required tariff reductions without compensatory revenue measures could lead to a worsening of the already alarming budget deficit. World Bank experts relentlessly pressurized the government to implement these reforms. Whatever the factors which held back the process of liberalization, the Bank persisted with its well-tried tactic to enforce compliance. It decided to hold up the concessional aid and waited for India's credit options to sufficiently narrow down so that sal/sac remained the only alternative.

The process of climinating foreign credit options was already underway in late eighties. The Aid Indian Consortium (AIC), a rich nations' club, was included to determine its aid pledges in the light of the World Bank's recommendations. Until 1987, it offered higher credit than that recommended by the World Bank in response to India's acceptance of the suggested economic policies. In 1988 and 1989 when the process of liberalisation slowed down, the flows recommended by the World Bank were slashed by almost 25 per cent. In 1990, AIC refused to pledge itself to maintaining even the 1989 level of concessional credit, itself a sharp reduction over previous year's levels. In fact, it put a great deal of pressure without offering additional credit. Commenting on the decision taken by the AIC in June 1990, a reporter stated: The Consortium tightened the scews, demanding policy reforms in the industrial, fiscal, trade, and financial sectors and making future aid flow contingent on their implementation. The US delegation declared that India probably cannot rely on historical levels of concessional assistance which is likely to remainsatic because of new claimants but her task is 'removal of barriers of foreign direct investment, trade and modern financial markets and ensuring fair competition.'

The external commercial credit also declined. The Economic Survey of 1990-91 states that 'the increasing trend in approvals of external commercial borrowings withnesed during 1987-88 to 1988-89 was reversed in 1990-91 owing to the fall in the overall availability of international credit and downgrading of India's credit rating for long-term funds by international rating agencies.

The pressure of foreign creditors was so great that the NF government's attempt to change the policy package turned out to be a fiasco. The policy package it proposed was similar to that of the Janata party in 1977. With a view to increasing employment potential and reducing the rural-urban disparity in infrastructure, it advocated that 50 per cent of planned investment be allocated to agriculture and rural development and production of basic consumer goods be reserved for the cottage and small-scale sectors. It 'assured farmers of guaranteed remunerative prices for their produce. It also proposed to 'reduce the role of multinationals in Indian economy activate import substitution strengthen FERA and MRTP Acts to ensure that opportunities for expansion are not misused for creating monopolies. It was of the view that 'in the name of technological upgradation the liberalized import of capital goods and turnkey projects has blocked indigenous enterprises for the development of industries on a self-reliant basis. In order to discourage this tendency and improve the balance of payments position, it advocated strict controls on inessential imports; and proposed a sharp reduction in defence and other non-development expenditures for reducing the budgetary deficit. The NF policy package was orthogonally different from that of the World Bank. But after coming to power in 1990, the National Front government found it difficult to implement a its own policy package owing to the resource crunch. In his presentation of the government's first budget the Finance Minister pledged to freeze defence expenditure, but two months later the defence budget was raised by Rs 500 crores. The new government's intention of allocating half the investible resources to agriculture also did not translate into practice. The approach paper to the Eighth Plan ostensibly shifted the emphasis of planning from growth of GNP to employment generation through decentralize planning and public participation in rural development. It apparently proposed to allocate 50 per cent of plan outlays to rural development and agricultural activities; shift investment in favour of product lines with low capital-intensity except in infrastructure, key intermediate manufactures and high the industries; and enlarge the share of small-scale industries in the production of consumer goods.

From the NF party manifesto to the approach paper, however, there was a distinct shift in emphasis with respect to rural development. The manifesto gave a higher priority to the proposed increase in the allocation of public investment to agriculture than to the policy of remunerative prices of agricultural goods. This preference was presumably based on the consideration that the latter would raise the cost of living of rural and urban workers. But after coming to power the NF government reversed the order. The procurement prices of wheat, rice and several other agricultural commodities were sharply raised—almost restoring the parity wit the prices of industrial products—whereas the plan allocation to agriculture increased only marginally; from 22 per cent to 25 per cent for 1990-91.

In fact, the official statistics on planned investment in rural development were fudged. In order to convey the impression that the government had kept its election promise regarding allocation of public investment for rural development to the extent of 50 per cent, the definition of investment in agriculture was changed. The union budget, implicitly, and the approach paper, explicitly, redefined the plan outlay on agriculture by 'including investments in fertilizers, pesticides, diesel oil. Electricity, transport and other infrastructure which facilitate better distribution of inputs and marketing of rural products. This definition, by doubly counting the investment in rural inputs to bloat up he allocation of planned investment to rural economy, it obviously spurious. If a consistent procedure is followed, that is, investments in inputs to the industrial sector are included in the plan outlay for industrial development, just as investments in inputs to bloat up the allocation of planned investment to rural economy, is obviously spurious. If a consistent procedure is followed, that is, investments in inputs to the industrial sector are included in the plan outlay for industrial development, just as investments in inputs to the rural economy are included in the plan outlay for rural development, then the increase in each case will tend to cancel the other out. The government's three year export-import policy was also at variance with the spirit of the manifesto. It enlarged the quantitative dimensions of the policy instruments used during the last decade 'to encourage rapid and sustained export growth. One of the principal instruments of export promotion was the so called Import Replenishment (REP) Licensing Scheme for replenishing the raw materials and components used in the manufacture of exported goods. The provisions of this scheme had been so diluted since 1982 that REP licences (and imports against them) could be transferred, at a premium, even to those producing for the domestic market. This practice had taken the teeth out of the protective system. In 1990, the scheme was made even more flexible. The specified lists for REP licensces were widened to include all items in the limited permissible section of the canalized list. Thee licences, whatever the export products against which they were issued, could be used to bring into the country any item whose import was permitted. The 'actual user' condition (for import) was also dropped and trading of imported items was officially allowed.

Capital goods licencing was virtually abandoned. Imports of non-OGL capital goods were allowed to export houses up to 15 per cent of their licences and to manufacturer exporters against their REP licences. Although the customs tariff barriers on capital goods were much lower than those on raw materials, they were further reduced in many cases. For manufacturer exporters, the import a duty was reduced to 25 per cent (compared to the ordinary rate of 85 per cent) on all types of capital goods—restricted, OGL and non-OGL—as long as he importer exported three times the value of import. And paradoxically, the import of second-hand capital goods, which were otherwise on OGL, was brought within the purview of the licencing system, restricting the advantage of low cost imports to the economy. The advance licensing scheme, which allows duty-free import of raw materials against export obligations, was redrawn with even more liberal provisions.

Although marginal, these changes clearly increased the access to imports of exporters and via the, of producers for the domestic market. They were, prima facie, more beneficial to big than to small companies. Big companies did not have much to show by way of exports. This was indicated by the fact that when companies with annual turnovers of Rs. 500 crores and more were listed in thousands, only three units in the entire country apparently qualified for inclusion in the newly created category of Star Trading Houses and only one of them, Tata Exports, was identifiable with big industry. Raising the limits for export houses excluded about 950 small exporters from availing of the facilities meant for export houses. The Industrial Policy Statement issued on 31 May 1990 further extended the logic of import liberalization. It provided for the automatic clearance of capital goods imports, up to 30 per cent of the ex-factor value (excluding the excise duty) of output, and foreign investment, up to 40 per cent equity participation; and 'if import of technology is considered necessary by the entrepreneur, he can conclude an agreement with the collaborator without obtaining any clearance from the government, provided the royalty payment does not exceed 5 per cent on domestic sales and 8 per cent on exports' (unpublished document, para 15). There were of course other changes, such as exemptions from requirements of licensing/registrations for small and export-oriented industries.

It is quite clear from these policy initiatives that the NF government was unable to arrest the ongoing process of liberalization and industrial delicensing. Its attempt to raise the priority of agriculture in plan allocations proved abortive. Nor was it able to promote small-scale industries. It could not withstand the pressures from multinational corporations; Pepsi-Cola was allowed to set up an agro-based industry in Punjab. The NF government had barely prepared a legislation for the Right to Work when it fell under the impact of its internal contradictions which, paradoxically, reached a flash-point on the question of providing job reservations to backward castes.

Meanwhile, the international environment had drastically altered. There was a new conjuncture in global relationships. The socialist bloc, following its capitulation to the capitalist world, was no longer a countervailing power in the world economy. The First World consequently acquired an unchallenged influence over the developing countries. Operation Desert Storm in the Middle East clearly established the unequivocal supremacy of the US on the international scene. In the 1950s and 1960s, India could play USA against USSR to strike a bargain for foreign credit; she could get loans from both with minimum political interference. The detente between the superpowers changed this condition in the early 1970s, Since then her political leverage has been declining; it reached its nadir with the fall of the Wall of Berlin in 1989 and even that bottom fell after the operation Desert Storm and the collapse of communist states the Operation Desert Storm and the collapse of communist states in USSR and East Europe in 1991.

The new world order increased India's vulnerability by adversely affecting her prospects of trade and aid. The move towards total integration of the European market was expected to not only divert European trade from developing countries to East European countries, but also make the latter a major destination of American, Japanese and West European investors. Under these conditions India could hope to get only a small fraction of the new trade generated by foreign investment and upgradation of technology in East Europe. This incremental trade would be offset by the diversion of foreign capital to East Europe.

Another important aspect of the international environment was the change in development ideology. Reagan and Thatcher inheited a world in which the 'development consensus' had already broken down and the Bretton Woods institutions had come under enormous strains. Internally, in the OECD countries, western capitalism had begun to shed well farism and turned its back upon full employment. This new aggressive self-confidence was consolidated in the eighties with a massive armament drive in the US and privatization in the UK and West Europe. Thus, the new international balance of power reduced the prospects of concessional and commercial foreign credit and consolidated the ideology of a new policy regime in the image of the West. This was the external backdrop to India' big push towards the policy of globalisation. The decisive moment, however, came when the foreign exchange crisis threatened default on debt servicing in 1991.

Crisis Foreign Exchange

The balance of payments (BOP) crisis had been deepening since the second oil shock in 1980. It worsened after 1985 owing to significant imports of military equipment (about $18 billion from 1985 to 1988). The government increasingly relied on borrowings from private international banks. As a result, the total external debt outstanding and disbursed increased from about $41 billion in 1985 to $70 billion in March 1991, raising the ratio of DOD to GDP from 10 per cent to 25 per cent. Much of this borrowing was in the form of relatively short-term and potentially volatile instruments such as foreign currency bank deposits from NRIs, with two to three years maturity. Since NRI bank deposits can be withdrawn on demand (with only a small penalty), the weight of these deposits and short-term commercial bank debts in the total stock of debt (about $18 billion or 25 per cent of DOD in March 1991) made the country extremely vulnerable to a liquidity crisis stemming from the loss of private creditor confidence abroad. These latent weaknesses were revealed at the time of the Gulf face-off in 1990. This crisis disrupted the supplies and increased the prices of oil and petroleum products. It raised the country's cost of POL imports by 72 per cent, deepening trade deficit by Rs. 4,400 crores. The direct and indirect effects of the Gulf crisis were estimated at $2.9 billion (equivalent of Rs. 5,200 crores). In view of the worsening BOP deficit, some international agencies suddenly lowered India's credit rating, restricting her access to the global money market. This drying up of international commercial credit occurred at a time when concessional credit was not available and the Gulf crisis had adversely affected the country's foreign exchange reserves.

In any case, the foreign exchange crunch was so severe that even after using the reserve tranche position in the IMF, amounting to SDR 487.26 million (equivalent of Rs 1,173 crores) from July to September 1990, the external payments situation did not stabilize. Reserves declined to $1.2 billion on 31 December 1990, equal to about two weeks' imports. On 18 January 1991, the government was forced to borrow against from the IMF, this time SDR 1.23 billion (equivalent to $1.78 billion or Rs 3,334 crores). Subsequently, he decline in commercial credit and withdrawal of deposits by NRIs created pani, leading to a de facto depreciation of he rupee in the Havala market.

The government resorted to emergency measures with respect to the BOP crisis beginning January 1991. First, it availed itself of Fund resources, drawing almost $1.8 billion from the contingency Compensatory Financing Facility (CCFF) and a first tranche stand-by credit. Secondly, it adopted import compression measures such as an increased interest rate on bank credit for imports.

Despite these initiatives, the decline in foreign exchange reserves continued unabated. By March 1991, the reserves plummeted by $1.4 billion, an amount almost equal to the reduction in commercial bank loans over the year. As the country's credit rating continued to fall and foreign banks refused lending, the cost of short-term loans rose to 1.25 per cent above LIBOR (standard reference interest rate in the international money market) by May 1991. The government also explored the possibility of fast disbursement of loans already sanctioned. In 1990, IDA—the soft lending affiliate of the World Bank—had cancelled some project loans. Still, credit of about $10 billion by the Bank and IDA for 120 projects was in the pipeline. Of these sixty-seven were in power, irrigation and rural development. Loans for these projects were not disbursed, presumably because the credit agencies were not satisfied with the project implementation. This might be due to the lack of necessary infrastructure or the resource crunch or the government's beginning indifference. Whatever the reasons for the unsatisfactory project implementation, the fact remains that close monitoring of these projects would have enabled the government to draw upon $10 billion worth of credit by 1990.

In January 1991, the government initiated discussions with the Bank for utilization of the undisbursed IDA loans ($3.3 billion). But the Bank indicated that important bases for fast disbursing assistance could be 'reform measures contained in the 1991-92 budget, and in any policy related statements. Nevertheless, it organized an informal donor's meeting in April 1991 to mobilize support conditional on the country's willingness to adopt a structural adjustment programme. However, since the caretaker government was not able to decide on policy reforms, neither the Bank released any portion of the undisbursed credit nor did any donor provide new loans.

The April denial was sufficient to transmit shock waves to NRIs, who love their money more than their country. Gripped by panic, they began to transfer their deposits to foreign banks. The outflow from NRI deposits was $952 million in April-June 1991 and continued, albeit at a reduced rate of $200 per month, in the next quarter. With this continuous attrition the rupee depreciated by 16 per cent in five months, from mid-January to mid-June 1991.

The fourth fire-fighting operation on the BOP front was the sale of twenty tones of gold valued at #200 million. But this, too, was insufficient to break the spiral of expectations generated by crawling depreciation and the possibility of further devaluation. These expectations, by shortening the period for the payments of imports and lengthening that for the realization of export proceeds, exacerbated the foreign exchange shortage. Reserves dipped again in June 1991. They fell below the previous bottom to $1.1 billion—less than sufficient for two weeks of import requirements. Since the next installment of CCFF withdrawal was to due till July 1991, default on deposit withdrawal and repayment of short-term loans loomed large on the horizon. The government was indeed pushed to the wall and in desperation decided to pledge an additional forty-seven tones of gold to garner $400 million in July.

Thus, the recurring current account deficit was exacerbated by the Gulf war which contributed to a higher oil bill and a temporary loss of export markets and remittance earnings. The flight of NRI deposits made the situation hopeless at a time when international commercial credit was not available (since the country's credit rating had already been scaled down in late. Foreign exchange reserves dwindled to $1.1 billion, barely sufficient for two weeks imports. Default on debt servicing was imminent. This was the moment when all foreign credit options of the country were foreclosed. Default could be avoided only if credit was made available from the IMF or the World Bank.

Liberalisation and Globalisation in India

Some of the visible changes are better services in the communications sector, such as telephone facilities, availability of colour television sets and other electronic goods at low prices. Many food processing companies such as Pepsi, Coca Cola, have entered the country and taken over the market for soft drinks and some food products. Some of the invisible changes in the economy.

India's share in the trade of goods and services in the world has increased marginally. However, compared to other developing countries, our progress is very slow. Investment from other countries (also known as foreign direct investment) to produce goods and services in India had increased from Rs. 174 crore in 1991 to Rs. 9338 crore in 2000. We need foreign exchange reserves to pay for our imports. This had increased from Rs. 4822 crore in 1991 to Rs. 152924 crores in 2000. The price rise in 1990-91 was about 12 per cent, and it has slowly declined to around 5 per cent in the late 1990s.

One of the objectives of the new policies is to generate employment. Though new jobs are being created in the economy, it is not sufficient to meet the increasing job requirement in the country. The new policy has failed to generate additional employment opportunities, particularly in rural areas, where 75 per cent of the population live. Though the industry has shown some growth during 1991-2001, it has not yet reached the expected level.

World Trade Organisation was set up in 1995 by the member countries of the United Nations to promote trade among countries. The headquarters of WTO is located in Geneva. It has significantly influenced the liberalisation and globalisation processes in most of the developing countries, including India. WTO aims at conducting international trade among countries of the world in an open, uniform and nondiscriminatory manner.

Cornered by the NRIs, foreign commercial banks and the World, the government approached the IMF and the Bank for a structural adjustment loan/credit (sal/sac). The IMF insisted on a nominal devaluation of 30 per cent--its leading weapon to test the government's pliability. With the rate of inflation projected at 17.2 per cent, this implied a real devaluation of 13 per cent which was not acceptable to the 'new' government. The aversion to devaluation was not based on the philosophy of self-reliance. By 1991 'ideology' had been pushed to the political back water, after a near-fifteen-year atrophy of self-reliance, globalisation had become the most cherished slogan. But devaluation of that order in 1991 would have upset the political (minority government's) apple-cart. The problem for the 'autonomous' decision-makers of this nation was, therefore, how to persuade the bank and the Fund to agree to a politically acceptable rate of exchange. The burden of salvaging the politically acceptable rate of exchange. The burden of salvaging the politics of devaluation fell on the Finance Minister, Manmohan Singh, who cherishes market friendliness, notwithstanding his oft-quoted speech on behalf of the South-South Commission, accusing the North of unfair trade practices. His early researches on India' exports, conducted in Oxford University, were widely acclaimed, and his articulation and personal contacts with international academic bureaucracy were unparalleled in India. He thought he would get away with 9 per cent devaluation announced on 1 July 1991. But it was wide off the mark; it fell short of the World Bank target even without adjusting for inflation. Simple rationalisation that the contemplated tight fiscal and monetary policies could reduce inflation was obviously unacceptable to the foreign bankers unless, of course, the target rate of inflation was put on paper.

The Finance Minister could do not better than fix the target of inflation at 9 per cent wit a stipulated reduction in the budget deficit equivalent to 2 per cent of GDP by March 1992. Arithmetic was then simple. A real devolution of 13 per cent with 9 per cent targeted inflation required a 22 per cent nominal devaluation. Within two days of the first devaluation the rupee was again devalued, so that on 3 July 1991 foreign currencies appreciated by exactly 22 per cent. The step immediately raised the ratio of external debt to GDP, which indicates the grip of external debt on the economy, from around 25 per cent to 31.4 per cent in 1991.

On 4 July, the government announced a trade policy reform package which, together with supplementary measures announced on 13 August 1991, aimed at significantly reducing the quantitative restrictions on imports of intermediate and capital goods, lowering the tariff rates, substantially eliminating the state monologue on imports and exports and making the rupee convertible for trade transactions in three to five years. On 24 July 1991, the union budget as well as a 'Statement on Industrial Policy' was presented to Parliament. The budget announced the devolvement's intention of reducing its fiscal deficit by more than two and a half percentage point of GDP in 1991-92, despite the fact that only two-thirds of the fiscal year remained at the time. The new industrial policy eliminated investment licensing requirements for all but eighteen industries, estimated at about 20 per cent of the existing manufacturing output. It drastically reduced the number of industries reserved to the public sector; eliminated restrictions on investments and mergers of large concerns under MRTP Act; and opened up an extensive positive list of industries in which ownership up to 51 per cent (and up to 100 per cent in special cases) by foreign companies was freely permitted. At the same time, the mandatory convertibility clause, under which financial institutions had the eight to convert a proportion (up to 20 per cent) institutions had the right to convert a proportion (up to 20 per cent) of their loans to the business sector to equity, was abolished for new projects. Thus, the new industrial policy marked a functional break with past practice of capacity planning and entry regulation. It was also announced that there would be no further phased manufacturing programes (PMP) for new projects, and in October some initial steps were taken to remove constraints on firms already operating under PMPs. This process, taken to its logical completion will leave all decisions on the sourceing of inputs to individual firms, subject only to any remaining controls ion imports, inputs and tariffs. So much was done in such a short period; and more was promised. While the government recognised the need for further concessions to foreign investors, because of the delicate BOP situation, investors still required licence to import capital goods for projects in which the foreign exchange content was over 25 per cent of total investment or Rs. 2 crores; unless foreign exchange supply was ensured through foreign equity capital. Again reflecting the acute BOP pressure facing the economy, dividend repatriation by companies with up to 51 per cent foreign ownership was linked under the new rules to their export earnings. Nevertheless, the government was aware that incentives for foreign direct investment would have to be strengthened, and planned to remove the provision linking dividend repatriation to export earnings once the external payments situation showed some improvement. It also realised that the all equity financing requirement on capital goods imports needed to be modified to allow debt as well as equity financing in order to facilitate financing of large investment projects. The government also promised to put in place a plan for comprehensive deregulation of the steel industry, the most important subector still subject to price and distribution controls. It also promised to devise appropriate amendments to the Sick Industrial Companies act of 1985, improve its functioning and streamline and facilitate its procedures in order to strengthen the BIFR. The government's commitment to economic reforms facilitated the IMF approval of the second drawing of the CCFF for SDR 166.2 million on 22 July 1991. The Bank subsequently organised a lending programme spread over the next four year period, 1992-95 comprising the following:

1. World Bank lending of up to $2.0 million per annum.
2. IDA resources of approximately $0.9 billion per annum
3. IDA resources of $0.65 billion from replacement of funds cancelled from the current IDA portfolio as proposed in the Board Paper R91-241 [IDA/R91-149], dated 12 November 1991.

It should be noted that the last facility constitutes about 20 per cent of the undisturbed IDA credit that was denied earlier and was extended after the Finance Minister submitted his letter regarding Development Policy on 11 November 1991. This is the Bank's first policy-based loan, amounting to $12.25 billion spreaders four years, to India. Its objectives are to support 'India's efforts to restore macro-economic equilibrium, accelerate structural reforms, and regain access to private credit markets abroad. These objectives will be ensured through a time-bound monitoring system.' The Bank would also 'closely coordinate' its evaluation of India's economic and sector progress and its policy dialogue with Fund staff, regularly review Fund staff briefing papers and reports and frequently exchange view son recent development and policy options.

As soon as the Bank agreed to lend, other creditors took their cue. AIC gave positive but niggardly response to the request for exceptional financing--about $6.7 billion in overall pledges, an increase of about 6 per cent over the previous year's level. Pledges of quick disbursing balance of payments assistance amounted to $2.3 billion. Some creditors, especially Germany, expressed interest in associating their fast disbursing assistance with the proposed SAP. Several major MNCs such as General motors, IBM and Henel (of Germany) also responded enthusiastically to India's liberalised foreign investment regime. The Government of India, on its part, did not fail the donors. In order to ensure continuing foreign assistance, it intensified the policy of reforms. In spite of a sizeable budget deficit, direct taxes were reduced. The exemption limit of personal income tax was raised form Rs. 22,000 to Rs. 28,000 and income tax slabs were reduced; capital gains were linked to inflation and the tax rate on inflation-adjusted capital again was fixed at 20 per cent; the exemption limit on wealth tax was also raised, with the overall wealth tax being reduced to 1 per cent; and wealth tax on shares, securities, bonds and bank deposits was abolished. The foreign trade regime was made 'market friendly.' Almost all quantitative restriction on imports were eliminated; customs duties were significantly brought down in April 1993--in the case of certain capital goods to the level proposed by the World Bank (1990); the rupee was made convertible on the trade account in two steps; significant tax concessions were provided to foreign institutional investors such as Pension Funds, Mutual Funds, Investment Trusts, etc., investing in the capital market (tax rate on them was reduced to 20 per cent); and the FERA regulations were diluted to such an extent as to render the Act deunct.

These policy decisions made it crystal clear to the World Bank and the IMF that the Indian government was committed to the SAP. Noting the 'irreversibility of structural reforms,' AIC pledged $7.2 billion of assistance for 1992-93, an increase of $500 million or about 7.5 per cent over that pledged in 1991. The quick disbursing component of this assistance was $1.79 billion, about 25 per cent of the total aid, which could be utilised straightaway. But it should be noted that in spite of an increase in the aid pledges, the rate of disbursement was quite low. In spite of the larger pledges from the Aid India Consortium donors this year, the disbursements have been running at a much lower level than last year. Up to December 1992, the gross disbursements have amounted to only US $2 billion against US $3.16 billion during the same period last year—36.7 per cent lower. As a result, for the first three quarters of 1992-93, net capital transfer under external assistance has been zero. This is in spite of the drawl of about US $625 million fast-disbursing funds during April-December 1992—US $200 million as the last tranche of World Bank's SAL, about US $100 million from World Bank under Social Safety Net Loan, US $150 million from ADB under Financial Sector Loan, US $125 million from Japan under Hydrocarbon Sector Loan, and about US $50 million from Germany during 1992-93 up to December 1992.

Thus, the economy was caught in a cycle of debt. To tide over the crisis caused by the first phase of liberalization, fresh injections of external life-saving aid were required. The World Bank loan was contingent on the acceptance of SAP. With the progressive adoption of the policy of reforms, the loan was released in doses. This cycle of external debt-SAP-debt is likely to continue until 1995 when the SAP is expected to complete its course and the loan will dry up.

5

Measurement of Poverty is Major Challenges Before Indian Economy

Introduction

Poverty is one of the most important problems that India is facing today. Poverty is a situation in which a person is unable to get minimum basic necessities of life, i.e., food, clothing and shelter for his or her sustenance. For instance, some of our neighbours finding it difficult to get food even twice a day. Some children in weak and highly malnourished because they do not get sufficient and nutritious food. They may not even be having enough clothes to wear. You may also see many children to working in canteens, hotels, dhabas and other shops instead of coming to school. In economic terms they are called poverty-ridden and are people living below poverty line. When a larger section of the people in an economy are deprived of these basic necessities, that economy is said to be in mass poverty. During 1999-2000, approximately 26 crore people in India are reported to be poverty-ridden. This proportion is nearly equal to the total population living at the time of India's Independence.

Measurement of Poverty

It has to take certain steps, to developing an appropriate mechanism to identify the poverty-ridden people, referred to in economic terms as poverty line. The second step is to estimate the total number of poverty-ridden persons with the help of that mechanism. There are two approaches by which the number of poor is estimated. In the first approach, expenditure incurred by a family on various items is used. In the second approach, the income earned by a family is used. For each person, the minimum nutritional food requirement for survival is estimated. We know that whatever we eat has some energy. This energy is measured in calories. The total minimum food requirement is first measured in calories and this calories amount is then converted into equivalent money value i.e., in rupees. Apart from food, we also need money to buy clothes and other requirements. In India, the daily minimum nutritional requirement for a person has been fixed at 2400 calories in rural areas and 2100 calories in urban areas.

Measuring Poverty is difficult because of conceptual problems and data deficiencies and because all definitions of poverty involve social judgements. While measuring inequality involves parallel difficulties also Absolute poverty is defined by comparing personal or household income or expenditure with the cost of buying a given quality of goods and services, relative poverty by comparing that income with the incomes of others, and subjective poverty by comparing actual income against the income earness expectations and perceptions. there is at present no specifies scientific, unequivocal definition of who is and who is not poor.

Basic needs are those things that an individual must have in order to service as a human being. The basic needs includes air, water, adequate and balanced food, physical and mental rest, and culturally and climatically appropriate clothing and shelter. In this article, effort has been made to analysis the causes of poverty, what is development, status of population and poverty in the World Economy and gaps in per capita income.

We know that measuring poverty is difficult enough even in a stable economy with regular and continuous statistics. Transition economies pose additional major measurement problems. Money data on income and consumption are highly questionable, not least because of serious deficiencies in the conduct of household surveys and because of growing informal activity, which goes unrecorded. Inter station is further complicated by huge changes in relative prices and by that increased availability of goods that accompanies shift to the market. Improving the quality of data can itself create problems.

Sign of Poverty

Following are the major indicators of poverty:-

Malnutrition	Low Income	Lack of clan Water
Illiteracy	Lack of Transport	Low productivity
Poor Sanitation	Over population	Poor Housing
Laziness/Idleness	Drunkenness	Superstition
Backwardness	Hunger	Corruption
Drought/Floods	Indebtness	Exploitation
Deforestation	Lack of tools	Unemployment
Lack of Markets	Low Prices	Lack of Skills
Colonialism	Poor Management	Lack of Industry
Traditions	Lack of credit	Lack of Initiative
Lack of Capital	Mistrust	Lack of Cooperation

In other words, we can say that poverty is undergrowth industry. The poor countries/people are laid above mentioned indicators and they have to improve the above cited indicators of poverty. Hence, we can say that poverty is a growth Industry.

Vicious Circle of Poverty

To understand the poverty more precisely, it would be more appropriate to explain here the vicious circle of Poverty as Figure 12.1

Gaps between the Low Income Countries and Industrial Countries in per Capita Income

In Table 5.1, details of per Capita Income of Low-Income

Countries, Industrial Countries and gap between these groups of countries has been explained in Table 5.1. From the above figures, it may be observed that year after year the gap between the Low-Income countries and Industrial Countries is widening i.e. between the Rich and Poor Countries gap in the average per capita income is increasing.

Table 5.1: Average Per Capita Income

(US $)

S. No.	*Year*	*Low-Income Countries*	*Industrial Countries*	*Gap*
1.	*2.*	*3.*	*4.*	*5.*
1.	1950	164	3,841	3,677
2.	1980	245	9,648	9,403
3.	1990	353	20,173	19,820
4.	1993	380	23,090	22,710
5.	1994	380	23,420	23,040
6.	1995	430	24,930	24,500

Source: Compiled from the Various Development Reports of the World Bank.

Number of Countries in Rich, Middle and Poor Groups

The Poor countries demand a "New International Economic Order (NIEO), which they hope will result in the transfer of Wealth away from the rich countries to the Poor countries. The Industrialised countries have responded with "Foreign Aid Programmes" that, by all accounts, can only hope to make a small dent in the problem of eradication of poverty. Indeed, some argue that Foreign Aid actually exacerbates the gap. Within the developing countries, domestic stability is frequently tenuous at best as victims of the yawning gap between the Rich and Poor (alongwith their sympathisers) seek redress through violent means. Thinking and research on the international and domestic gaps between Rich and Poor has been going through a protracted period of debate that can be traced back to the end of World War-II. "Classic Thesis", suggests that the gaps are temporal and will disappear overtime. Simon Kuznets have been associated with this School of Thought.

Growth of Gross Domestic Product (GDP) in World Economy

The Economy-wise share of Gross Domestic Product (GDP) and Population for the years 1965 to 1995

Performance of Special Employment and Poverty Alleviation Programmes in India

Indian Government have organised various special employment and poverty. Poverty alleviation programmes and target has been fixed for these programmes. In a recent Rajya Sabha Starred Question No. 2270, the Ministry of Finance, Government of India submitted the information to Rajya Sabha about the total subside extended under various developmental schemes for eradication of poverty in border sense.

The main problem of the Third World Countries is the wide-spread appalling poverty, their main thrust—its planned eradication and spreading economic development. Throughout the last 50 years, it has been realised that the problem is touched marginally, so far. The Governmental and Non-Governmental Organizations (NGOs) in various countries are therefore in search of identifying the factors of failure and build new strategies to alleviate poverty.

Direct attach on poverty and identification of some crucial factors affecting the elevation/eradication of poverty in the need of hour. It has been observed that from community development experiment to target group and special delivery systems, the plight of poor has been marginally affected. The work done by the NGOs, though effective, remained short-term and sporadic. So far India is concerned and overwhelming majority of the Indian population lives in the Rural and Semi-urban areas. Most of them suffer from object poverty. This multi-dimensional sydrome comprises wide-spread unemployment, disuised unemployment and udner-employment, very low-income, low standards of living, lack of ownership of productive assets, inadequate productive skills, malnutrition, morbidity and lower-life expectance and illiteracy.

The Government of India and NGOs have taken a general as well as specific programmes of development to alleviate poverty. These includes improvement in the conditions of living, raising productivity, improving levels of consumption and generating more employment opportunities in the provanious parts of country. These programmes were developed and implemened with the idea to eradicate rural and semi-urban areas poverty and generate more income, specially for the poorer sections of the society. For eradication of Urban poverty also many programmes were implemented. The author is of the view that linking threshold of poverty line incomes to social security needs, and price rise phenomenon alongwith minimum consumption levels should be the main thrust for alleviation of poverty.

For Urban poverty, as it is of a transitional nature/ phenomena, a strategy of investment, away from expenditure oriented Capital Investment and subsidies, favouring upgradation of self-employment capacities which would pay current expenditure out of future earnings should be put into practice for implementation. Some the Economists has suggested that it would be more appropriate to disagregate life expectancy data in various economic and social categories to fix-up the target groups and to broaden the battery of poverty alleviation instruments by including instruments for delivery of health services, health education, family planning, sanitation, etc. alongwith the existing economic instruments of poverty eradication programmes.

It will be more appropriate to organise and education urban poor for greater participation, if bureaucratic- cum-political corruption is to be controlled in a better manner. It may once again be reiterated that 'Poverty is a Curse'. A very poor person is hardly alive. There is no difference between a poor man and a dead man. Hence, removal of poverty and in its place "to bring Growth" is the prime duty and responsibility of all the State Authorities, Planners and Administrators. Even in this process, the role of the beneciary is not less important. They should create some developmental assets instead of spending/ eating whole the subsidised amount for drugs and adding more population to the National without discharging their role to break the vicious circle of poverty.

If the poverty eradication/development programmes are implemened in right spirit they can have the break-even effect on the eradication of the "Vicious Circle of Poverty" more aggressively in India and other Low-Income Countries in the World.

World Labour Market and International Migration

Labour market is an imaginary situation in which a worker or group of workers provide their labour to employers in exchange for some payment. When a labour contractor or a house-owner employees workers at the construction sites, we can term that situation as construction labour market. When farmers employ agricultural labourers in their lands, we can term that situation as agricultural labour market. When countries around the world exchange their labourers, we term that labour market as the world labour market. This takes place in the form of migration. Let's look into the issue of migration at the international level briefly. Migration of persons from rural to urban areas or from one region to another region within the country for employment is quite common. However, this phenomenon also takes place across national boundaries. Such movements take place in course of international trade, business, and pursuit of academic professions. In recent years, migration has been marked by the movement of highly skilled person across nations. The migration of skilled people to other nations in search of better opportunities and employment.

Annexure I

Group of Economy/Selected Country-wise Exports During the Year 1980, 1990, 1993 to 1995 and Their Respective Market Share in World Exports

(Million US $)

S.No.	*Group of Economies/ Selected Countries*	*1980*	*1990*	*1993*	*1994*	*1995*
1	*2*	*3*	*4*	*5*	*6*	*7*
I.	Low-Income Economies Of Which:	84.204	141,176	156.474	202,239	245,456
1.	Nepal	80	162	390	363	348
2.	Bangladesh	793	1674	2272	2661	3173
3.	Kenya	1250	1033	1374	1609	1878
4.	India	8590	17,967	21553	25000	30764
5.	Pakistan	2620	5,590	6636	7370	7992
6.	China	18100	62091	91744	121047	148797
II.	Middle Income Economies	586567	491128	648218	826822	893331
	Of Which:					
1.	Indonesia	21900	25553	33612	40054	45417

6

The Organisational Structure of Public Sector Banks in India

The organisational needs arose on account of the increase in the level of consumer/customer's education, increased expectations from banking clients, technological development, information based functioning, new generation of human resources and changing priorities of unions and management. This fact coupled with ever changing expectations of customers has a bearing on the organisational needs. The Banking Organisations were built on formal authority structures and have well defined the system based on authority delegation.

However, now due to growing technological and information contents, the Banking Organisations are not able to cope up itself with only authority structures in the recent years. The leadership concept in Banks will have a reorientation towards guiding and following simultaneously. The Banking system in India have the distinctive attributes like; large number of branches, large variations in size of the branches, large information requirements of outside agencies, high diversity in product mix, locational diversity and disadvantages, rapid obsolescence of data, need of qualitative information, pressures on Management Information System not one at a time or individually separately etc. The last 23 years saw quantitative expansion in Banking Industry, where the physical dimensions of banking grew multifold including the manpower. This continued upto early eighties and thereafter on realising the diminishing potential the space of quantitative expansion slowed down. The latter half of eighties saw banking consolidating itself and developing skills for managing the change. Further, the vast human resources acquired during seventies were to be inducted, trained and mended into the main organisation.

Now the situation has to survive with grace the Banking Organizations need to develop marketing management concept. Marketing does not mean aggressive selling. Marketing really is identification of ever changing customers' needs and then developing appropriate service packages, to suit the changing needs and cater the customers to their entire satisfaction. These days the Banking services packages needs to be reviewed with the active achievement of Government authorities and Reserve Bank of India and then it has to be done in co-ordination with the Research and Development Authorities to facilitate marketing. Indian Banking Association (IBA) at the behest of the Govt. conducted a study on impact created by Publicity Programmes of various institutions.

The survey revealed that there is a need for concerted planning and greater involvement of Bank staff in publicity programmes.

There has been a spectacular expansion in the geographical coverage and spread of Banking System in India after the Nationalisation of Banks in 1969. It has contributed significantly in increasing the rate of economic development of the various sectors of the economy. However, in the recent years, some rigidities and weaknesses have developed in the public sector banks and a need is felt to enable the banks to play its role in a more efficient and competitive manner.

In this paper, an effort has been made to make the critical evaluation of the working of the Public Sector Banks in India from 1969 onwards.

- Deals with the Nationalisation of Banks.
- Critically evaluate the achievements made by public sector banks.

- Critically analysis the organisational structure of public sector banks.
- Deals about the concept of marketing in Banks.
- Makes the indepth study of competition and Regulation in public sector banks.
- Makes the critical analysis of Profitability of public sector banks.
- Deals with Organisation, Personnel and Housekeeping aspects of the banks.
- Makes the critical analysis of mechanisation in public sector banks.
- Makes the analysis of the steps taken by public sector banks to reverse the adverse trend in various sectors.

In the last, conclusion has also been drawn.

Nationalisation of Banks

The idea of Social Control on Banks gained sudden importance on the eve of general elections in 1967. The election manifesto of the Indian National Conference declared, it is a necessary to bring most of the Banking Institutions under Social Control in order to serve the cause of economic growth; and fulfil our social purposes more effectively and to make credit available to the producers in fields where it is needed.

Social control was something short of Nationalisation exercised complete control over the lending policies of Private/ Foreign Bank; and directed them to follow the directives issued by the Government to change the credit pattern.

Thus, the Bank's role changed from Commercial purpose to "removal of poverty" without caring for "Economy of Scale of the working of Banks in India. When Mr. Morarji Desai in 1969 introduced the concept of Social Banking", little did he visualised the scale and complexity that Social Banking assured in less than 23 years time.

The criteria laid down by the Bureau of public Enterprises in their Report in 1987-88 about public sector is as under:

1. To help in the rapid growth and industrialisation of the country and create the necessary infrastructure for economic development;
2. To earn return on investment and thus generate resources for development;
3. To promote redistribution of income and wealth;
4. To create employment opportunities;
5. To promote balanced regional development;
6. To assist the development of Small Scale and ancillary industries; and
7. To promote import substitution, save and earn foreign exchange for the economy.

Achievements of Public Sector Banks

The Nationalisation of Banks on 19th July, 1969 has achieved the major objectives of Nationalisation, viz. Socialisation Bank Credit, Expansion of Banking Network, Mobilisation of Resources and trapping of domestic savings. Banking Institutions are the premier financial institutions which perform a pivotal role in the economy of a country. But, it was a sugar coated pill.

The Nationalisation of Banks has been hailed by the people who believe the domestic socialism can improve the economic condition of the masses.

There are at present 28 Public Sector Banks incuding State Bank of India and its 7 associate banks and 20 Nationalised 369 districts in the country. Aggregate deposits of the Scheduled Commercial Banks as on 22nd March, 1991 stood at Rs. 1,91,189 crores and total advances of all the Commercial Banks stood at Rs. 1,16,184 crores.

The credit deposit ratio works out to 60.77%. The total net work of branches in the country is about 60,000 out of which 58% are rural branches. This has helped to reduce the population per branch from 65,000 in 1969 to around 116000 as per 1981 census. The outstanding deposits and advances of all scheduled commercial banks as on last Friday of Sept. 1991 stood at Rs. 2,13,024 crores and Rs. 1,31,827 crores, respectively.

Social Banking has led to the attainment of the objectives of providing greater funds at reasonable rates to priority sections of the economy like agriculture, small industries, small business etc. which were previously neglected and which the priority sector banking is cost-effective and viable.

The cost benefit analysis of Indian Public Sector Banking is pointless for the simple reason that once the decision to extend banking to the Priority Sector was taken, the required Branch Expansion took place. Further, it is an other ticklish question to revert to the golden days, when banking was essentially commercial in character and metropolitan-urban in its character.

With the introduction of "Social Banking" a whole series of branches often called rural, semi-urban, urban, metro or small industries, overseas, Industrial Finance or even other activity based branches came into existence.

As a matter of fact, the failure of Private Banks to serve the common man and the country compelled the then Government to Nationalise the Banks. With all these developments, Banks faced changes during the recent years, 60th in their macro and micro economic environment. The economists cannot experiment to test their theories. The nearest approach to an experiment occurs when a Government adopts the new policies. Even then there is a need to have more critical examination of ideas and premises of banking economists who help in making economic policy as there is only a team of economists who are playing the Government's game.

As a result of deliberate policy pursued vigorously since the nationalisation of banks, there has been a spectacular progress in territoral coverage by banks in the country. No system is perfect in itself. Hence, the concept of Public Sector Banks is not an exception to this.

Competition and Regulation in Public Sector Banks

Competition and regulation are not alternatives to each other. A growth oriented and efficient financial sector needs a measure of regulation especially during the periods of growth and development of money and capital markets. The degree of such regulation would of course vary depending on the stage of country's development. Growth oriented and efficient financial sector would also need a measure of competition.

Owing to these too many problems which emerged during the 1st 23 years after Nationalisation of Banks in the Indian Banking scene like poor customer service, complaints, to dispose large credit application, to deal with sick units, rescheduling and providing reliefs to units, Industrial Relations and personnel related problems, development of multitier system, reversal of decision making process to higher authorities etc.

To cope with this situation, some of the largest banks in India acted as under:

* Participative strategy formulation;
* Delegation of authority for decision making upto a significant limit to lower tier of management.
* Preparation of operational budgets, reflecting the strategic Plan in respect of the permanent Centre.
* Preparation of budget-based performance report and review.
* Preparation of various manual, guidelines procedures etc. for use of lower levels of management and performance levels for ensuring uniformity of operations,

and

* Introduction of modular structures like Regional Office's heau as Assistant General Manager and at big branches Chief Manager etc.

The problem of size are clearly becoming unmanageable. Volume of transaction increased substantially, particularly with the spread of banking habit among the massess.

These days profitability is one of the major criteria for evaluating the performance of Banks. But it is not a mere post-nationalisation or a wages-and-productivity problem. If profitability has to be planned and imporved detailed systematic and objective analysis is necessary. For this the detailed analysis of what factors determine profitability, how, they behave, how they are related to each other, and how valid inter-bank and Inter-temporal compassions are to be made.

An outsider may use published data and arrived at broad and general conclusions. Financial analysis is largely based on ratios as tools for making fare comparison. There is nothing wrong with ratios as tools. The problem lies with the selecting of ratios. To be really helpful and practically useful, the package of selected ratios should be small, simple and logically consistent, so that valid and fare comparison can be made and useful results are obtained.

In the absence of information regarding the demarcation of resources held by banks against their demand and time liabilities, it seems appropriate to choose M III as a measure of money stock of control. In India, high powered money emerges as an important deteriment of M III with CRR and SLR already nearing the sealing levels i.e. 15% and 38.5% respectively, the banks are left with small amount for lending purposes. Government and RBI have taken a series of conflicting measures to improve that profit earning capacity of the banks. Further, the partial deregulation of interest rates put the banking industry at a disadvantage. It is doubtful whether financial institutions in any other country in the world offer assistance on a liberal terms as they do in India.

RBI have drawn the attention of the banking authority from time to time to the need to augment the bank's profitability and strengthen their financial base by generating enough surplus to provide for the estimated loan losses and other contingencies. Banks were advised to observe prudent accounting standards and guidelines for classification of advances under health codes as also for stopping the application of interest. For the purpose of augmenting profits, banks have to consider seriously improving the volume of business, concentrating on effecting quicker recoveries of bank's dues ensuring.

To further improve the profitability the steps includes augmentation of bank's capital, rationalisation of service charges and interest rates structure curtail ment of staff growth and levy of commitment charges on nutilised portion of operating limits.

It is heartening that the performance of the banking industry measured in terms of profits, despite heavy odds, has been encouraging. Reduction in interest rates on agriculture advances and export, enhancement of direct agriculture advances imporved the profitability. Banks fulfilled these targets. But what about recovery of advances. The main draw back in priority sector advances was fixing targets without making any indepth study of cost benefit analysis. Increased targets coupled with reduced interest rate puts sever strain on the earnings of banks, or the Government should have provided adequate subsidy to banking sector to Inspite the banks to promote experts.

The implication of the mix of social and commercial objectives of public sector banks is that the profit criteria used here is not good enough to measure their performance, as it gives little weight to social obligations.

Further, the problems of rural banking like under utilisation, lower productivity, dearth of investment opportunities, inadequate infrastructed etc. also effected the banks profitability to a great extend.

As at the end of March, 91 total paid up capital of all nationalised banks stood at Rs. 200.Crores and the share capital of 7 associate banks of SBI stood at Rs. 113.05 Crores. During the year 1989-90, total published profits of 26 public sector banks were of then order of Rs. 366.88 crores compared to Rs. 291.83 crores for the year 1988-89. The nationalised banks are bankrupt in all but name after being pillaged by political forces for more than two decades. This has eroded profitability, while political directives have fixed banks to keep lending to unviable units and bogus enterprises in loan meals.

The Narasimhan Committee rightly emphasised the need to slash the same ratios, something that should follow anyway from the Governments as commitment to slashing its fiscal deficit. This will leave for more money for lending to entrepreneures, in keeping with the liberalisation ethos. To improve the profitability of the banks the following points like funds management, cash management, recovery, cost-effectiveness and control proper pricing of services to improve productivity and diversifaction of activities have significant role to play.

Organisation, Personnel/Housekeeping

Reserve Bank of India also emphasised the need of the effectiveness of the performance of controlling offices by making critical review under relevant parameters regularly and to improve their performance. In the case of smaller banks, it does not seem to be worthwhile to have a four-tier organizational structure and such banks should consider if they revert to the three-tier structure, in the interests of saving costs as well as for improving the speed and effective of the decision making process.

With the job security after Nationalisation of Banks in India, the follow up and supervision by the staff deteriorated continuously. Owing to this, the customer service was affected adversely to a great extent and work started accumulating in the Branches.

In the following areas, the house-keeping was affected very much, when paying the overtime in the Public Sector Banks was stopped to a great extend in 1981:

(i) Regular balancing of individual accounts with subsidiary books and collectively with general ledger balance book;

(ii) Reconciliation of accounts;

(iii) Prompt and accurate preparation and submission of control and other returns;

(iv) Observance of systems/procedures and manual of instruction;

(v) Physical preservation and accessibility to vouchers and books of accounts;

(vi) Control over advances which encompass scientific appraisal, judicious exercising of discretionary powers: perfect and proper documentation, regular review, follow-up and recovery, etc; and

(vii) Proper follow-up of audit/Inspection.

There is no doubt that smaller branches are still providing a satisfactory customer services. While the delays, refusal of service, behaviours of staff and inflexibility in rules have further deteriorated the House Keeping in the branches.

Further, instead of the present rigid organisation structure common to all branches spread over the nook and corner of the country, it is the right time to consider a flexible structure which may be more suitable for accomplishing the task of achieving targets, both quantitative as well as qualitative. The contribution of employees is not merely in terms of performing the existing roles better but in terms of capability to perform newer functions and roles in an organisation. The above can be made more effective if the Indian Banking Association and Govt. of India/RBI at the time of next wage revision and at the time of signing the bipartite settlement are able to add the right of transfer of all employees from one State to another State. For the slackness, shown by this group of employees in the past, they should be made agreeable to bear the cost of default in the years to come.

Normally, in Banks' there are three tier of officials, namely (i) front line-Clerical staff; (ii) Officers; and (iii) the Branch Manager. As and when some customer comes to the Bank first of all he meet the front line management and he forms the opinion about the Bank from the first contact. The main impressions made by the public about the Banking Customer Service uptill now is based on the basis of frontline experience. To overcome this problem, the author is of the opinion that in the banking Sector the Clerical staff should be named as another Junior Class Officers to bring them under the purview of transfer policy from one State to another and make them more responsible to the Customer as well as to the Management.

We borrowed the ideas of hierarchy and nomenclatures from British Raj. The same continued to influence the present day Banking Organisations. Now, it is the right time to have a rethinking over this for scraping of reduntal levels. This concept would certainly face a stiff resistance from the Unions but nevertheless sooner the redundant levels are abolised better is the future of the Banking Organisations in India.

Information linkages, technological linkages and upward and downward organisational communications will establish commitment and cohesiveness in the organisations than authoritity tie ups. Banking sector organisations must strive for better organisational cohensiveness would certainly mean a lot of psychological resistance from the existing human resources in the higher echelons who have spent considerable number of years in the organisations. Computers will have a good role to play in this regard.

While the Banks are making some progress in the installation of ALPMS at branches and mini-computers at controlling offices, it has been observed that full advantage is not being derived from them. It is necessary for the Bank Management to ensure the optimum utilisation of the systems installed. This needs to be pursued as otherwise there would be mismatch between customers expectations and Banking Organisations' delivery of service.

India has just awakened to the new technology and lacks the necessary infrastructure in banking Industry. Lack of E.D.P. expertise, is a major handicap. Moreover, supply of trained EDP personnel is no where near the demand. There is also the specialised nature of this job which involve a large time frame before one can really master the machine.

Further, it has been observed that in majority of the Banks Human Relations Development Department could not make the job rotation in EDP so far.

Steps Taken by Public Sector Banks

Some of the Banks introduced the series of reform measures to rectify the adverse trend in their Banks. A major cause of poor performance of some of the Public Banks in India is that Government as owners do not restrict their role as do the owners of private and Foreign Banks. A sure way of improving the performance of Public Sector Banks is to expose them to competition by lifting compulsion on advances to priority sector advances and reducing the SLR and CRR to a reasonable level.

Though, no proper time and motion studies have been made out so far, it is estimated that Banking transactions now claim only 60% of the total manhours, while the remaining time is spent on compilation, amalgamation and follow-up of statistical information of all sorts. Further, the format designing in Banks is still in a primitive stage and statements require to be compiled regularly are cumbersome, involve wasteful duplication and repetitions and do not take into account the existing accounting procedures which form the basis for all statistical information.

Some of the Banks have already initiated the steps to improve Banking Service by taking corrective measures in the field of discipline and punctuality, posting talented and honest staff at Controlling offices, environment studies, arranging awareness Programmes and public relation meetings in co-ordination with staff, SWOT analysis of branches, action

Plan/Long Range Plan (LRP), insisting moral and social responsibility, to upgrade the unsatisfactory branches, to develop model branches, etc.

Further, it is imperative for Banks to endeavours for constant improvements in the area of presanction appraisal and post-sanction follow-up and supervision of credit. The higher management should insist and should take strict action against the tendency for officials at various levels to frequently exceed their discretionary powers and makes delays in getting the confirmation of the same from the higher authorities.

Indian Banks may adopt the methodology/procedure adopted by the Foreign Banks in management of SLR and CRR. A professional Banker, therefore, has to understand the dynamics of the new developments staking place in the field of Commercial Banking and international financial markets and has to equip himself with the professional skill and competence to be able to operate in the changing environments. To operate in a changing environment requires professional skill and competence to be successful.

Presently, the environment in the Banking sector is becoming day by day more open and competitive than before. The Commercial Banks have diversified from their traditional areas of operation and their business has become more competitive. Therefore, greater stress is being laid on efficiency in Banks. Liberalisation and competition generate pressures on the profitability of Banks. Therefore, there is a need to pay greater attention to improvement in their financial viability. Under these circumstances, it becomes necessary to increase the capital base of banks, to enable them to absorb shocks. On the one side, Reserve Bank of India is continuously striving for improvement in technology in financial operations, institutional development and liberalisation of the regulatory framework, on the other side, these banks should gear themselves to meet the challenges of the changing market environment. For this, the Management, all staff working in the Banks and the Officers Associations and Unions should come closer to each other and should work out the action plan to enable the Public Sector Banks to face the changing market environment and to make the Banks available unit once again.

Taking a global outlook, the environment for banking has rarely been worse. Most of the favourable cartel arrangements have broken down and the market environment due to the transformation in technology and the globalisation and unity of financial markets has made the competition intense, at the same time the regulations still seems scrappy and the prevailing Monetarist Economists' sentiment on bailing out failing banks is uniformly grim.

So far merger of Public Sector Banks is concerned, there is a good evidence to show that organisation structure and management systems beyond a certain level of organistional effectiveness becomes ineffective as the human systems linkages begin to break down like state bank of India. Hence, the concept of merger of Banks needs detailed analysis and through discussions so that before taking any concrete step in this direction, suitable effective organisational structure is chalked out.

Of late, one School of Thought of Banking Economists have come up with the idea of denationalisation of Public Sector Banks. In this direction, the Govt. and the RBI have also initiated half hartedly few steps on structural changes in the Indian Banking System. The changes involve mainly among others is the gradual privatisation of Public Sector Banks.

Banks were nationalised in 1969 to expand Banking infrastructure to unbanked rural and semi-urban areas and to reorient the entire banking system for serving the poor and downtrodden. It was also expected that banks would upgrade the lending techniques from security oriented to purpose oriented lending by ensuring economic growth and social justice. It is commendable to note that during the 23 years, the Public Sector banks have achieved by and large, the objections for which they were nationalised. However, there has been a steady erosion of profitability of commercial banks as explained earlier for which also Public

Sector Banks are to solely responsible. For that some responsibility also lies to Government/Politicians, Reserve Bank of India and local/State Governments.

Instead of privatisation, the Public Sector Banks should be freed from the stronghold of political interferece and bureaucratic contracts. They should be left completely free and made responsible to manage themselves effectively.

Operating in such a changing environment of banking, requires the right type of personnel and manpower to handle it. There is a need to train manpower and proper post training utilisation, so as to improve the productivity of the capital and labour in Banks and to continue the implications of strategy for training and productivity. Therefore, it is necessary to evolve an appropriate training strategy, which would enable the manpower to obtain necessary skills to operate in changing environment efficiently. Banking is marked by changes in policy, environment and operations. Operating in such a changing environment involves risk and one cannot afford to loose money while operating in the changing environment whatever be the nature of risk. Hence, to bear the external and internal shocks, internal remedies to Banking Industry and self-imposed conditionally is a preferable step. It is more important to restore credibility to the Public Sector Banking System, but political will is necessary to achieve that objective.

Despite several constraints, the Public Sector Banks have played a major role in fuelling economic development in India and in future have to perform still a better role according to the desire of the customers. One must end somewhere, even if an end suggests only the possibilities of a new beginning. The Central theme of this paper is the need to develop a more articulate notion about the working of Public Sector Banks after Natonalisation.

7

Implications of Globalisation for Agriculture Crises in India

The Rural elite obviously did not agree to the principle of land reforms and co-operative farming. They perceived the entire development strategy as an organisational device for weakening their economic, social and political power. Hence they did not accept the strategy of rapid industrialisaiton and its complementary programmes of rural reorganisation.

Their opposition was articulated by the Ministry of Food and Agriculture and the state chief ministers. India is a large continental economy, and the development process has to take account of the various parts of growth and structural changes in the economy. In this process, there may be diversity in terms of resource endowments, manpower development, institutional framework, governance, other parameters of development and to bring about reductions in disparities. We know that the liberalisation of the Indian economy during the early nineties gave increasing hopes to the Agricultural Sector. History was created at Marakesh Ministerial Meeting, when Ministers from 117 countries put their seals of approval on 15th April, 1994 to the final text what is now known as "*GATT Agreement, 1994*". This biggest ever trade accord was signed to "smash the barriers of Export and boost Global Prosperity." While, on the one side India's subjection to the Accord was considered as the reversal of our economic policy of self-reliance, protectionism and anti-Multi-nationalism. At this juncture, many people thought it as gradual loss of economic sovereignty and consequently the political subservience of the nation—as Indians can never forget the pernicious role played by the East India Company. While on the other side, the supporter camp considers it as the beginning of a progressive era of New World Economic Order (NWEO) leading to nation's advancement for prosperity and mass well being. We know that first wave of Globalisation, in the form of Western Colonialism, swept through Asia and Africa, overwhelming all resistance. It was a Globalisation far less sophisticated that phenomenon we are witnessing with the establishment of WTO in 1995, but in its own time was predicted on similar inequities in technological progress between East and West.

Developed Countries were able to subjugate the developing World by virtue of their superior production techniques, mobility, communications and technological development. Today, the quest to open up new markets and new opportunities for investment is once again sweeping the globe. The difference this time around is that no coercion by force of arms is involved. Instead, all member countries of the WTO are competing to open up their economies to free flows of trade and investment even in the Agriculture sector also. The root cause of the crises which emerged during the last 3-4 years was inadequate preparation by the developing countries for the global economy. Although, with the WTO's Agreement on Agriculture, the members country were deepening integration of member countries into the global economy, it remained still a superficial sort of integration.

World Trade Organisation was set up in 1995 by the member countries of the United Nations to promote trade among countries. The headquarters of WTO is located in Geneva. It has sgignificantly influenced the liberalisation and globalisation processes in most of the developing countries, including India. WTO aims at conducting international trade among countries of the world in an open, uniform and non-discriminatory manner. The GATT Agreement 1994, aimed to further develop the World Trade and Free Flow of goods and services among the World Trading Nations. It was also to ensure free flow of goods and services with the least pressure of Customs, Tariffs and Trade Barriers as well as Non-Tariff Barriers (NTBs). Even, prior to the creation of WTO, the World Trading Nations were trying through different phases of Trade Negotiations had witnessed unprecedented ups and down in its proposal on account of addition of newer and diverse trade, as well, trade related matters within the ambit of trade negotiations under the umbrella of GATT.

The signing of the GATT Agreement also signalled the setting up of the World Trade Organisation (WTO) from 1st January, 1995. The GATT Agreement 1994, tried to do the "Bilateral basis" to "Multilateral basis" so that each country does not have to enter into separate agreements with another country. For example, if India had not been a part of GATT, we would have to enter into 3800 Agreements with different countries in the World for trade. By agreeing to join GATT, India could do away with a more or less with one agreement for International Trade. GATT Agreement would have been basically to monitor that tariffs are removed or slowly and gradually reduced. Any trade barrier, which also could be NTBs, like a quota system, were to be slowly abolished. With this, it was expected that Developing Countries will get a chance to develop and eventually come to the status of Developed Countries. But, after the Uruguay Round of Negotiations, seven new things came up. which are as under:

- The Agriculture;
- Textile;
- Trade Related Intellectual Property Rights (TRIPs);
- Trade Related Investment Measures (TRIMs);
- Services;
- Retaliatory Measure i.e. if any body got out of line; and
- Foreign Investments and Institutional matters.

We know that the economic and institutional integration of developing countries is a major challenge for International Cooperation. To foster such integration , concrete economic and social policy measures are required to promote competitiveness, stimulate investment, develop human capital and facilitate the exploitation of trading opportunities resulting from the Uruguay Round of Trade Negotiations and Agreements. In this direction, measures were also need to be taken to strengthen the effective participation of developing countries in the Multilateral Trading System (MTS), as it has emerged from the Uruguay Round and to minimise the risks of new imballences and instabilities, including International Financial Markets, and the potential marginalisation of the Least Developed Countries (LDCs) and other Weaker economies. The Integration of Developing Countries into the World Economy and Trading System to ensure equitable and sustainable development was to be seen as an inherent component of the Future Trade Initiatives.

World Trade Organisation (WTO) placed the International Trading System (ITS) on a firm Constitutional footing. For the first time, the pillars of the International Trading System (ITS) were put on a full-fledged International Organisation, and with an International Legal Personality. The main objectives of the WTO are to ensure reduction of tariffs and other barriers to Trade; and the elimination of discriminatory treatment in International Trade relations. Alongwith the above, WTO was to ensure the following:

— Higher Standards of Living

— Full Employment

— A Growing Volume of Real Income and Effective Demand

— Expansion of Production and Trade in Goods and Services.

Thus, WTO is a catalyst and harbinger of "Rule based International Trading System" for global peace, prosperity and equity distribution. In other words, we can say that WTO is a significant step for pulling- out the developing countries from the paradoxical rapture of "No Rule Situation" on access to the International market, ensuring their Comparative Advantages and better Competitive environment. The GATT 1947 alongwith its Seven Understandings emerged as a "GATT 1994 Agreement," which became the part and parcel of World Trade Organisation in 1995. With the Liberalisation & Globalisation of Trade, comparative costs, production efficiency, technology and quality of the produce are having the major edge over the others in having greater market share in the International Trade.

In an imperfectly competitive setting, potential gains from trade may flows from the elimination or reduction of distortions' that result from "Market Power" and from an increase in the size of produce by means of increasing returns to scale technologies. Trade, however, does not necessarily lead to an expansion of these sections. Transportation costs including crop lost in spillage and transport works out to 2% to 5% by the time it reaches the mandi where, once again, fees and commission charges have to be paid. The transportation & storage facilities at all stages are very inefficient leading to significant degradation in quality, and losses to spillage, pests and insects.

At UNCTAD IX, the International Community, recognised that its main role in the field of trade in goods and services should help to maximise the positive impact of Globalisation and Liberalisation on sustainable development of assisting in the effective integration of Developing Countries into the International Trading System. The degree of a country's integration within the International Trading System can be measured in relation to its ability and capacity on the following parameters:

- To identify and take advantage of the trading opportunities;
- To meet its multilateral trade obligations;
- To formulate and pursue development strategies within the framework of those obligations;
- To defend its acquired trade rights; and
- To set trade objectives and effectively pursue them in trade negotiations.

Meeting the captioned challenges effectively will require a substantial strengthening of Institutions and Human and Financial Resources in the Developing Countries and in Countries which are in transition. Moreover, Global Integration of Developing Countries is also an issue of special interest to the Developed Countries. The gains to the Industrial Countries from increased trade integration with Developing Countries are potentially larger than the gains from additional integration among themselves. Trade integration arising from the ongoing liberalisation process and from its extension to new areas, such as services, is likely to generate dynamic gains from the increased market size, Competition and Technology Transfer. It has been projected and forecasted by the leading International Trade Authorities that Developing Countries are expected to grow about twice as fast than the Industrial Developed Countries; and countries in Transition will develop stronger supply capacities and become more competitive internationally, the dynamic gains from increasing trade with them are likely to be especially important. The realisation of these gains, will depend on the extent, to which the adjustments required by the process of integration are carried out. International Trade can only fulfil its potential as an "Engine of Global Economic Growth" if the necessary reallocation of resources in line with countries' different and changing Comparative advantage is allowed to take place; and if the inevitable frictions and protectionist pressures that will arise in implementing the appropriate structural adjustment policies are resisted.

In this process, there may be supply-side constraints, as well as the constraints of external economic environment, for Developing Countries. While, for Developed Countries would entail "Adjustment Costs," for example, shutting-down the "Sunset Industries".

In the light of foregoing discussions, it is expected that agricultural sector in Developing Countries are going to witness major changes as the Multilateral discipline underlined by the World Trade Organisation (WTO) is extended to this Sector. The critical elements of policy adopted in the WTO regime pertaining to Agriculture form parts of several key agreements discussed and formalised at the conclusion of the Uruguay Round of GATT negotiations. The Agreement on Agriculture states that it seeks "to establish a fair and market-oriented Agricultural Trading System." Thus, the primary focus of the Agreements is to evolve a discipline pertaining to the Agricultural Sector that would best meet the stated objective. While, the Uruguay Round witnessed substantial shifts in the positions taken by the countries mainly involved in the Agricultural Policies. Thus, the Agreement arrived at UR appears to be only a small step in the direction of liberalisation of Agricultural policies. However, the issue of price support was only one of the aspects of the negotiations covering agriculture. The Agreement on Agriculture covered several other areas, covering: (i) Market Access; (ii) Public stock- holding for food-security purposes; and (iii) The Agreement on Trade Related Aspects of Intellectual Property Rights (TRIPs) and Sanitary and Phytosanitary measures, which would determine the future of agriculture in developing countries. While, the former aims at extending patent or a patent-like protection to agriculture, the latter seeks to introduce strict health and safety regulations. Through, these Agreements, norms and standards as already existing in the Developed Countries are being extended to Developing Countries.

Globalisation and Agriculture Crises in India

Thus, the critical analysis of the WTO Agreements from the view point of their impact on the developing countries and specially its implications on India has revealed that it become more imperative and important owing to the following reasons:

(i) India need to take on board the challenges that she would face in meeting the requirements of WTO regime. For this, considerable changes will have to be effected by India in its domestic policies to bring harmony and conformity with the WTO requirement.

(ii) The problems which India and other developing Countries will encounter in meeting the WTO Commitments need to be focussed on the review provisions that l. ive been in built in the Urguay Round of Trade Negotiations and Agreements.

Such provisions need to be taken care of by developing Countries, especially, India in order to minimise the burden of adjustments as they increase their engagement with the Global Economy.

The Indian Agriculture is facing new challenges and opportunities from the Competitive International Trade regime like challenges to draw new investments, producing Competitive crops and exporting as well as withstanding the rigour, of the WTO regime, Agriculture in India, needs a great deal of realism and this can be given only by those people who work on the fields and the Business Sector. There is no doubt that the experts opinions' are quite valuable, it is however the 'Market realities' that give us the Competitive spirit, which mainly drives the Global Economies. India is the second largest producer of wheat in the World with an output of more than 70 million tonnes. While the fact is that our average productivity per hectare is only 2.7 tons, which is significantly lower than the best yield of 7 tons of per hectare. Even in Punjab we could reach only 4.3 tons of per hectare. Thus, there exist significant potential to improve productivity and to reduce the cost of production per ton.

The emphasis on drawing the Private Sector Companies into Agriculture in India is based on the belief that the future of Indian Agriculture depends very much upon farmers investing in agro-ventures and Private Sector and Investments in new and innovative fields like floriculture, agri-business activities in a large number of Agri-products and services. With this, we will be in a position to bring paradigm shift in Public Opinion about the Agriculture and its role in National and International Affairs. Thus, Indian Agriculture needs a more realistic focus. Agriculture cannot continued to be "Grandma's tale" or a "Folk tale". In India, We still talk of Agriculture as, if it is a grand theme or a Government's exclusive preserve because Agriculture has for long been used farmers as a machines to produce food for others. There is much show of Food Production Targets and "Green Revolution theme" is again to brought by all the farmers in all the States on a sustainable basis. It should not be only managed by big actors and few States as a one time show.

It has been observed from the Plans' Allocations to the Agriculture sector, that inspite of the fact that Agriculture is India's largest sector of the Economy, yet the allocations to agriculture are miserable. Details may be seem from the Annexure-I. Further, unspent funds abound in this sector and agriculturists are still treated in a condescending manner. In other words, we can say that Agriculture as being basically farmers, their hopes and aspirations and frustrations needs, proper approach and outlook, to overcome the challenges and to over come the prevailing crises in Agriculture Sector in India successfully. One important factor among many, is the World Trade Regime. The post- GATT WTO regime is here and India is a signatory to the Trade Regime. Moreover, India stands to benefit by various developments, coming with the global developments and latest techniques in Agriculture Sector from which, India can get the benefits, to increase its production capacity, yield and quality. Further, India can benefit from the least cost techniques and strategy adopted by other countries, to produce agriculture products at competitive prices and with a higher yield for marketable surplus to exports.

WTO Agreement on Agriculture

The main features of the WTO's Agreement on Agriculture are given in brief as under:

(i) Discipline in the Subsidies regime;

(ii) Enhanced Market Access through increased Tariffication of Non-Tariff Barriers (NTBs) and establishment of minimum access opportunities for imports where it is, below 3% of domestic consumption during the period 1986-1988;

(iii) Discipline on Public Stock Holding of grains for food security;

(iv) Adoption of Health and Safety Regulations in accordance with the established International Standards; and

(v) Strengthening of Intellectual Property Protection, even including the introduction of Intellectual Property Rights in Agriculture.

During the period of liberalisation of the Indian Economy in the early nineties, it was expected that it will help the agricultural sector to a great extend, with increased exports. It was expected in December, 1994 that the signing of GATT accord would be a great instrumental in promoting multilateralism and in increasing International Trade in Agriculture, other commodities and services. It was further expected that the reduction or complete withdrawal of domestic and export subsidies by the Developed Countries would result in raising prices which will bring immense increase in Agricultural exports of the Developing Countries. It was also expected that agricultural products being "Labour - Intensive" would help in increasing employment and in reducing poverty. At the time of signing the GATT accord, it was further assumed by developing countries that 'increased prices' combined with 'efficiency of production' would lead to increase in Private Investment leading to increase in aggregate agricultural output.

The Agreement on Agriculture (of WTO), as a package provides, basically, the following 3 commitments:

(i) Commitment on Market Access;

(ii) Domestic Support Measures; and

(iii) Measures on Reduction of Direct Export Suboidies.

Trade in Agricultural Products

It has been observed that with rising incomes, consumers are shifting demand toward high-value-added agricultural products and away from frozen, canned, and processed homogenous goods. By increasing the variety of agricultural products available, advances in bio-technology may have an important impact on developing countries, whose climates sustain only a narrow range of basic agricultural crops. But exports of agricultural products can be constrained, if a country's domestic infrastructure and trade regulations do not permit speedy delivery. Further, it has been observed that fears about product safety that lead to calls for banning imports of certain foods can also constrain exports from the Developing Countries.

The Uruguay Round's agreement on trade in agricultural products laid the foundation for future liberalisation in this sector. Member Countries agreed to convert Non-Tariff Agricultural Barriers into Tariffs and to set the latter at or below a certain level. Similar, ceilings were agreed upon for export and domestic subsidies. The advantage of this approach is that it converts a wide range of Trade distortions into the following trade policies, with maximum levels that can be negotiated down over a period of time. Unfortunately, many countries took advantage of this opportunity to convert their NTBs into extremely high bound tariffs. It has been observed that for three widely traded commodities—rice, coarse grains, and sugar, many countries set, the maximum tariffs well above the actual tariffs collected in 1986-1988.

These tariffs are highly damaging. First, by raising domestic prices above World Prices, they make food more expansive for consumers. Secondly, they increase the costs of domestic food-processing firms, making them les Competitive in export markets. Third, the artificial expansion of the domestic agricultural sector boosts the demand for resources, making the latter more expensive for the rest of the economy. These economic costs may be added to those created by export subsidies for agriculture and the taxes that Finance such subsidies.

The Agricultural Exports growth rate over the previous year increased 16.71% in 1990-91, 33.13% in 1992-93, 38.21% in 1995-96 and came down to negative growth rate of 15.48% in the year 1999-2000. Further, the share of Agriculture exports to

GDP which was 25.74% in 1985-86, came down to 12.46% in 1989-90, increased to 17.20% in 1996-97 and decreased continuously and sharply to 11.31% in 1999-2000. This reflects a very critical position of the performance of Agriculture sector in India, on which 70% of the population depends.

Table 7.1
India's Agricultural Exports' Share in Total Exports

(Rs in crores)

Year	*Agricultural & Allied Products*	*Total Exports*	*% of Agricultural Exports to Total Exports*
1	*2*	*3*	*4*
1990-91	6317	32553	19.41
1995-96	21138	106353	19.88
1996-97	24239	118817	20.40
1997-98	25419	130101	19.54
1998-99	26104	139753	18.68
1999-2000	24576	162925	15.08

Source: Compiled from the Monthly Statistics of Foreign Trade Exports and Reexports. March issues of Director General of Commercial Intelligence and Statistics. Calcutta and Economic Survey: 2000-2001, Govt. of India. Ministry of Finance. New Delhi.

From Table 7.1 i.e. India's Agricultural Exports' share in total exports, it may be observed that in 1960-61 Agricultural and Allied Products' exports from India's to total exports worked out to 44.24% in value terms. It declined continuously to 19.88% in 1995-96 and then further came down to 15.08% to total exports in the year 1999-2000. The other details may be seen from the Table 7.1.

After a period of one decade of economic liberalisation, it has been observed that instead of experiencing and unprecedented boom in growth, Agricultural sector in India is facing some of the serious problems. These problems can be summed in brief as follows:

- Farmers in India are mostly uneducated and does not have access to best practices which are being followed in agronomy in the leading countries;
- Low incomes and limited capacity to invest in output;
- Absence of support services in India;
- The growth rate of agriculture products in terms of Gross Product and output has decelerated during the last 4-5 years;
- The diversification of the cropping pattern from coarse cerels towards Oilseeds Crops has slowed down, considerably;

— The initial spurt in agriculture exports after liberalisation in dollor terms has now come to a stagnant position. The exports of Agricultural products though in Ruppee terms which were Rs. 6,317 crores in 1990-91 increased to Rs. 24,576 crores in the year 1999-2000. The same may be seen from the Annexure II and Table 1.2.

— Further, it has been observed that despite a fairly high growth in GDP i.e., 10.62% at the current prices, in the year 1999-2000 over the previous year, the process of shifting away of Labour Force from Agriculture to Non-agriculture has not gathered any momentum.

— It has been also observed that there has been back tracking on many Institutional issues like Land Reform, Ceilings on holdings and on security of land tenure in India. Owing to absence of a cohesive and strong peasant movement, enabled many of the State Government to bring retrogressive legislation.

The GATT Agreement on Agriculture, ephasises the importance of trade in improving performance of agricultural sector in WTO Member Countries, it nonetheless highlights the need to give due recognition to various Non-Trade Concerns (NTCs) in this sector. Further, for the developing countries like India, providing food security to its population is one of the most critical problem. Hence, it is necessary for such countries to focus on the domestic foodgrains sector to ensure food security. Such, problems are visualised, when the policies governing the Agricultural sector are currently passing through a series of changes the World over. And member countries of WTO are making, attempts to fulfil their commitments, under the Uruguay Round's Agreement on Agriculture. The Agreement on Agriculture seeks primarily to remove the distortions existing in Agriculture Trade by introducing two sets of disciplines. First of all, the barriers affecting "Market Access" are to be lowered. To adopt this, involved the elimination of all NTBs and replacement thereof with Tariffs. However, the latter would, in turn, have to be progressively reduced in a time bound period. As a measure to give further fillip to Agricultural Trade in general, provisions for establishing minimum access opportunities for imports have also been provided for in the Agricultural Agreement. While, the second set of discipline. that the Agreement on Agriculture seeks to introduce. is in the area of the "market distortion subsidies." For "domestic support" as well as "export subsidies" are to be reined in within a stipulated time frames laid down by the WTO. From the above it is very clear that the central focus of the "Agreement on Agriculture is the introduction of mechanisms, *which would ensure a better climate for agricultural Trade.* Alongwith, the above implications, the several non-trade concerns (NTCs) would have to be taken for implementation by the WTO member countries. These non-trade concerns include "food security" and "protection to the environment" among others. The NTCs also find its mention in Article 20 of the 'Agreement on Agriculture', wherein the need to continue the reform process, that it has initiated, has been emphasised, explictly. Moreover, existing provisions in Agreement on Agriculture do not provide any clear guidelines with which to address these concerns except the food security' issue that too in a very perfunctory manner. For name sake, the only support for measures aimed at ensuring security appears in the form of an exemption from the calculation of Agreegate Measure of Support (AMS) i.e., the expenditure made on public stock holding of food grains. Under this, the expenditure made for accumulation and holding of stocks of products would be exempt from the Aggregate Measure of Support (AMS) only if these activities form an integral part of a "Food Security Programme'. Further, the stockholding activities for food security have been subjected to several additional conditions, which seems to be difficult to put them into implications in a country like India i.e., such as environmental protection, Market failure, large-scale out-migration, substantial employment opportunities, maintenance of phytosanitary environment and to restore efficiency. Under these circumstances, improving productivity, enhancing income levels, reducing vulnerability to market fluctuations and ensuring stability of prices of agricultural commodities, among others. Hence, there is an urgent need to further encourage the domestic production for a country like India for the realisation of the objective of "Food Security". In India, we have already experienced many times that inadequacy of availability of food stocks have been put under strain. These types of adverse environmental conditions have affected agricultural production many time. The same trend has also been observed, in several of the populous Asian Countries, in the recent years.

In the beginning most of the developing countries expected that once Foreign Direct Investment (FDI) accelerates, then Globalisation process will further be an inevitable response to faster economic growth to become sustained, quickly.

Under Globalisation, there are many other scenarios, where developing countries, specially India has to act in a very systematic, planned and result oriented manner, in the following areas:

— India to become more Competitive.

— To seize the opportunities arising out of a more Free

Trade Regime,

— India must learn to live, survive and develop like a mature adult nation,

— To play role as an equal player and not on any other terms in the long-run period,

— To improve the inefficient supply chain,

— To adopt effective strategy for reduction in cost of production,

— To reorient all our policies from managing shortages to promoting efficiency and value addition,

— To create Common Indian Market for all States in India,

— Revolutionisation of agriculture in India by creating a more vibrant food processing industry. Further, there is an urgent need for improving all round productivity in agriculture.

India's Experience in Globalisation and Emerging Agriculture Crises

Data for the years 1990-91 to 2000-2001, reveals that Indian Economy as a whole, and Agriculture Sector in particular, is not growing at a rate that is considered reasonable. By reasonable, we mean, to satisfy the aspirations of all sections of the economy especially Agriculture production. Indian Economy in the last about 50 years grew at a rate less than 4% a year, which even the late Prof. Raj Krishna called the Hindu Rate of Growth and had come to symbolise all that was bad in India's Economic Planning. The World Bank in its report (India: Achievements & Challenges in Reducing Poverty") has predicted that with a growth of 7% P.A. World Bank is enough to wipe-out India's poverty by 2005. If India maintains the average growth rate of 7 per cent per annum and income distribution at current levels, the country's "incidence of poverty' can plummet from its current rate of approximately 35% to a mere 6.3% by 2005. The Author is of the view that even this rate of economic growth is not enough to put India in the *"Asian Tigers"* league table. For that, India have to achieve a still higher rate of growth, say of 8% or 9% a year.

Further, subsidies in agriculture of all kinds are attracting lot of flake in the new World Trade Order (WTO) regime. These are being condemned for creating distortions in the other-wise Competitive Economy. Competition is seen as a "Boon," while subsidies have become a ban for moving to a more integrated and open World Economy (i.e., Global Economy).

It has been observed that the Developed Countries are maintaining surplus food production at very heavy cost. For all OECD Countries, the producer Subsidy Equivalent (PSE) constitute about 45% of the value of production at the Farm Gate. As compared to these figures, the subsidies to the Farm Sector (i.e., Fertilizers, Water, Electricity, etc.) in India are insignificant. Moreover, these subsidies are in fact, transferred to Consumers because the Commission for Agricultural Costs and Prices (CACP), in its calculation of the "Cost of production of different crops," considers the actual i.e. subsidised prices/rates paid by farmers for these inputs. The author is of the view that if OECD countries withdraw subsidies to their Farmers, the World Prices for different Agricultural Commodities will rise abnormally and then Farmers in India and other developing countries, with any subsidy, can compete, successfully in the Global Market. If, we do not protect our Farmers from the evil impact of Agricultural Policies followed by OECD & Developed Countries, we may soon find our country again becoming food deficit and, in time, subject to unwanted pressures.

The Rule Based WTO Agreement on Agriculture is

going to do maximum good to the maximum number of countries. As for the Developed Countries, the Agreement stipulated that within 6 years, direct subsidy has to be reduced by 20%, Export Subsidy has to be reduced by 36% and tariff on Capital Goods has to be reduced by 38%. As against this, the developing countries, like India, it has to be reduced only by 13.3% in 10 years. So, India got extra time and extra protection for gradual reduction in Tariff Barriers. While, Farm Subsidy were to be abolished in a phased manner in Developed Countries. Whereas, India being a developing country was allowed to have subsidy upto 5.2%. *It was expected that this will provide an impetus to the developing countries to compete with Developed Countries in the Farm Sector.* Indian Farmers were expected to have easy access to the World Market and they will increase their export earning. In NTBs, mainly the following barriers are covered ie. Quota, Subsidies, Voluntary export restraints, Counter-vailing duties and Dumping measures.

The success of bringing agriculture under WTO is a significant achievement for developing countries, as a whole. The Developed Countries finally agreed to substantially cut their subsidies on agriculture consequent upon the new accord. So, *it was expected that the agricultural prices in developed countries will increase.*

We can sum-up the benefits arising out of the WTO's rules for Globalisation with the Agreement on Agriculture as under:

- World Trade Organisation will help the developing countries boost their agri-exports to Developed Countries as their competitiveness will increase,
- This opens up "Market Access" and "Opportunity" for India's exports as well.
- With more exports at higher World Prices, Agricultural Terms of Trade will improve, which will improve the level of farmers' Income.

— The limit of agricultural subsidy as granted by the GATT Agreement was much higher than that prevailing in India. Hence, India was not to reduce the same, immediately.

— There was also an additional safeguard of GATT Agreement's Provision that the subsidies given to Marginal and Small Farmers can be excluded in calculating the limit. It may be mentioned that the burden of Agricultural Subsidy doesn't depends on WTO's Agreement on Agricuture limit, but on the Capacity of the Country's Fiscal System to pay. So, far as "Farm Seeds" were concerned (forming part of the provisions under the IPR), it was expected by the Critics that it may pose a threat to the Third World's Food security.

However, seed patenting was not compulsory. A farmer can choose the seed he likes, can store it from one Crop and use the same for replanting. He can sell his surplus seed but, not as branded seed in case of a protected variety.

But, the Technological gap between the domestic Industry and Global Economy emerged to be the biggest constraint on the growth of India's Exports. Since, 1991, India has been speeding up the process of "Globalisation". A "Globalised Economy" must have "Global Outlook" to compete in the "Global Markets." The Agreement on Agriculture of WTO regime, have the following disciplines:

— Production Subsidy Disciplines

— Export Subsidy Disciplines

— Imports Access

— Sanitary/Phytosanitary measures

— Dispute Settlement

Thus, on the whole, the WTO's Agreement aimed to

minimise agricultural subsidies and accelerate the opportunitities of Markets Access in Developed Countries with the strategies to be adopted by Developed Countries for minimisation of Agricultural subsidies, some obstacles to the Developing and LDCs as under:

* The subsidisation in rich countries proved strangle hold to the Developing Countries,
* Subsidisation in Developed Countries resulted in lowering the prices of agricultural products, by which the Developing Countries became unable to compete with the agricultural commodities of Industrial countries;
* Subsidisation in Developed Countries exterminated the chances of Developing Countries and LDCs' Agricultural Commodities access from the Market of Industrial Developed Countries; and
* Subsidisation in Developed Countries procured dumping of their agricultural commodities in Developing Countries either through direct commerce or in the name of aid, and underlined the self-reliance and livelihood in developing and LDCs.

Now, we can sum-up the reform made by WTO Agricultural Agreement specially concerns on the following vital issues:

— Reduction of Agricultural Subsidies in Developed Countries,

— Removal of NTBs through Tariffication,

— Concession on Tariffication to Developing Countries in comparison of Developed Countries,

— It has discouraged CAP practised by EU,

— Exclusion of some domestic support policies from the reduction commitments,

— Greater de minimise allowance on domestic support,

— Developed Countries members' responsibility to take account the needs of LDCs,

— Exclusion of some export subsidies to LDCs from the reduction commitments,

— Special and differential treatment on Developing Countries and LDCs is accorded; and

— LDCs are required to undertake no reduction commitments.

Implications of Globalisation for Agriculture Crises

The increased pace of Globalisation of trade in agricultural commodities which was expected with GATT 1994 Agreement is not likely to be fully realised in view of the experience of the implementation of the Accord across countries. The adverse impact on Indian agriculture which was feared seems to be unfounded given the inherent competitiveness Indian wheat has over the imported Wheat. Enough, safeguards are available to counter the threat of cheaper imports. However, greater attention needs to be given to the provision of inputs such as seeds, fertilizers and uninterrupted power supply to the sector to further boost Agricultural production. With the integration of Indian Agriculture in the 'Global Trade', a competitive trade scenario can be realised and maintained by reducing the domestic cost of production through proper measures, which ensure increased productivity and control procurement and distribution costs.

It has been observed that the Globalisation of Trade in Agriculture will makes the States losing the ground reality of power and decisions involving States' future. Indeed, the future of the whole of the Planner, are taken outside Government Institutions. As a consequence of this Power Pathology, some States and Regions become marginalised and their reactions might take on any one of a number of forms of religious fundamentalism based on violence. Hence, peace and justice seem full of contradiction in 'Global Society' of 'global Villages. Further, Globalisation of Trade in Agriculture can brings forth manifold risks to all the Member Countries of WTO. Moreover, Globalisation of Trade-in Agriculture in future can arouse certain fears as to eruption of major conflicts, resulting both from differences in economic, technological and Industrial levels of might in different countries. Capital's inherent tendency to create a World Market in Agricultural products, replicates vertical division of Labour in the National class-structure. Further, Globalisation of Trade in Agriculture generates dependency in the sense of the asymmetrical distribution of opportunities to pursue one's interests. Domination is the key analytical category for understanding this World Trading Society. The concept of Globalisation of Trade in Agriculture or World Trading Society belongs to the critical tradition of theories of Comparative Costs, imperialism, and focuses above all on the negative aspects of International Trading Society - formation. The ideological onslaught against the Welfare of Developed and Developing Countries has made many countries unable to respond to the domestic needs of a more integrated economy. Open trade conflicts with social contracts that protect certain activities from the relentless of the free market access. This is a key tension of the Global Trade in Agricultural products. While, Globalisation of Trade in Agriculture removes barriers between Nations, it, thus, erects new barriers within Nations. In other words, it responds not only to the needs of people alone, but also the rights of Corporations which are the main focus of politics in the area of Globalisation.

Following are the major expected challenges of Globalisation of Trade in Agriculture production:

(i) All the Member Countries to ensure that the implementation is done fully both in spirit and letter of Uruguay Round of Agricultural Agreement. It has been observed that despite the commitment made to reduce subsidies, the countries in some form or the other are continuing their agricultural subsidy programme The EU Countries are increasingly adopting the "Green Box measures of the Agreement which are exempted from the subsidy reduction commitments. With the continued increase in the exposure of domestic agriculture to International unfair competition would imply considerable damage to the Indian Agricultural Sector. It is, therefore, utmost necessary that an integrated strategy for the agricultural sector is adopted in India in the context of new Trading System.

(ii) The future negotiations should be able to phase out "Amber-Box" production subsidies, even in developing countries where those resources can typically be put to better use elsewhere. And they should be able to shrink the "Green-Box" of permitted supports, marking sure they have removed elements of support that should perhaps have been in the "Amber" category i.e., subject to the WTO discipline.

(iii) The next challenge for the future Negotiations will be to move the reform process forward, in all the areas mentioned in the GATT Agreement 1994.

(iv) Tariffs are to be reduced dramatically as per WTO's rules by all the concerned Member countries. By the end of the implementation period for this new agreement all Agricultural Tariffs should be brought down below an agreed minimum level."Stratospheric" tariffs in agriculture should become only a memory in the near future.

(v) The future negotiations need to amend the Sanitary/ Phytosanitary Code based on the implementation experiences under the Uruguay Round of Trade Negotiations on Agriculture. People every where should have access to ample supplies of wholesome foods. Food Safety will become an increasingly important issue, and that will put the WTO Sanitary/Phytosanitary Code in the limelight. We must insure that it does its job, and does it well.

(vi) There exists a strong case for increasing investment in Rural infrastructure. It is essential to accord very high priority to Public Sector investment in agriculture, which has been neglected during the last two decades in India.

(vii) India being a founder member of the WTO, is bound to undertake further economic reforms in agriculture. These would include the removal of barriers to internal trade in agricultural commodities, abolition of Zonal/Regional restrictions, compulsory procurement procedures, opening future markets and protection of patent rights, etc. On the other side, India should also do hard bargaining on the issue of "Market Access" and removal of subsidies by the developed countries.

While, India can derive the real gains from trade in agriculture commodities only by improving its competitiveness by increased productivity at Comparable Cost. For this, there is an urgent need for a large investment in Rural Infrastructure, in agricultural Research & Development, in Biotechnology and creation of institutional arrangements for providing benefits of research & development to all the farmers including the Small and Marginal Farmers.

(viii) Further, there is an urgent need to-proceed further with the consolidation of holdings and other Land Reforms in the country.

(ix) Reforms in Agricultural Sector are likely to open-up more export possibilities. So, there is an urgent need to design a pro-active policy to foster exports and to involve all types of farmers in increasing productivity. Such efforts should be supplemented by creating support services Institutions like Trading Houses, Market Intelligence services, creation of net work of information on National and International Prices, to create necessary infrastructure in processing, marketing and grading of produce.

India has done well in observing its Commitments to WTO under GATT, GATs and Trips. Broadly, these relate to the removal of quantitative restrictions and tariff restructuring, simplification of Customs procedures, evolving International Standard in Trade and Industry, Agriculture, Textiles, IPR. Trade related Investment Measures, Anti-Dumping Measures and Safeguards, Services Sector and so on. While, in contrast to this, many of the Developed Countries did contrived or lackdaisical implemention on these commitments.

However, it is a little pre-mature to make a judgement, at this stage, essentially because things have just started evolving. A clear picture will emerge well after all agreements on agriculture are implemented world-wide, net of neutralisations and modifications a that might come off because of the voices being raised by the developing Countries. With the Globalisation and Liberalisation of Economy, the Indian Agriculture is facing many Challenges and Crises since the last decade specially from 1995 onwards. This has happened owing to the facts that the growth in agriculture has decelerated and stagnated during the period under reference, owing to lack of any major technological break-through.

This resulted into a stagnation in yield levels of various crops. Such type of situation have very serious implications for a country like India. Hence, there is an urgent need to accelerate growth rate of agricultural production, for feeding the continuous increasing population and to increase exports in a big way. For exporting the Agricultural produce, India needs adequate marketable food surpluses. The crises in Indian agriculture is being further aggravated owing to lack of diversification shift in cropping pattern and continous increasing burden of Workforce on Agriculture Sector. While, it has been seen in the US that the generalised income support provided through deficiency payment have significant impace on the increased agricultural production. It is mainly owing to the following encouraging points: (i) Such type of support enable the Farmers to operate at a higher levels of Average costs; (ii) It is based on the Farm Area; and (iii) The payment under the Support Scheme are linked to the production of a Specific Crops. To have the exports benefit in Agricultural commodities India have to develop a strong platform of Product Production and Marketable surplus to export. Despite the decline in foodgrains by about 10 million tonnes, there is little scope for speculative uptrend in Agricultural products, as the Country is fortunately perched on an unprecedently large Public Stocks of nearly 45 million tonnes of foodgrains. Moreover, for the increased production, the forward linkages such as agro-processing industres;

storage; transportation and marketing and export of agricultural produce, will have to be strengthened to enable the farmers to realise remunerative prices and return for the increased production. The Textile Industry is set to face tough times with the prospects of cheap imports under WTO Agreement coming into force in 2005. This will be a major challenge to the Indian Textile Industry affecting its trade prospects in the future. The Indian Textile industry have to bring Comparative efficiency in its production units like weaving, knitting and texturing at the earliest. WTO serves the developing countries' interests by facilitating trade reform, providing a mechanism for settling disputes, strengthening the credibility of Trade Reforms, and promoting transparent Trade Regime which lower transaction costs. Thus, we can conclude that all countries have much more to gain than to lose from opening-up their Markets. It is an encouraging step that the Indian Govt. after taking a cue from the EU and the USA, has proposed for the first time to give direct subsidies to Exporters of all agricultural commodities dis-advantaged in World Markets owing to minimum Support Prices (MSP). These subsidies would be paid once approved by the Parliament, through a savvy new mechanism compatible with GATT 1994 Agreement on Agriculture. This means traders which export commodities with an ever-increasing MSP like wheat, rice, sugar and pulses would be paid back the difference between their total costs and the Final Realised Export Price. Further, India is vehemently opposing attempts to link environment and Labour Laws with Trade. Further, India is also of the strong argument that inclusion of Non-Trade Issues on the WTO Agenda would only create Trojan Horses of Protectionism which will be used to distort Competition and Undermine Comperative Advantage of developing Countries. If, we are to emerge from such types of Agricultural Crises and get ready to take on the challenges of the Globalisation era, the above types of attitudes will have to be adopted by the Indian Government.

Further, there is an urgent needs for the Floriculture Industry to gear itself for Global Competition by improving productivity and reducing production Costs. Moreover, there is an urgent need on part of Government to mobilise the developing Countries around the agreement that a New Round of Trade Negotiations should only be launched once all the issues of GATT 1994 Agreements are implemented as agreed by the Member coteries of WTO. Thus, from the above discussions, it becomes very clear that Globalisation has brought both ample opportunities, risks, challenges and few crises to the Agriculture Sector in India also. The key to this problem is to Manage Crises, not Whether to crises. Contesting the Planning Commission's claim that hoarders and speculators were responsible, the Ministry of Food and Agriculture pointed out that the price rise was due to scarcity conditions; the real solution for which lay in increasing the commitment of resources to agriculture rather than in state trading and price controls.

The began the estrangement between the rural elites and the central planners. During the second half of the fifties, when the government allocated the major share of available resources to industry, the states refused to mobiliser resources for development and sabotaged the rural reorganisation programmes. subsequently, when the centre soft-pedalled land reforms and co-operativisation but tried to regulate prices, the states resisted the implementation of price controls and state trading in foodgrains.

REFERENCES

Asif H. Quershi, "The World Trade Organisation: Implementing International Trade Norms," : Manchester University Press, 1996.

Baxi, Upendra, "Global Neighbourhood" and the "Universal Otherhood": Notes on the Report of the Commission on Global Governance, (Manuscript with author) at 12, 1996.

Biswajit Dhar and Sachin Chaturvedi, "WTO Agreements and Agricultural Sector: Implications and Options for India", RITS, New Delhi, 1999.

Christopher Arup, "The New World Trade Organisation Agreements: Globalising Law Through Services and Intellectual Property," Cambridge University Press, 2000.

8

GATT and International Economy

Despite inauspicious beginning, the GATT has been remarkably successful during its nearly five decades of its operations. Partly, this is because of indigenous and pragmatic leadership in the GATT, particularly in its early years, as the GATT struggled to fill the gap left by the I.T.O's failure. As the decades passed however, there was recognition that the GATT system was being increasingly challenged by the changing conditions of International Economic activity, including the greater "Inter-dependence" of National Economies and the growth in trade of services. With that the concern developed that the GATT was too handicapped to play the needed role of complementing the Bratten Wood System as the "Third Leg", alongside the IMF and World Bank.

The major problems and birth defects before GATT were as under:-

— Provisional application and Grandfather rights exceptions embraced by the protocol of Provisional Applications.

— Ambiguity about the powers of the contracting parties to make certain decisions.

— Ambiguity regarding the waiver authority and risks of misuse.

— Murky legal status leading to misunderstanding by the Public, Media, and even Government officials.

— Captain defects in the dispute settlement procedures.

— Lack of institutional provisions generally, so constant improvisions.

The new WTO and the results of the Uruguay Round are both a modest step forward with regard to the Institutional structure, and a watershed for the International economic system. The modest step can be seen in the WTO charter. The watershed, however, is the more fact of creating a definite institutional arrangement combined with the extraordinary expense of the Uruguay Round substantitive negotiations. Clearly, this marks a considerable departure from the hesitancy, tentativeness, and 'provisional' nature of the GATT system. It puts in place a structure that will necessarily have to face an increasing number of problems during the next few decades.

In Kaleckian Model, the author had concluded that the Developed Countries owing to a limited supply of labour, their growth rate depends upon:-

- The rate of growth of Labour Supply.
- The rate of growth of labour productivity, given no change in the Capital/output ratio.
- An increase in labour productivity arising from the substitution effect.

According to Kalecki, there are 3 major obstacles to the development:-

1. A shortage of Natural Resources and Human skills, the production of Capital goods;
2. An inadequate supply of wage goods to satisfy the demand arising from increased employment; and
3. The private investments may not be forthcoming at a sufficiently high rate.

Kalecki emphasised that investment should be planned with very little capital per worker and all investments should press on food supply i.e. by giving higher priority to increasing food production.

The paradigms of International competitiveness is a difficult subject because it is excedingly complex. It encompasses policies, competition, and business practices with respect to trade, investment, technology and regulation. It is also inherently linked to tax, fiscal and monetary policies which affect them.

The globalisation has encouraged greater interaction across the National boundaries and affects many aspects of International Economy by encouraging the following:-

* Intensification of competition in the International economy.
* Encouraged the value added process.
* A strong incentive for transnational Corporations to minimise cost.
* Encourages better global network of services facilities.
* Encourages innovations in Institutions and Instruments.
* The trend towards urbanisation.
* Movement of capital, goods and services has been paralled by the movement of labour.
* Persistent disparities.
* Individual countries have little choice than to participate in these processes since an insullar approach is likely to marginalise them further.

The theory of comparative advantage and factor proportions could be elaborated, refined, or patched-up to handle the new problems. The paradigms of comparative advantage, after all, is effective in analysing many critical problems. It is possible to share-up factor proportions theory by adding more "factors" i.e. human capital and technology. Even Leàntief himself felt that his paradox could be explained through examining human capital. Technology can also be treated as a factor of production. Like human capital, it alters the relation of land, labour and capital.

For about fifty years, the GATT sponsored trade negotiations that dramatically reduced world trade barriers, from tariffs to procurement laws, and spurred global economic growth. GATT's record of success did not inspire overwhelming public support. The GATT was simply a temporary multilateral agreement designed to provide a framework of rules and a forum to negotiate trade barriers reductions among nations.

World Trade Organisation (WTO) to replace the GATT took place on January, 1995. The WTO will provide a permanent arena for member governments to address international trade issues, and it will oversee the implementation of the trade agreements negotiated in the Uruguay Round. Inspite of the many advantages associated with international cooperation in financial affairs action on this front alone is not sufficient to solve some thorny problems confronting the World Economy these days. Additional International cooperation is needed to resolve one of the meet important of these problems, the impediments to the free flow of trade.

The economies of the EEC, EFTA, and OPEC, are foreign trade oriented and highly dependent upon the rest of the world as a source of raw materials. These Regional groupings are too small in scope by themselves to provide member countries with completely adequate resources and product markets. As the scale of living is advanced n conjunction with the greater productive efficiency, these areas are expected to become increasingly dependent upon international exchange. The growth in their income may serve to make them better markets for foreign production. As a result, the majority of the world developing countries may gain by the removal of obstacles to free product and factor movements on a global scale. Globalisation is an other steps towards this direction. The NAFTA debate centred primarily on the import on job of free trade with a developing, lower wage country, while the Uruguay Round debate focussed largely on the sovereign powers and the ability to control its own economic destiny.

Multinational Corporations in International Economy

Paradigms of Multinational Corporations has added now and interesting dimension to International economies. The new theory and data on-able us to define and to some extent predict divergence between the way in which the International Multinational Corporations, firms and domestic firms may react to a particular market situation or policy decisions.

Multinational Corporations/Firms generates the following types of economies:-

(i) Profit maximisation.

(ii) Multinational firms are a product of eligopolistic forces.

(iii) MNFs towards New explanations—The International Thesis.

(iv) MNFs, trade and proper allocation of resources.

(v) Issues raised by MNFs:-
- The Transfer Price Issue.
- Labour issues.
- MNFs and Governments.

(vi) MNFs can bring Capital to the heat countries.

(vii) MNFs use Capital and Labour more efficiently than domestic competitors.

(viii) Advanced Technology flows better through MNFs.

The successful MNFs know that product design must follow consumer preference, and both vary from market to market around the World. These firms recognise that local market require a local presence, which has led to wider distribution of the assets of many MNFs. But local presence, even manufacturing, does not often translate into local technology development, which has remained-with a few important exceptions-stubbornly resistant to the globalisation phenomonen.

There appear to be at least three factors which unambigously promote intra-firm trade. These factors are as under:-

1. A novel division of labour;
2. Problems of quality control; and
3. Large non-recoverable investments, or any other commitments which adversely affect bargaining power.

The impact of Regional Trade Liberalisation on the rationalisation of industrial growth seems to be owing to the following:-

— Product specific economies of scale involving the length of product can be important sources of cost reductions.

— Economic recession or slower than anticipated economic growth can play havoc with expected cost reductions arising from rationalisation.

— Rationalisation does not necessarily occur some after trade liberalisation took place, even where potential economies of scale are large and transportation costs are low.

Integration of World Economy

For Integration of the World Economy, some of the policy responses a theoretical paradigm, though has yet to emerge which in its own internal logic provides a role for intervention and an explanation for the failings of liberalisation. Rather traditional theoretical foundations are paid lip service to and developing countries which are able to undertake independent decisions have become increasingly pragmatic. Hence, what is needed is a rethink of developing countries' monetary policy which can provide an alternative paradigm explicitly accounting for the economy's starting points. This alternative paradigm can then be used to develop a sharper policy and growth. Such a theoretical paradigm can build on the insight provided by new structuralists and the micro economic foundations of Stiglitz and Weiss, to capture the experience of development.

The Trade Policy never restrict our exports, while in the recent years we have been badly hurt by the ever more harmful trade policies of other countries. Further, exports create jobs in the country, and on the other side imports destroys them. The excessive dependence on import is harmful to the nation's security. Further, the recent theory of strategic trade policy recognises that the World market place is not one of perfect competition and there are a number of market imporfections which necessitate the adoption of certain strategic policy interventions with a view to appropriating to oneself, maximum share of the rents created by market imperfections. The World Trade Organisation was finanalised after a long period of seven years of negotiations. With the WTO coming into being at the beginning of 1995, the critical phase of implementation of the Uruguay Round agreements comenced. The functioning of the WTO could be further impaired by the growing tendencies at regionalism through the formation of various trading blocs.

After thirty-five years of successful post war trade liberalisation in the Developed countries., during which round after round of Negotiations under the auspices of GATT had slashed tariffs to unprecedented lows, and the threat of protectionism has resurfaced. Though, the trading system is vulnerable to protectionism, but it also offers new opportunities to combat it. These opportunities must be seized by means of bold, imaginative, and perhaps difficult institutional changes.

In the long-term interest of the International community and smooth development of the World economy, it is essential that the developing countries are given adequate facilities and assistance to secure a fair share of the World export which in turn could help them to balance their foreign trade, to accelerate industrial development and to increase their per capita income. The globalisation and interdependence in the international economy are creating interests favourable to freer trade, through trade and direct foreign investment. Economists have tried in various ways to analyse what determines the amount of trade that is conducted, but they have focussed primarily on the determinants of national and bilateral commerce rather than on total global trade. However, a number of economic variables appear likely to influence the value of the ratio of global exports to total production.

There is a growing asymmetry between trade and Competition policy. While, trade policy, formerly the domain of governments, is increasingly tackled in multilateral fora (like the WTO), competition policy is still formulated domestically. This situation could be lead the nations where competition policy sticks out like a serethumb, blacking trade instead of facilitating it. With globalisation companies taking a beating in export markets may indulge in anticompetitive activities in the domestic market by reducing market access to foreign competitors. Further, transitional mergers and international cartels fixing prices pose new challenges and serious threats to the smooth functioning of the multilateral trading system. The author is of the opinion that when WTO is focusing on services and Trade Related Intellectual Property Rights (TRIPs), the competition policy should also be covered by it in the subsequent rounds of negotiations, At present, WTO has a working group on trade and competition policy looking at trade-related aspects and Inter-linkages. Hence, at this juncture, WTO as the platform to address this sensitive issue may be inappropriate. Moreover, the developed countries at present are not much keen on multilateral competition policy. At present half of the members countries out of 132 of WTO, do not have domestic laws on competition, hence making them to agree on multilateral principles would therefore, jumps the gun, and might be resisted by developed countries.

The main emphasis in the theory of International Economy, which is emerging is generating the feeling, is that the World Economy has to become and should function like a national economy. Economic laws governing equal levels of development in different parts of the World Economy in a context of full capital and labour mobility will have to characterise the working of the International Economy. It is a challenge before the economists to find out the ways and means to have control over the sudden flight of foreign capital and foreign funds and to avoid the adverse effects of globalisation and liberalisation. Its

Offects on the small scale sector, unorganised producing sectors and the Least Developing Countries (LDCs) in the World Economy. On these aspects, UNCTAD, IMF, World Bank and World Trade Organisation (WTO) should work out the modalities for homogenous trend in stock markets, fear of increasing unemployment and to avoid adverse impact of globalisation and Multinational Corporations' on the domestic industrial units of the developing countries. The author is hopeful that these organisations will workout the strategy and action plans to have an other rounds of negotiations to ensure rapid industrial growth of exports of developing countries which will help the developing countries to improve their exports in the World Economy.

Nations seems to have intended that mutual dependence should units all the inhabitants of the earth into one commercial family. Far this purpose, nature has indefinitely diversified there own products in every climate and in almost every extensive district.

For this purpose, also, nature seems to have varied so extensively the wants and the productive powers of the different races of man. The superiority of modern over ancient wealth depends in a great measure on the greater use we make of these varieties.

International Capital Movements

Under the mercantilists, gold and silver were hold to be the international balancing items on a nation's balance of trade. If a country ran a surplus on its current account they believed that it received gold and silver from these nations having a deficit with it. Conversely, if its current account should a deficit, they held that it shipped gold and silver to these countries with a surplus.

It is a fact that surpluses and deficits on these accounts also were financed by international capital flows. Nations with current account surplus were held to be creditors, investing capital in countries experiencing deficits and these with deficits borrowed from nations which had surpluses. Thus foreign capital movements, in addition to international specie flows, were balancing items and the term creditor or debtor nation reformed inte. -changeably to a country's situation on its current accounts and to its lender or borrower position on the capital flows.

Globalisation essentially implies increasing cross-border movements of goods, services, finance and factors of production. Effective participation in the globalisation process requires a certain degree of stability in the basic macroeconomic paramaters of price level, exchange rate and interest rate. Further, reforms and liberalisation associated with globalisation and Regionalisation may worsen the current account deficit position. The developing countries like India, should focus in strengthening the country's production base by building internationally competitive capacities and reducing the cost of transactions through improved infrastructure. Such type of countries should adopt the approach of stability even if it reduces the higher rate of growth to slower growth. Fighting in the International market trends and holding the National currency at artificially at high levels would only sow the seeds of a major crash on a later data as happened in the Asian Currency crisis. Such country should learn the lessons from the Asian Currency crisis. Ones, the national currency finds it own level, the danger of volatility could be avoided. To have and maintain edge in the International economy, the developing countries must remain and continue to become increasingly competitive on an on-going basis and should reflect the improvements in the following areas so that they are able to face them in an aggressive manner:-

- Competitiveness should be rejected with their improved market share in the World Trade.
- Should be capable to capture the big emerging markets, and to face on a new competitive challenge boldly. For that adaptable workforce should be there.

As you are all aware, the successful completion of the Uruguay Round of Trade Negotiations and the emergence of new trading system under the aegis of the WTO have generated a number of new apportunities as also challenges for development in the International Economy. Further, the author has observed that the new trading system under the WTO has diluted various lements of the Part IV of the GATT and has consequently taken away from the policy realm of the developing World, a number of policy options which were open to them earlier.

REFERENCES

Balassa, Bela (1971), *The Structure of Protection in Developing Countries*, Baltimore, Johns Hopkins University Press.

Baldwin, Rober, (1985 a), "Inefficiacy of Protection in Promoting Social Gals, " World Economy 8.

Borner, Silvio, (1986), *Internationalisation of Industry*, Berlin: Spinger-Verlag.

Brander, James, (1986), "Rationales for Strategic Trade and Industrial Policy," In Krugman, 1986.

World Bank (1997), *World Development Report*, 1986, New York.

9

Role of Insurance Market in India

Insurance is a Co-operative device to spread the risks; the system to spread the risk over a number of persons who are insured against the risk; the principle to share the loss of each member of the society on the basis or probability of loss to their risk and the method to provide security against losses to the Insured. We know that Insurance has some peculiar characteristics, which are generally observed in the case of Life, Marine and General Insurance. The present economic reform in India has been in 1991 with the 1st Generation Reforms i.e., "Crisis Driven" in the Balance of Payments and increasing Fiscal Deficits both at the Centre and State levels. In brief, the main diagnosis of the crises in one sentence i.e. India was-living beyond its means." While, in the 2nd Generation Reforms, the main emphasis shifted from "Crisis Driven" to a "Development Driven Reforms". These peculiar characteristics can be summed up as under:

* Sharing of Risk,
* Cooperative Device,
* Value of Risk,
* Payment at Contingency,
* Amount of Payment,
* Large Number of Insured persons,
* Insurance is not a gambling, and
* Insurance is not a Charity.

Classification of Insurance

Insurance can be classified from two angles as follows:

(i) From the Business point of view; and

(ii) From the risk point of view.

Features of the Life Insurance Contract

The Insurance Contracts are based on certain fundamental principles. These principles are common to all types of Insurance with the exception of the principle of indemnity which is not applicable to a Life Insurance contract owing to a contingent nature. These principles are as under in brief:

(a) Insurance Interest

(b) Utmost good faith

(c) Warranties

(d) Proximate cause

(e) Assignment and Nomination.

The word Insurance and the need for insurance are not understood by many as we find the level of understanding in the Western countries. From the data, it came to light that only 18% of the population in India is insured, rather we can say that it is under insured. Even among the insured, the understanding of insurance is very poor. It has been observed by the author that nobody is made-aware by any particular agency to create awareness and thinking that the insurance benefits in the following areas:

1. Insurance protects the families,
2. The old population,
3. The infirm,
4. The widows and the orphans, and
5. Properties.

An Insurance Company makes promises to meet contingencies and to indemnity the insured against risks, which are specifically agreed to between the parties to be covered. The Insurance by its very nature provides a number of concomitant benefits as follows:

1. Insurance provides capital in such cases where assets covered by a risk Insurance get destroyed.
2. It assures a protection to a businessman or a trader, the security of his assets.
3. Insurance activities a Capital Market on which its Investments are deployed.
4. Insurance protects lives in cases of a Life Cover which is assured of payment on death or a repayment on maturity of the Policy.
5. The Insurer also provides a safety cover, a social net in case of old age by providing a pension.
6. Insurance protects persons of fail and indifferent health for the payment of a small sums called premium.

Hence, there is a utmost necessity on our part to think broadly in visionary manner about further development of Insurance Business in India.

The Insurance Sector has been opened up to the Private Sector, with a view to marking available long-term funds for:

1. Infrastructure;
2. Introducing new and innovative products; and
3. Effecting improvement in Quality of Service to Customers.

Moreover, Life Insurance Corporation of India (LIC) is dominant in the following two aspects:

1. Pooling and re-distributing risks across millions of Policy Holders, and
2. Performing Financial Intermediation.

The phenomenon of "risk" as calculable and Insurable uncertainity pervades economic and social life everywhere.

The conventional theory of Competitive Markets does not apply directly in the study of Insurance Business in less developed economics where credit and Insurance Markets are either "thin" or "non existent".

The main principle underlying Insurance is "the pooling of risk", a large number of people contributing to a fund out of which compensation can be paid to those experiencing a particular type of loss. Plan the past experience, the probability of many risks can be calculated with great accuracy. Some of the commoner risks which it is usual for businessmen and private individuals to Insurer against are the destruction of property or stock of fire, losses arising from burglary or other causes, goods in transit, motor vehicles, and "third-party" claims arising out of accidents, marine insurance forms a separate branch of Insurance on account of the many special features involved. However, it has been observe that the Insurance Mechanism, *per se*, fails to protect agents from future contingencies leading to "Critical Market Failures".

Scope and Need of Insurance

Need and desire for insuring risks whether of life or non-life viz. real-estate, plant and machinery, vehicles, etc. have been felt for ages. But the business of insurance on commercial basis started with the establishment of "Oriental Life Insurance Company in Culcutta in 1818. The first Indian Insurance Campany" Bombay Mutual Life Insurance was established in 1870 to cover Indian lives at normal rates. The year 1870 also saw the enactment of the Insurance Act. Therefore, many insurance companies, both life and non-life, came into existence.

The Life Insurance Industry was nationalised as on January 1956 where covering of all 154 Indian Life Insurers, 16 non-Indian insurers and 75 provident societies were vested with Govt. of India's Custodian.

The process of Nationalisation of Insurance Sector

became complex with the nationalisation of non-life insurance industry in 1972 on the basis of recommendation of the Planning Commission of India. This lead to the advent of GIC as a holding company of 4 companies viz National Insurance Co. Ltd.; The New India Assurance Co. Ltd.; The Oriental Insurance Co. Ltd. and United India Insurance Co. Ltd.

Since, then the Indian Insurance Companies are operating under a monopolistic conditions though there is some competition amongst the four general insurance companies. Because of this none-too-existence of competition, the said companies not only charged/recovered high premiums for the inefficient and inadequate services provided to the insuranced. Because of the 'PSU' character and absence of any competition, the insurance companies could not come, out with the products customised to the needs of the customers at attractivable prices thus leaving the vast potential untapped.

"Financial Sector Reforms"

Foreign exchange crises of 1991, forced the planners to think of new vista to uplift the sagging Indian economy. This gave birth to the process of "LPG" i.e. liberalisation globalisation and privatisation. Financial Sector reforms started in the Insurance industry, which is a part and parcel of financial sector, couldn't escape from the process of liberalisation. R.N. Malhotra Committee on Insurance sector reforms was setup in April 1993 which submitted its report in January 1994. On the basis of the recommendations of 'Malhotra Committee', opening up of the insurance sector was announced in Union Budget in June 1998, and IRDA bill was passed by the Parliament in December 1998. As per the regulations, foreign insurance companies can pick up stake up to 26% of the equity in an Indian Insurance Company.

The Malhotra Committee in its report recommended for Privatisation and Foreign participation in the Insurance Sector. Apprehension is there that this will upset the required balance between economic and social objectives of the Insurance Sector in a country like India. Therefore, privatisation needs to address the following critical questions:

1. Why do we need privatisation of the (Life) Insurance Sector?

2. What needs to be done prior to privatisation of the (Life) Insurance Sector

3. How should (Life) Insurance Sector reforms proceeds?

LIC assumes critical importance with a dominant position in the Indian Economy in two ways:

1. As a National Insurance Agency, it seems to pool and re-distribute risks associated with the death of earners (Policy Holders) in millions of house holds. Insurance is thus important from the "Social Point" of view.

2. As a major Collective Savings Institution, the LIC is a dominant financial intermediary in the economy, channelling investible funds to productive sectors.

However, inspite of above facts, there is an urgent needs on the part of LIC to make a "SWOT" analysis of its working.

Privatisation of Insurance Business

It is believed that Private owners will:

— Maximise profits instead of engaging in political patronage, as a result, it is believed that productive efficiency and economic growth will increase. Consequently, consumers will enjoy a higher standard of living, better quality and services of goods at lower prices. This entails, atleast the following reforms:

— Property rights within each firm/company should be re-established so that owners enjoy full residual rights of control in their firm/company.

— Outside the firm/company new owners must face "Hard Budget Constraints". That is new owners should not have the power to either extract fiscal transfers or obtain bail outs.

— A non-corruptible judicial system and transparent bankruptcy procedures that are free from political pressures should be established.

Thus, policy makers can be assured that privatisation of Insurance Business will increase efficiency only if the above conditions are satisfied. Unfortunately, not all of these conditions have been satisfied in many of the countries they have implemented privatisation programmes. Now, the question arises as to what course of action should be undertaken in such cases.

— Should one wait until the Government has the capacity to implement the required reforms?

— What, if privatisation have only a small window of opportunity?

— Either they privatise hastly today, or not at all. Should they go ahead with privatisation and hope that the newly privatised companies will create demand for good laws?

These issues can be analysed by the LIC/GIC in details by improving the operational and productive efficiency of all the levels of Management in their respective organisation:

Level I: Routine operations and reflects actions;

Level II: Well defined management operations; and

Level III: Strategic planning and creative decision marking

For changing the emphasis, Management have to ensure to undergo shift in the following directions:

1. Securing the future.

2. Dynamic leadership on a continuous and consistent basis.

3. Managing constant organisational change.

These steps will help the LIC/GIC to ensure the following aspects:

— Constant and broad-based insurance business growth.

— Increase in Market share in Insurance Business.

— Increased customer base on a continuous basis.

— To take decision whether to continue with more emphasis on intermediation or go for dis-intermediation.

Potential of Insurance Industry in India

Insurance Industry in India is mainly divided into two segments viz. Life Insurance' control by Life Insurance Corporation of India and 'Non-Life' by GK and its four subsidiaries.

Life Insurance Business: Growth and Prospects

With population crossing 1000 million mark, India is emerging as a major Insurance Market. The India's Infrastructure report estimates the size of life insurance market, in terms of premium, to increases to Rs. 456 billion (at 1995-96 prices) by 2005-06, from a level of Rs. 130 billion as on 1995-96. At a growth rate of 18% the LIC is able to sell 15 million policies, at present. Only 25 percent of insurable population (around 312 million) have got life insurance till date. It has been estimated by Financial Time that out of insurable population of 312 million 50 million have the capacity to pay a premium of $300 (Rs. 10,500/-) per year, 100 million have the capacity to pay $ 200 (Rs. 7000/-) per year and 162 million have the capacity to pay $ 100 (Rs. 3500/-) per year.

The LIC has posted a record growth rate of 65% in first premium income (premium on new business) during the year 2000-2001 over the previous year. It increased from Rs. 3796 crores in 1999-2000 to Rs. 6262 crores in 2000-2001. This is mainly on account of the good result of the Bima Nivesh Policy (i.e. a single premium product with a certain degree of returns). In this insurance scheme LIC collected Rs. 1541 crores during the year 2000-2001.

After the cent of interest rate in the Public Provident Fund (PPF), the Bima Nivesh Policy has emerged as an attractive alternative to the PPF. Now, the average size of a LIC Policy has grown around 17%, with average sum assured per policy at Rs. 63,332. At the same time, the number of policies sold has also grown by 16% to over two crores policies during the year 2000-2001. Other products of LIC which surpassed targets were individual pension schemes which grew by 80% to Rs. 563 crores. Individual Assurances scheme also grew by 63% to Rs. 570 crores in the year under reference. It is expected that LIC's Life fund may touch to Rs. 1,92,000 crores.

It has been conceived by the Author that after 1980s, LIC operations grew owing the following facts:

1. Growth of Industry in India,
2. The capital market,
3. Infrastructure Development; and
4. Savings rate including Financial forms of savings and Capital Formation.

A vast potential still exists for LIC/GIC to explore in India, owing to the following points:

— Lower population coverage till date.

— Per capital premium

— Contribution to employment and Percentage of Insurance Business to GDP is still very low as compared to developed countries.

LIC and GIC still fall short much below the International Standards in the following parameters.

1. Technical and Managerial skill;
2. Cost Efficiency (higher premium);
3. Product range; and
4. Innovation.

That there are still vast potentials in this sector in India which are yet to be explored. Even the new private sector which will have to face competition "Branch Equity of LIC" may find the field of life insurance more lucrative as the tendency of claims (in case of LIC) is 5% which is very close to global average of 3%.

Table 9.1

Type of Insurance Business during the Years 1996-97, 1997-98 and percentage increase thereof

(Rs. crores)

Class of Business		*1996-97*	*1997-98*	*increase over previous year*
1.	Fire	1719.14	1916.10	11.5%
2.	Miscellaneous			
(a)	Motor	2334.80	2585.02	10.7%
(b)	Aviation	193.02	167.46	(-) 13.2%
(c)	Engineering	635.40	644.84	1.5%
(d)	Other Misc.	1148.35	1396.43	21.0%
3.	Marine			
(a)	Marine Cargo	764.57	764.36	0.0%
(b)	Marine Hull	261.31	225.87	15.7%
		990.44	1025.67	3.6%
All Classes		7021.15	7735.52	10.2%

Source: The Insurance Times.

Growth and Prospects of General Insurance in India

Non-Life Insurance Industry has registered tremendous growth ever since GIC and its four subsidiaries came into being on January 1, 1973. Total premium received was Rs. 17 crores in 1950 which increased to Rs. 7700 crores approx, in 1998-99. Portfolio wise non-life direct premium written in India in 1997-98 has been shown in Table 9.1.

The growth of insurance products in commercial and personal lives are much better in Indian market as compared to other parts of World as this market has lot of new vistas which are yet to be tapped. This is evident from the data given in the table 9.2.

Table 9.2

Growth of Insurance Products in some of the Countries

Country	*Year*	*Growth Motor*	*Growth Personal lives*
Japan	1998	-4.4%	5.3%
Scuth Korea	1998	2.4%	20.5%
UK	1995	15.0%	17.5&
Germany	1997	-4.4%	3.7%
China	1997	14%	18.0%

Source: The Insurance Times.

As per projections of Confederation of Indian Industries (CII), non-life premium is expected to rise from the current level of Rs. 8000 crores in the year 1995 to Rs. 37500 crores in the year 2009-2010.

Insurance sector also plays an important role in country's infrastructure building. As of 31.3.1997 investment made by LIC and GIC was as under:

Name of Corporation	*Investment (crores)*
LIC	82665.17
GIC & Subsidiaries	15500.00

Rakesh Mohan Committee estimated that there is a total need for infrastructure investment at around Rs. 7,50,000/- crores (US$ 215 bn) over next five years (2001-05).

Thus, insurance sector, both life and non-life, not only will provide opportunities for insurance business but also opportunities to invest in profitable infrastructure projects.

Life assurance is in a different category from other types of Insurance, since, sooner or later, the risk is certain to occur, whereas in other cases the centignency insured against may never occur. For this reason, a distribution is often made between Insurance (i.e. where there is no certainty) and Assurance (i.e. where there is no certainty) and only uncertainity being the time of occurrence). In addition to those enumerated, many other risks can be insured against. While in U.K., Insurance Business is conducted by Insurance or Assurance Companies and by Under-writers who are members of Lloyd's. Insurance against sickness, unemployment and old age is undertaken by the state in many countries these days.

In brief, future insurance market will be influenced by the following:

Govt. Policies,
Regulatory Authority,
Forces of Globalisation,
Inter-Company relationship within the Industry,
Quality of work force,
Competitive edge in relation to products services and technology used on a continuous basis,
Dynamic Marketing strategies, and
Proper and efficinet distribution channel.

Role of Intermediaries in the Insurance Industry

The Insurance Campanies play the role of "Interme-diaries'. These intermediaries pool funds from set servers and lend them to finance expenditures of Business Firms and local bodies to obtain funds from the savers, the intermediaries issue and sell "Indirect securities" i.e. Insurance policies. Insurance Companies mainly buy bonds and sell Insurance Policies.

We have seen earlier that LIC/GIC are playing a dominant role as an inter-mediaries in the Insurance Business by pooling and re-distributing risk across millions of Policy Holders; and by discharging the role of Financial Intermediaries. Insurance marketing has some unique features. It has to identify uncertainties in the operations of an Economic System and to create general awareness to cover these uncertainities by selling insurance products.

Further, we know that credit institutions require insurance protection for the economic activities supported by them. Individuals and families need cover to sustain their standard of living upon death or disablement of the bread winner. They may also require "Insurance Linked" Savings with reasonable returns for their consumer needs, rainy days, and old age. Moreover, Social regulations in many societies require employers to secure lives of their employees by obtaining for them "Group Life Insurance" covers. Yet, in a majority of cases in both life and non-life areas, ambiguity prevails over the necessity of obtaining Insurance Covers. Lift to themselves, economic agents-whether individuals or groups would rather carry their risks than buy Insurance. Thus, Insurance Intermediaries-agents, brokers, etc. have probably a more onerous marketing job than their counter-parts in many other trades and services.

In this directions, the R.N. Malhotra Committee vide paragraph 12.3 in its report recommended that the Central Offices of LIC/GIC should basically concentrate on:

(a) Policy formulation, review and evaluation;

(b) Product Development, pricing and actual valuation;

(c) Investments;

(d) Personnel Policies;

(e) Systems Development; and

(f) Accounts of the Corporate.

The Committee also recommended that the organisational structure of Zonal/Divisional Officers and supervising Branch Offices/Branches to be improved in such a way that the real effective operational efficiency of the LIC/GIC improves substantially in various business parameters.

The Committees incuding the Rakesh Mohan Committee which looked into infrastructure development plan for India, had emphasised the need to have large term resources to be ploughed into the basic infrastructure areas like roads ports, airports, communication transport, etc. and such long term resources would became available only by developing a "Vibrant Insurance Market". This view is mainly based on the fact that it is only from the Insurance Market particularly the Life and Pension segments that long term resources are further generated in the years to come. Thus, the Insurance Market is only a part of the overall financial sector which has in the recent past gone through a transformation, a change which had taken its place from a position of assumed "complacency" to Vibrancy" and "Vitality" which it lacked earlier.

Financial Intermediaries

A term that can be taken to include all Financial Institutions engaged in some form of Borrowing and Lending. In this broader sense, it would include all commercial banks but it is more usual to restrict the term institutions other than the Commercial Banks, Saving Banks, building societies, hire-purchase finance companies, insurance companies, Pension Funds, Investment Trust, and factoring Companies.

The Redeliff Report (1959) noted the growing importance of these Financial Intermediaries which by action as alternative sources of Finance to the Commercial Banks tended to render less effective any restrictions on credit imposed on the banks by the Monetary Authorities.

National Insurance

The principal benefits under the Great Britain's National

Insurance (known since 1966 as the Ministry of Social Security) include:

1. Retirement Pensions;
2. Unemployment benefit;
3. Sickness Benefit, i.e. payment while the insure person is unable to work, medical attention is being provided by the National Health Service, the cost of which falls entirely on the State;
4. Maternity grants; and
5. Industrial Injuries.

The traditional Insurance products are Whole Life Assurance, and Endowment Assurance. Now, there are many Insurance Products such as Money Back, Term Assurance, Annuity, Pension Plan and so on. Strong presence and dependence on "Traditional Products" may not have helped introduction of new products in a bigger way in India. Owing to paucity of time, now I sum up in brief the present and future expectations from LIC/GIC in discharging their role of Intermediaries in the insurance industry successfully as under:

- Accountability and responsiveness to the public.
- Concern for value of Public Assets and Funds
- Professionalism and Team Work
- Link business strategy more effective with technological reality.
- To manage system investments by adopting simultaneously tight-loose policies.
- Treat routine automation differently from distinctive automation.
- To consider industry system's capacity when making product decisions.
- Focus, focus, focus: Get rid of those huge shared cost structure.

- Risk Management.
- Corporate Governance.
- Legal framework.
- People Management.
- Customer Focus.
- Proper monitoring and control of public investment.
- Insurance Regulations.
- Transparency and disclosure in LIC/Insurance.
- Challenges before the LIC/Insurance Sector in India.
- Competition between New/Private Sector/Foreign insurance companies entrance.
- Bank's entry in insurance in India.
- Foreign Insurance Companies and Intermediate's Role.
- More efficient intermediate role is the expectation of the future from Insurance Sector.
- Market Oriented approach.
- Efficiency, speed and decisiveness.

It has been observed from the Annual Reports of the LIC/GIC that majority of the complaints received from customers pertain to the following areas:

- Lack of proper compliance in the fields of issue of documents; and
- Settlement of claims.

This speaks of the truth and actual position of the grass root level working. Such types of complaints by the customers in the general people determines the "goodwill" or "efficiency" of a service organisation i.e. Insurance Industry. Further, it has been observed that innumerable complaints are in the areas of:

* non-issue of policies and notices for payment of premium,
* non-receipt of policy documents,
* non-issue of claim forms, and

* non-payment of claims promptly.

The Insurance Regulatory and development Authority (IRDA) which was set up on April 19, 2000 is empowered with the following tasks:

* To regulate the investment to be made by the Companies from out of the Premium money collected from Customers.
* To specify the Life Insurance and General Insurance to be undertaken by the Insurers in the Rural and Social Sectors.
* To Control and regulate the rates, advantages, terms and conditions that may be offered by the Insurers in respect of General business not controlled or regulated by the Tariff Advisory Committee which sets premium rates for most policies; and
* To issue licences to undertake Insurance business in India.

The Globalisation and Liberalisation in the World Economy stressed the Indian Government to open the Insurance Sector to the Private Insurers. The main objectives behind this are as under:

1. To provide better coverage to the Indian Citizens; and
2. To augment the flow of long term Financial resources to finance the growth of infrastructure.

Penetration of Insurance in India

LIC and GIC could not ensure very fast growth of Insurance in India even in a long period expanding over four decades. Hence, the penetration of Insurance is low in India. Which is more clear from the following indices:

1. Per Capita Insurance Premium in Developed Countries is very high, while is quite low in India, For instance, per capita insurance premium in India

in 1999 was only US$ 8 while it was $4800 for Japan, $1000 for Korea, $ 887 for Singapore, $823 for Hong Kong, $144 for Malavsia.

2. Further, the penetration of Insurance is also assessed by the ratio of the Insurance Premium to the Gross Domestic Product (GDP) in a country. The Insurance premium as a percentage of GDP was 14% for Japan, 13% South Africa, 12% for Korea, 9% for UK and France, while it was only around 2% in India in the year 1999. It is very clear from the same that the penetration of the Insurance is low in India.

3. The penetration of Insurance is also assessed by a ratio of the Insurance Premium to the Gross Domestic Savings (GDS). The Insurance Premium as a percentage of GDS was 52% for UK, 35% for other European and American Countries, while it was only 9% in India in 1999.

4. The share of India in World Market in teams of Gross Insurance Premium is very small in India. For example, in Japan it is 31%, European Union 25%, South Africa 2.3%, in Canada 1.7% share of the Global Insurance Premium, while it is only 0.3% in case of India.

5. In the sphere of Life Insurance, only 25% of the Insurable population of India i.e., around 314 millions in 1999 have been able to get Insurance cover. Such Insurance cover in the, Developed Countries of Europe and America has been extended to around 90 to 95% of the total population.

The Insurance Regulatory and Development authority (IRDA) has twin roles i.e. Regulation as well as development. It is said that no game is possible without rules but too many rules spoil the game. Hence, the Regulator had to ensure a balance in the enactment of the regulations. The Insurance Regulation can be classified into:

(a) Licensing of New Companies; and

(b) Supervision of Existing Companies.

The major findings of the Advisory Group on Insurance Regulation: Standing Committee on International Financial Standards & Codes, submitted its report in September, 2000 to the Deputy Governor, RBI. The major findings of this report may be seen from the Annexure I. The Insurance Industry for its effective development needs fair competition. This has to be ensured by the regulator and LIC and GIC. Further, a large number of Insurers with initiative, commitment and financial resources should be encouraged to enter the Insurance Market. The entry rules should be easy and simple so that compliance may be easier by the potential insurers. Moreover, the safety if the life fund will be a concern of the regulator. Owing to this, a prudent solvency reserve should be enforced but at the same time, it should be realistic. The regulator has to create an environment, where insurers, consumers, intermediaries and other related groups can co-exist and operate for promotion of the Insurance. Hence, the regulator has to give synergy to this operation.

Further, Regulator should also put emphasis for the development of certain "niche markets" which are in the interest of the Consumers and may include Pension Market, Health Insurance Market, Rural Insurance and Insurance for Weaker Sections of the Society. Moreover, regulator should be perceived as an impartial authority to win confidence of all the concerned groups for achieving its objectives of regulation as well as development of Indian Insurance. The size of the existing Insurance Market is very large. It is also growing at the rate of 10% per year. Further, estimated potentiality of the Indian Insurance. Market in terms of premium is about $80 billions in 1999. While, only 10% of the potentiality has been tapped by LIC and GIC and the 90% of the market potentiality is yet to be tapped. Such a vast potentiality can be tapped only by a large number of Insurance. To serve a population of more than 1027 million, Indian Insurance Market can easily sustain atleast about 100 Insurers. Owing to this, regulator should issue licences to a large number of Insurers, if the Insurance Market has to grow at a fast rate.

Further, with the increase in the span of life at 61.1 years and disintegration at the Joint family system, each individual now has to arrange Insurance cover for himself and for his family. The huge Life Fund can be utilised for financing the infrastructure industry as well as a support for other industries in the country. Thus, Insurance Industry is likely to play a key role in changing the economic landscape of the country. However, the success of the Insurance Industry will primarily depend upon meeting the ever rising expectations of the Consumers who will be real kings in the liberalized Insurance market in future.

Ten Life Insurance Companies and six General Insurance Companies have been granted certificate of Registration, out of which 12 Companies have commenced business. The Capital base of Private Insurance Companies and its comparison with that of GIC and its subsidiaries as March, 31, 2001 may be seen from Annexure I.

Thus, we can conclude that the future insurance will be impacted by the Government Policies. Regulatory Authority, Forces of Globalisation and Decentralisation, Inter-company relationship within the Industry, Quality of Work Force, Competitive edge in relation to products, Services and Technology, and Distribution Channel. Moreover, the Challenges Inter Insurance Market would be from the following:

1. Changes in the external environment for the Life Insurance Market:
2. Changes in the Population Structure;
3. Changes in the Structure of Personal Financial Assets, The Government economic policies with regard to price stability; expenditure control; investment promotion; and taxation, These would affect the Product Cost;

4. Customers' Expectations i.e. Return on Investment;
5. Methods of conducting Business; and
6. Developing Insurance conciousness amongst the community

These challenges and forces that inpede progress need to be critically appreciated. However, the Competitive Strength of the Insurance Industry would be seen only from the following factors:

1. A large Insurance Market Share:
2. Sustainable Low-cost Operations;
3. Ability to differentiate in the Market;
4. Adopting perspectives and dynamic strategies; and
5. Speed, Flexibility and Development of Capabilities, technological upgradation of operation process and other Competencies to have edge over the private and Foreign Insurance Companies.

Thus, at this stage where the Insurance Industry is on the front line and is poised for challenges, changes and survival LIC and GIC and its subsidiaries will have to set their game plans and strategies in such a way and to make the different portfolios, self-sufficient and to meet all these challenges of Competitive threats successfully and to improve the Market share in Insurance Business.

However, I am hopeful and believe that the Controller of LIC/GIC, IRDA and other regulatory authorities will not fail to come up to the expectations of Customers/Insurers. In this backdrop, Globalisation, Decentralisation, Privatisation and Liberalisation is a fact of life for the conscious and long term survival of the Organisations in a competitive environment, I am grateful to all of you for inviting me to this gracious occasion. It has been both a privilege and an honour for me. Thanks all of you.

Annexure I

Report of the Advisory Group on Insurance Regulation Standing Committee on International Financial Standards and Codes, September, 2000

Major Findings of the Group

1. Regarding the Legal Form of Insurance Companies, in India, the Joint Stock Company route is followed, which is not inconsistent with the International practice. However, with a view to spreading Insurance business in rural areas the role of Cooperatives may not be ruled out in future (Para 1, a, 4).

2. Superannuation Business comes under the definition of Life Insurance Business in India. To protect the interests of the members of the superannuation funds, it is, therefore, necessary to bring these funds under some form of clear regulatory arrangements/mechanisms. There are many methods of achieving this, one such method could be through the formation of the Occupational Pension Board, as in the UK Para 1, a, 8).

3. An Insurance Company can be a domestic or a Foreign Company. The Foreign Company can operate either through a branch or on a service basis. This is the practice in most of the countries. Even though, Foreign Companies are not allowed to operate directly, they are permitted through Joint Venture arrangements with an India Company with a shareholding not exceeding 26% in the paid-up capital of the Company. Hence, this departure from the standard International Practice of allocing Foreign Companies to operate either through a branch or a service basis need not be considered as a material one (Para 1, a, 12).

4. Regarding the location of Head/Corporate Office at present, India's position is consistent with International practice although with Globalisation, Integration of markets and developments in Communication networks, this stipulation may not be effectively implementable in future (Para 1, b, 4).

5. With a view to conform to the International Practice, a section similary to Section 6(2) (h) of the LIC Act could be considered for incorporation in the Insurance Act 1938, which would enable Indian Insurance Companies to provide similar allied services to their customers(para 1,c,4).

6. In the field of specialisation, "Life" and "non-life" businesses are to be conducted by separate companies, IRDA has also decided not to permit formation of Composite Companies. However, it would be advisable to place an explicit restriction on the formation of Composite Companies (para 1,d,3).

7. It may be desirable to take a fresh look at the development in other countries and consider introduction of a more elaborate classification of life and non-life Insurance business (para 1, d, 6).

8. At present, the minimum Capital requirement is more than adequate as compared with best International practices (IP) (para 1,e,e, 5). The minimum Capital levels may be fixed fo reach class of business on a scientific and on a more transparent basis (para 1,e,9).

9. The Indian practice in respect of deposit requirements is in conformity with the best intenational Practices (para 1,f,3).

10. The Business Plan required to be submitted alongwith the application for Licence is quite Comprehensive in India at present and is consistent withthe international best practice (para 1,g,3).

11. With a view to enhancing transparency, the regulator may, as a general rule, ascertain the names of the natural and Legal persons holding a direct or indirect qualifying participation in the applicant Company and more importantly, make this knowledge Public while granting the Licence (para 1, h, 2).

12. With regards to suitability of owners', the group is of the view that the sound reputation of owners my be ensured on a continuous basis (para 1,h,6).

13. White discussing the suitability of Directors and or Senior Management, the Group observes although the resent position in India is different from that of Current international Practices, necessary steps could be undertaken, in future, to ensure the fulfilment on a continuing basis. Accordingly, the information system needs to be modified and maintained (para 1,i, 4).

14. Regarding outsourcing, it is the Group's view that it would be desirable to follow the International Practices as also other Indian Industrial practices, by considering outsourcing of various functions of an Insurance Company in view of the economies of scale and scope (para 1,j,7).

15. There is no Uniform International Practice as regards the design of products. The Group is of the view that the Certificate, incuding the basis of premium given by the actuary may be treated as a public document and be made available, on demand to other Companies and any practising actuary. Further, the premium rate table and the benefit design may also be treated as "Published Information". A similar procedure could be considered for group business and also for general Insurance business (para 1, k, 3 and 4).

16. The Group considers that with a view to ensuring uniformity in the design of products terms and considerations and marketability and also to bring about a level playing field between Insurance Companies and mutual funds, there is a need Co-ordination between Regulations of these two segments of the Financial Sector (para 1,k,6).

17. It is recommended that the Regulator may make available a recommendatory standard format of articles of incorporation (para 1,1,3).

18. The group is of the view that a firm of Consulting acturaries may be considered for acting as appointed actuaries as per the practice obtaining in most countries. Furthermore, the condition that a "Certificate of Practice" has to be obtained each year from the professional body is not present in respect of any other profession. The group feels that this needs a relook (para 1,m,6).

10. In the field of reinsurance, the Group feels that:

(i) The stipulations regarding reinsurance appear to be adequate for ensuring healthy reinsurance arrangements and are mostly in line with International Practice (para 1,n,6).

(ii) The Indian prescription of having compulsory cession of risks to Local reinsurance may appear to be against the recommendation of the IAIS. However, this prescription may be continued till a satisfactory solution is found for the problem of International reinsurers converting local Insurance Companies in to brokers (para 1,n,12).

(iv) Since, it would take quite sometime to develop necessary International contract and build a reliable database on the activities and strengths of various reinsurers, the existing domestic expertise could be nurtured and strengthened for this purpose (para 1, H, 14).

Annexure II

Capital Base of Insurance Companies (paid up Capital and Free reserves)

S.No.	*Name of Insurance Company*	*Amount (Rs. crores)*
1	2	3
1.	GIC	2.662.04
2.	National	1.052.93
3.	New India	3.066.28
4.	Oriental	918.86
5.	United India	1,177.63
6.	Private Companies*	1,862.50

*Note: Only Paid up Capital.

Source: Economic Survey. Govt. of India.

Glossary

Agricultural Resources. Gifts of nature that include fertile soils, water for irrigation and favourable climatic conditions for the growth of plants

Balance of Trade. The difference between the total value of a country's exports and imports. An excess of export over import makes a favourable balance of trade and the converse an unfavourable balance.

Basic Industries. Industries, whose finished products are used as raw materials in other industries.

Economic Environment. The interaction of all phases of the economy in which a marketer conducts business. Such factors as national income, economic growth, recession, inflation and depression must be taken into account by the marketer since they affect the success or failure of the firm's marketing strategy. For example, during a period of recession, depression or rapid business decline customers curtail their purchases or stop buying a product completely. This will cause the marketing strategy to fail, no matter how well planned it may be. Similarly, the shortage of natural resources needed by the marketer (such as energy resources) will affect the manner in which the marketer conducts business. For example, an energy crisis will cause consumers to seek out and purchase more fuel-efficient automobiles or use their automobiles less for trips to shopping malls and other retail establishments. The availability of the natural resources or raw materials needed in the production of a product will also affect the marketer. For example, during

World War II, when available silk was needed to produce parachutes, hosiery manufacturers were forced to switch to nylon for women's stockings. See also *technological environment*.

Economic Forecasting. The use of changes in the national and international business climate to predict the effects of those changes on specific industries. For example, changes in the Gross National Product (GNP) are said to affect changes in U.S. automobile sales. When the GNP increases (indicating prosperity), auto sales are said to rise accordingly. Commonly used predictors or indicators are the GNP, the unemployment rate, the increase (or decrease) in average weekly hours worked, the increase (or decrease) in the employment cost per man hour, gross private domestic investment, corporate profits, housing starts, interest rates, disposable personal income, consumer price indexes and retail sales etc. These indicators are compiled and published in the United States both by the government and by outside organisations such as banks, brokerage houses and universities. Economic forecasting may be used to predict impending changes in the demand for both consumer and industrial goods. See also *forecasting*.

Economic Goods. The goods that are so scarce relative to human wants that human effort is required to obtain them.

Economic Indicator. The data collected over time that reflect economic activity and general business conditions.

Economic Infrastructure. The internal facilities of a country available for conducting business activities, especially the communication, transfortation, distribution and financial systems.

Economic Order Quantity (EOQ). The optimum size of an order, calculated to minimise carrying and procurement costs, especially the cost of frequent re-ordering, while maintaining sufficient quantities to meet the average level of demand. An EOQ model is the technique used to balance the costs of holding inventory against the costs involved in placing orders.

Ecosystem. The complex of interactions of all the organisms with their environments and with each other. Technically, it is a subunit of the biosphere or a unit of a landscape. The interactions of members of a distribution channel or the interaction of a company and its products with consumer environments are examples of marketing applications.

Federal Food and Drug Act (1906) Federal legislation which prohibited the manufacture, sale or transportation of adulterated or fraudulently labeled foods and drugs in interstate commerce. The Act was replaced by the Food, Drug and Cosmetic Act (1938), amended by the Food Additives Amendment (1958) and the Kefauver-Harris Drug Amendments to the Food and Drug Act (1962). Also called the *Pure Food* and *Drug Act* (1906).

Federal Hazardous Substances Labelling Act (1960). Federal legislation requiring manufacturers to place warning labels on all items containing dangerous household chemicals.

Federal Regulatory Agencies. Administrative agencies that create and enforce the bulk of the laws that make up the legal environment of business. More than one hundred federal agencies exercise some degree of control over private economic activities.

Federal Trade Commission (FTC). A regulatory agency of the federal government charged with policing anti-monopoly laws. In the 1970s, the FTC emerged as a protector of consumer rights by regulating children's advertising, cigarette package labeling, the funeral industry, etc. See also *Federal Trade Commission Act (1914)*.

Federal Trade Commission Act (1914). Federal legislation which established the Federal Trade Commission (FTC) and empowered it to enforce the Sherman Antitrust Act (1890), the Clayton Act (1914) and subsequent related legislation. The Act made it illegal for anyone to commit an unfair or deceptive act of commerce or to engage in deceptive business practices. Amended by the Wheeler-Lea Act (1938).

Financial Institutions Marketing Association (FIMA). An association of individuals involved in marketing, public relations, sales, advertising, and/or consumer research in the banking industry. The Chicago based association publishes *Financial Marketing* (monthly) and *Marketing Alert* (bimonthly), an annual *Membership Directory*, and specialised manuals and books.

Global Brand. A brand that is marketed according to the same strategic principles in every part of the world.

Global Corporation. A stage of development of a company doing business outside the home country.

Global Direct Marketing. Direct marketing across national borders.

Global Marketing. 1. (Global marketing definition) A marketing strategy that consciously addresses global customers, markets and competition in formulating a business strategy, (consumer behaviour definition) An approach to international strategy that argues for marketing a product in essentially the same way everywhere in the world.

Global Marketing Information Systems. A system designed to acquire, store, catalog, analyse and make available to decision makers information from global sources within and external to the firm for use as the basis for planning and decision making.

Global Product Portfolio. See *portfolio management*

Global Retailing. Any retailing activity that spans national boundaries.

Industry Forecasting. The practice of predicting sales expectations for a class of products (such as shampoos) rather than a particular product (such as Prell shampoo). Industry forecasting is based on the amount of industry-wide marketing activity as well as the prevailing social and legal climate of the marketing area. The goal of industry forecasting is to predict the share of income that consumers are willing to spend on a product rather than save or spend elsewhere.

Industrial Revolution. The change in manufacturing from hand-operated tools topower drivenmachinery beganin England durign the middle of eitheenth century.

Irrigation. The Distribution of watr on agricultural land by artificial mean in oder to enhance the growth of crops

Manufacturing Industry. Systematic production chracterised by division of labour and extensive use of machinery.

Privatisation. The sale of transfer of public assets to the private sector.privatisation increases efficiencyand raises revenue for the state, besides spreadding share ownership and depolarisingdecisio-making.

Shifting Agricultur. A method of farming in which a patch of ground is cultivated for a period of few years until the soil is partly exhausted or over run by weeks, and after which the land is left to natural vegetation while cultivation is carried elsewhere.

Sustainable Development. A development that meets the needs of the present without compromising the ability of future generations to meet their needs.

Terrorism. A Phenomenon in which serious acts of violence such as murder, blast, arson etc. are committed by an individual or a group in order to promote a political cause.

Urbanisation. A general movement of people from small rural communities or villages to larger towns, engaged in varied activities as governance, trade, transport and manufacture. It also indicates the concentration of an increasing proportion of total population in towns and cities.

World Trade Organisation (WTO). An international organisation set up to promote trade among countries. It aims at conducting international trade in an open, uniform and nondiscriminatory manner.

Bibliography

Aggarwal & Chowdhary, *Indian Economy Crisis and Reforms*, Shipra Publications.

Agarwal R N., Capital Market Development, Corporate Financing Pattern and Economic Growth in India, *The Asian Economic Review*, April, 2003.

A.H. Maslow, *Motivation and Personality* (New York: Harper & Row, Publishers, 1954).

Ahluwalia, I.J. (1991), *Productivity and Growth in Indian Manufacturing*, Oxford University Press, New Delhi.

Ahmed, J. (1986), "Import Substitution and structural Change in Indian Manufacturing Industry, 1950-1966,' *Journal of Development Studies*, April.

Aiyar, S.S. A. (1989), 'A Coup that Worked', *Indian Express*, 3 August.

Ajit Kumar Sinha, *New Economic Policy of India*, Deep & Deep Publications, New Delhi.

Alan Blaylock and Edwin H. Duett., The Declining Market Reaction to ADR Issuers in Emerging Markets, Global Business and Finance Review Fall 2004.

Amin, S. (1990), *Delinking: A Polycentric World*, Oxford University Press, New Delhi.

Amilan S., Consistency of Equity Returns with Corporate Fundamentals in India, *Indian Journal of Commerce*, Vol.57, No.4, Oct-Dec.2004.

Anderson, Robert J. (1990), 'Reform and Growth: Implications of Trade Reforms for the Growth of the Indian Economy,' A Background World Bank Paper for the 1990 India, Country Economic Reform Memorandum.

Arun K. Datta, *Government, Finance and Capital Market*, P.G. Book Market, Calcutta.

Asif H. Quershi, "The World Trade Organisation: Implementing International Trade Norms," : Manchester University Press, 1996.

Baxi, Upendra, "Global Neighbourhood" and the "Universal Otherhood": Notes on the Report of the Commission on Global Governance, (Manuscript with author) at 12, 1996.

Bagchi, A.K. (1971), "The Theory of Efficient Neo-colonialism," *EPW* (Special Number), July.

Bakke, E. Wright, "Concept of the Social Orgnization," *General Systems*, Vo. IV (1959).

Barach, Arnold B. "U.S.A. and Its Economic Future," *Twentieth Century Fund Report*. New York: Macmillan Co., 1964.

Banerjee, S. (1984), *India's Simmering Revolution: the Naxalite Uprising*, Zed Books Ltd, London.

Bardhan, P.K. (1973), "On the Incidence of Poverty in Rural Indian in the Sixties,' *EPW*, (Annual Number) February.

Bardhan, P.K. (1978), 'Authoritarianism and democracy: First Anniversary of New Regime,' *EPW*, 18 March.

Baumol, William J. Business Behaviour, Value and Growth, New York: Macmillan Co., 1959.

Bhata, *Indian Economy, Issues and Policies*, Vikas Publishing House, New Delhi.

Bhagwati, J.N. and Desai, P. (1970), *India: Planning for Industrialisation*, Oxford University Press, London.

Bhorali, *GATT Agreement on Dunkel Draft Threaty: Its impact on Agriculture Industry TRIPs and TRIMs and Drug Industry*, Mittal Publications, New Delhi, 1994.

Biswajit Dhar and Sachin Chaturvedi, "WTO Agreements and Agricultural Sector: Implications and Options for India", RITS, New Delhi, 1999.

Buss, Perry, *Marketing and the Behavioural Science*, 2nd ed. Boston: Allyn and BCON, Inc., 1967.

Chandra, N.K. (1973), 'Western Imperialism and India To-day,' *EPW*, (Annual Number), February.

Chandrasekhar, C.P. (1988), 'Aspects of Growth and Structural Change in Indian Industry,' *EPW*, (Special Number) November.

Chandler, Alfred D., Jr. Strategy and Structure, Cambridge, Mass.: M.I.T. Press, 1962.

Christopher Arup, "The New World Trade Organisation Agreements: Globalising Law Through Services and Intellectual Property," Cambridge University Press, 2000.

CMIE (1991), World Economy and India' *Place in It*, CMIE, Bombay.

Datt, R. (1987), *India's New Economic Policy*, S. Chand & Co., New Delhi.

Dev Nathan (191), 'The State,' (mimeo), a paper presented at a seminar, The Problem of Violence, 9-13 September, at the Indian Institute of Advanced Studies, Shimla.

Dutt, R.C. (1969), *Report of the Industrial Licensing Policy Enquiry Committee, Main Report*, Government of India, Ministry of industrial Development, New Delhi.

Ernet. "Discovering the Inner Jones," *Harvard Busines Review*, Vol. XLIII, No. 3 (May-June, 1965).

Fazal, M. (1982), *Report of the Expert Committee of Public Sector Management and Performance*, Government of India, New Delhi.

Ferrer, Robert, And Wales, Hugh, G. (eds). *Motvation and Market Behavoiur*, Homewood, Illinoois: Richard D. (rwin, Inc., 1958.

Fischer D. E. & Jordan R. J., *Security Analysis and Portfolio Management*, Prentice Hall India, New Delhi.

Ford Foundation (1958), *India's Food Crisis and Steps to Meet It*, New Delhi.

Frankel, F.R. (1978), *India's Political Economy*, 1947-1977, Princeton University Press, Princeton.

Ghosh, A. (1992), *Planning in India: The Challenge for the Nineties*, Sage Publications, New Delhi.

Government of West Bengal (1981), *The IMF Loan – Facts and Issues*, Government of West Bengal.

Gottman, J. "Megalopolis: The Urbanized Northeastern Seaboard of he U.S., "*Twentieth Century Fund Report*, New York: Macmillan Co., 1961.

Gokarm.S: Indian Capital Market Reforms, 1992-96, *Economic and Political Weekly*, April13, 1996.

Gupta, S.P. and Raman, P.S. (1992), *Economic Liberalisation and Its Social Impact*, Indian Council for Research in International Economic Relations, New Delhi.

Gupta Shashi K. & Others, *Financial Institutions and Markets*, Kalyani Publishers, New Delhi, India.

Gupta. K.R., *Liberalization and Globalization of Indian Economy*, Atlantic Publishers and Distributors, New Delhi, India.

Gupta. S.P., *Liberalization: It's Impact on the Indian Economy*, Macmillan India, Delhi.

Gupta. L.C., The Changing Structure of Industrial Finance in India, Clarendon Press, Oxford, 1969.

Guruswamy S., *Financial Markets and Institutions*, Vijay Nicole Imprint, Chennai, India.

Harry P. Bower, Abraham Hollander, ad Jean-Marie Viaene: "Applied International Trade Analysis," Macmillan Press Ltd., London, 1998.

Hari Shanker Singhania, "Economic Issues Global & National", Vikas Publishing House Pvt. Ltd., New Delhi, 1995.

Hazari, R.K. (1967), *Industrial Planning and Licensing Policy, Final Report*, Planning Commission, New Delhi.

Herman E. Koenig, "Theory of Modeling Socio-Economic Systems," mimeographed paper. Department of Electrical Engineering, Michigan State University.

Hiro, D. (1976), Inside India To-day, Monthly Review Pres, New York

Hussain, A. (1984), *Report of the Committee on Trade Policies*, Government of India, Ministry of Commerce, New Delhi,

Jain, L.C. (1993), 'Turnaround in Industrial Growth: Hasty Claims for Liberalisation,' *EPW*, 20-27 February.

Jannuzi, F.t. (1989), *India in transition: Issues of Political Economy in a Plural Society*, Orient Longman, New Delhi.

Jagdish Bhagwati and Mathias Hirsch (Ed.), *The Uruguay Round and Beyond: Essays in Honour of Arthur Dunkel*, The University of Michigan Press, 1998.

Jha, L.K. (1985), *Report of the Economic Administration Reforms Commission on Government and Public Enterprises*, Government of India, Bureau of Public enterprises, New Delhi.

J.M. Clark, "Competition: Static Models and Dynamic Aspects," *American Economic Review*, Vol. XLV, No. 2, May 1955.

Joydeep Biswas, Foreign Portfolios Investments and Stock Market Behavior in a Liberalized Economy: An Indian Experience, *Asian Economic Review*, August Issue 2005,

Karanjia, R.K. (1975), *Indira-JP Confrontation: The Great Debate*, R.K. Karanjia, New Delhi.

Katona, George, "Rational Behaviour and Economic Behaviour," *Psychological Reveiw*, Vol. LX, No. 5 (September, 1953).

Kelley, Eugene J.: Lazo,Hector: Corbin, Arold:and Kahn, Edward. *Marketing Management: An Annotated Biblioraphy*, Chicago: american Mrketing Associiton, 1963.

Lewis, J.P. (1970), 'Wanted in India: A Relevant Radicalism,' EPW (Special Number0, July: also reprinted in C.D. Wadhwa, ed., *Some Problems of India's Economic Policy*, Tata McGraw-Hill, New Delhi, 1973).

Little, I., Scitovsky, T. and Scott, M. (1970), *Industry and Trade in Some Developing Countries: A Comparative Study*, Oxford University Press, London.

L.M. Bhole and Shreeya Pattanaik. The State of Indian Stock Market Under Liberalization, *Finance India*, Vol. XVI No.1, March 2002.

Marathe, S.S. (1986), *Industrial Policy in India – Retrospect and Prospect*, Sage Publications, New Delhi.

Malineau, Pierre, "Social Class and Spending Behaviour," *Journal of Marketing*, Vol. 23, No. 2 (October, 1958).

M. Francesco, Consumer Decision Processes: Marketing and Advertising Implications, Englewood Cliffs, New Jersey:Prentie-Hall, Inc., 1966.

Mundle, S. (1992), 'Employment Effects of Stabilisation and Related Policy Changes in India, 1991-92to 1992-93' in ILO-ARTEP, *Social Dimensions of Structural Adjustment in India*, New Delhi.

Myrdal, G. (1954), *Economic Theory and Underdeveloped Regions*, Orient Longman, New Delhi.

Nagaraj, R. (1990), 'Growth Rate of India's GDP, 1950-51 to 1987-88): Examination of Alternative Hypotheses,' *EPW*, 30 June

Nair, K.R.G. (1982), *Regional Experience in Developing Economy*, Wiley Eastern, New Delhi.

Nrasimhan, M. (1985), *Report of the Committee to Examine Principles of Possible Shift from Physical to Financial Controls*, Government of India, New Delhi.

Nayar, B.R. (1989), *India's Mixed Economy*, Popular Prakashan, Bombay.

Nayar, B.R. (1990), *The Political Economy of India's Public Sector: Policy and Performance*, Popular Prakashan, Bombay.

Nayar, D. (181), The IMF Loan and Its Conditions' in Government of west Bengal, The IMF Loan—Facts and Issues, Government of West Bengal, Calcutta.

Nayyar, K. (1971), *India: The Critical Years*, Vikas, New Delhi,

Neri, M. 9190), 'Abrasive Beginning,' *The Illustrated Weekly*, 15 July.

N.K.P. Sinha & M.B. Singh, "Industrial Development in India", Rawat Publications, New Delhi, 1993.

Patel, I.G., (1987), 'Free Enterprise in the Nehru Era,' in D. Tripathi, ed., *State and Business in India*, Manohar Publications, New Delhi.

Planning Commission (1969), *Fourth Five Year Plan*, Government of India, New Delhi.

------, (1990a), Approach to the Eight Five Year Plan. 1990-95, Government of India, New Delhi.

------, (1990b), *Employment: Past Trends and Prospects for 1990s*, Working Paper, Planning Commission, New Delhi.

Purshottamdas Thakurdas (1944), *A Plan of Economic Development*, New Book Company.

Rao, V.K.R.V. (1983), *India's National Income*, 1950-80, Sage publications, New Delhi.

Sathe, V. (1987), "Planning Process and New Directions of Policy" in R. Datt, India's *New Economic Policy*, S. Chand & Co., New Delhi.

Sen, A. (1990), 'How Is India Doing?' in Chaudhury, R.A., Gamkhar, S. and Ghose, A., *The Indian Economy and Its Performance Since Independence*, Oxford University Press, New Delhi.

S.K. Misra & V.K. Puri, *Indian Economy - Its Development Experience*, Himalaya Publishing House.

Drengupta, A. (1984), *Report of the Committee to Review Policy for Public Enterprises*, Government of India, Ministry of Finance, New Delhi.

Seshan, A. (187), *Burden of Domestic Public Debt in India*, Occasional Paper, Reserve Bank of India, Bombay.

Sidharthan, N.S. (1981), *Technology, Market Structure and the Decentralisation in the Growth of Capital Stock in the Indian Engineering Industries*, Institute of Economic Growth, New Delhi.

Singh, B.P. (1983), *Retrospect and Prospect of Indian Agriculture*, Federation of Indian Chambers of Commerce and Industry, New Delhi.

Swamy, D.S. (1980), *Multinational Corporations and The World Economy*, Alps International, New Delhi.

-----, (1983), 'Economic Trends in Indian Economy', in R. Dutt, ed., *Indian Economic Trends*, Radical Humanist Publications, New Delhi.

Tangermann, Kessing's Record of World Events, 1994-Except from Gill, Gerald J, *Nepal's Agricultural Trade in the New World Trading Order* , 1996.

UmaKapila, *Indian Economy Since Independence: The Ongoing Economic Reforms*, Delhi Academic Foundation.

Uruguay Round, Consolidating Economic Globalisation, (address by Peter Sutherland, to the Canadian Clumb Toronto), New of the Uruguay Round, NUR 083, 22nd March, 1994.

Various reports of the World Trade Organisation (WTO),

Varghese, *Indian Economy Problems & Prospects*, Ashish Publishing House, New Delhi.

Venkata Subramanian. K., *Policy and Performance of Indian Economy*, Manoj Prakasham Publications, Bangalore, India.

Vinod Vyasulu Hemalata Rao, *Indian Economy: Emerging Challenges*, Printwell, Jaipur, India.

Weiner, M. (1989), *The Indian Paradox*, Sage Publications, New Delhi.

World Bank, *World Development Report*, 1987, and 1992.